Published by Straight Talk Books
P.O. Box 301, Milwaukee, WI 53201
800.661.3311 • timeofgrace.org

Unless otherwise indicated, Scripture is taken from GOD'S WORD®,
Copyright © 1995 God's Word to the Nations. Used by permission of Baker
Publishing Group.

Scripture marked NIV is taken from the HOLY BIBLE, NEW INTERNATIONAL
VERSION®. NIV®. Copyright © 1973, 1978, 1984, 2011 by Biblica, Inc.™ Used
by permission of Zondervan. All rights reserved worldwide.

Cover image: © Riitta Kulinski for Champagne Studios

Printed in the United States of America

ISBN: 978-0-9904771-0-5

Dig In!

Family devotions to feed your faith

Foreword

What a pleasure it is for me to present Linda Buxa's devotional book to the world on behalf of Time of Grace. Linda has been a friend for many years and someone whose humor, insight, and passion I have appreciated the entire time. She brings a wealth of experience on living the Christian life, assisted by her amazing husband and three children. The voice you will hear in these wonderful devotions is the voice of one who has lived all over America—East Coast, West Coast, Alaska, and the Midwest—and who loves the Word and listens to the Word.

You may have come to know her from her weekly blogs on the Time of Grace website. Now you can enjoy her insights into family life as well through these daily devotions as you seek to let God's Word inform you on how you live. May Linda's joy in the Lord be yours too.

Pastor Mark Jeske

Speaker for Time of Grace
Senior pastor at St. Marcus Lutheran Church in Milwaukee, WI

Dedication

To everyone at Time of Grace Ministry . . . you accomplished what many wish they could do—left me speechless. Thank you for the humbling opportunity to share Jesus with so many.

To the kids who wrote the "By kids for kids" devotions scattered in this book . . . thank you for sharing Jesus with kids just like you. You are awesome!

To my husband, Greg . . . you are a man after God's own heart. Your dedication to making sure that family, friends, and strangers know about Jesus is a great example for our children and for everyone. I love you.

To my children—Abby, Lydia, and Ben . . . I'm often so busy reminding you to do your chores and eat healthy foods that I skimp on talking about what has been done for you. These devotions are what I most want you to know about the God who formed you, the Son who saved you, and the Holy Spirit who lives inside of you. God has big plans for you!

Introduction

These devotions aren't meant to be the only spiritual nourishment kids get. Most are like the ice cream on the front cover: a sweet dessert, simple encouragement that would be great as an after dinner treat or a bedtime snack. Some of these devotions, however, are meatier—big chunks of God's Word. I want you to dig in, to chew on God's Word on your own.

I pray that this book draws you closer to the living, powerful God who feeds you every day with his Word. Thank you for taking the time to "taste and see that the LORD is good."

Linda Buxa

January

Happy New Year!

All over the world people are coming up with resolutions, things they say they will do to make their lives better.

For kids, New Year's resolutions might sound like these:

1. **Do my best at school.**
2. **Be kind to others.**
3. **Eat ice cream every day.**

That's a pretty cool list, but maybe you're looking for some other ideas. About two thousand years ago, the apostle Paul gave a list of resolution ideas, and this list never gets old. See if anything jumps out at you.

"Brothers and sisters, we ask you to *show your appreciation for those leaders who work among you* and instruct you. We ask you to *love them* and *think very highly of them* because of the work they are doing. *Live in peace* with each other. We encourage you, brothers and sisters, to *instruct those who are not living right, cheer up those who are discouraged, help the weak,* and *be patient* with everyone. *Make sure that no one ever pays back one wrong with another wrong.* Instead, always *try to do what is good* for each other and everyone else. *Always be joyful. Never stop praying.* Whatever happens, *give thanks,* because it is God's will in Christ Jesus that you do this" (1 Thessalonians 5:12-18).

Chomp on this!

Which of the things on this list will you, with the Holy Spirit cheering you on, work on this year?

Seeing clearly

We're going to do a little experiment.

If you wear glasses, take them off.

If you don't wear glasses, borrow someone else's and put them on. (If no one has glasses, just squint really hard.)

What happened? It messed with your vision and everything got blurry, didn't it?

That's how our idea of heaven is right now. We sort of know what it might be like, but it's kind of blurry. In 1 John 3:2, we hear that when Jesus comes back, our vision will be clear: **"Dear friends, now we are God's children. What we will be isn't completely clear yet. We do know that when Christ appears we will be like him because we will see him as he is."**

Our human minds can't really imagine heaven because we have never seen perfection. Sin and sadness and hurts blur our minds.

In heaven, however, our vision will be clear. We will be like Jesus. We will be pure, holy, and sinless. We will love God and love each other perfectly. We will never again hurt others or feel guilty for hurting others. We will see Jesus face-to-face and live with him forever.

That's awesome!

Dear Father,

we can't wait to have clear vision. Right now this world is blurry and we stumble around trying to imagine what heaven is like. Help us trust that we will see clearly once we get to heaven. Thank you for letting us be like Jesus. Amen.

God loves you, Stinky Face

I Love You, Stinky Face is one of my all-time favorite children's books. Have you read it?

At bedtime, the sweet little child keeps asking the patient mom just how big her love is. "Mama, would you love me if I were a Cyclops? Mama, would you love me if I were a skunk? Mama, would you love me if I were a dinosaur?" Over and over the mom reassures . . . "Yes! I'd love you no matter what."

Maybe we wonder the same thing about God. Are we ever tempted to think that something can make God love us less? "Heavenly Father, do you love me even though I have problems in my life? Abba, do you love me even if I sometimes act on temptations? Daddy, do you love me even when I make bad choices?"

God's answer in Romans 8:38,39 sounds a lot like God's version of *I Love You, Stinky Face*:

"I am convinced that nothing can ever separate us from God's love which Christ Jesus our Lord shows us. We can't be separated by death or life, by angels or rulers, by anything in the present or anything in the future, by forces or powers in the world above or in the world below, or by anything else in creation."

Whenever you start to forget his love, read these words again. Because of what Jesus has done for you, nothing can separate you from his love. Nothing. Nothing. Nothing.

 ## Chomp on this!

Have there been times when you thought that God didn't love you?

In what BIG way did God show you that he loves you no matter what? (Hint: It happened way before you were even born!)

Temptation is coming

"There isn't any temptation that you have experienced
which is unusual for humans.
God, who faithfully keeps his promises,
will not allow you to be tempted
beyond your power to resist.
But when you are tempted,
he will also give you the ability
to endure the temptation as your way of escape"
(I Corinthians 10:13).

Signs all over Alaska warn drivers of trouble ahead. Avalanche
Area. Rock Slide Area.

There have been enough destructive snow slides and rock slides
that the people in charge of road signs there need to warn people
of possible trouble. They want the drivers to pay attention.

First Corinthians 10:13 is God's warning sign that you live in a
Temptation Area.

You see, sometimes you are tempted to hit, to fight, to disobey
your parents, to get involved in drama. Notice that God says,
"*When* you are tempted." It's simply a fact. You. Will. Be. Tempted.
You aren't the first one to drive down that road. Everybody who
has ever lived before you has faced the same temptations. (Believe
it or not, your parents face the same temptations too.) God wants
you to use today's passage as a reminder to pay attention to the
ways Satan, the world, and your own sinful thoughts want to bring
destruction to your life.

Don't forget, though, that God also says, "I. Will. Help. You." When
you face temptation, look for the escape route that he has provided.
Look for his Detour sign. See how he loves to protect you.

Be different

Lake Hillier in Australia is pink. Not simply light pink, but bubble gum pink, Barbie pink, cotton candy pink.

It looks even weirder when you see that just a small strip of trees and sand dunes separates it from the Southern Ocean (also known as the Antarctic Ocean), which is blue—like normal-looking water.

Scientists have a couple of guesses why the water is pink. Some think it's from a dye produced by microorganisms; others think bacteria live in the lake's salt crusts, but those are just guesses. Whatever it is, Lake Hillier is different.

You are like Lake Hillier. The Bible says, **"Don't become like the people of this world. Instead, change the way you think. Then you will always be able to determine what God really wants—what is good, pleasing, and perfect"** (Romans 12:2).

Faith in Jesus means that you don't look like the rest of the world. When other kids are disrespectful, you listen to your teachers. If someone is being bullied, you speak up. You help your older neighbors with chores. Faith in Jesus doesn't change only your actions, though, it changes the way you think. You do things for other people because you love Jesus. You stand up for what's right because Jesus watched out for others.

Just know that people around you will be studying you, wondering why you're different. Unlike the scientists who can't figure out Lake Hillier, you know exactly why you are different. And you can let others know. **"Dedicate your lives to Christ as Lord. Always be ready to defend your confidence in God when anyone asks you to explain it. However, make your defense with gentleness and respect"** (1 Peter 3:15).

In a world of blue water, be a pink lake.

 ## Chomp on this!

How does your faith make you different?

God knows the way

**"'For my thoughts are not your thoughts,
neither are your ways my ways,' declares the Lord.
'As the heavens are higher than the earth,
so are my ways higher than your ways
and my thoughts than your thoughts'"**
(Isaiah 55:8,9 NIV).

Kids sometimes drive their parents bananas in the car. They ask all sorts of questions:

"Are we there yet?"

"Are we lost?"

"How much longer?"

"Do you know where you're going?"

"Are you going to answer me?"

In your defense, you aren't sure where you are going and you just want your parents to reassure you. Maybe you're driving through a bad neighborhood, maybe you don't recognize where you are, or maybe you're just tired and want to be done. Your dad, who is wiser than you are, looks at you with compassion and says, "Don't worry. Trust me. I know exactly where I am."

Sometimes we do the same thing to God. We ask questions like, "How much longer until this gets better?" "God, are you sure this is the place I'm supposed to live?" "God, it seems like you're not answering my prayers. Are you even listening?"

Through the words in Isaiah today, God reminds you that he is wiser than you are. He's telling you to look at him through his Bible and see his compassion for you. Today, ask God all the questions you want. Then listen when he tells you this: "Trust me. I know where I'm going."

To the best of my ability*

**"Do you not know that in a race
all the runners run,
but only one gets the prize?
Run in such a way as to get the prize"**
(1 Corinthians 9:24 NIV).

It's tough to run long distances. You might start with a great mind-set, believing you can pull through the race with flying colors. But as you get farther along, you get tired and just want to finish—no matter what place you end up in. You stop caring about the prize.

You and I often find ourselves falling into this pattern in our everyday tasks too. We start with the idea that we will do them to the best of our abilities, to glorify and honor God. But as we get worn down, we don't care about the end result or if what we do honors God. I might start the school year doing my homework faithfully, but at the end of the year as summer vacation nears, I might struggle to finish the final worksheet. You might promise yourself that you will read your Bible or pray more, but after an incredibly long day, you might not care if you run the race to get the prize.

The good news is that the God who never gets tired forgives us through the tiring spiritual work that Jesus completed for us. He always lived for God's glory, he ran the entire race to get the prize, and he always focused on the end result. Because we get the credit for what Jesus did, we keep on running.

Dear God,

we know that you sent Jesus to renew and strengthen us. Thank you! Please help us complete our tasks as if always trying to get the prize. In Jesus' name we pray. Amen.

*This devotion was written by Karissa, a kid just like you.

BY KIDS FOR KIDS

What's your inStinct?

"Those who live by the corrupt nature
have the corrupt nature's attitude....
The corrupt nature's attitude leads to death....
This is so because the corrupt nature
has a hostile attitude toward God.
It refuses to place itself under the authority
of God's standards because it can't"
(Romans 8:5-7).

My yellow Lab, Rio, can't help herself. As a Labrador retriever, she has been bred and trained to chase, to fetch, to retrieve. This is incredibly useful when it comes to hunting. This was not helpful the day she was in our yard and a skunk ambled its way onto our property. Instinct took over. She chased. She didn't manage to fetch, though, because the skunk's instinct took over—and Rio got sprayed. We spent the next few days trying to get the horrible smell out.

You'd think she'd learn her lesson. But she is not able to think, "Oh, black-and-white furry thing = bad." Her instinct is still too strong. So, two months later, when another skunk visited our house again, she got sprayed—again.

Just as my dog's instinct is to chase, your corrupt nature is trained to do evil; it chases smelly skunks. You cannot train it to do good because it doesn't want to. It is hostile to God's ways.

This is the exact reason you need God. **"But if God's Spirit lives in you, you are under the control of your spiritual nature, not your corrupt nature"** (Romans 8:9). God has changed your instinct. Now you want what God wants. You do what God wants. Your spiritual nature is in charge.

Don't be quiet!

**"Blind and lame people came to him
in the temple courtyard, and he healed them.
When the chief priests and the experts in Moses'
Teachings saw the amazing miracles he performed
and the children shouting in the temple courtyard,
'Hosanna to the Son of David!' they were irritated.
They said to him, 'Do you hear what these children are
saying?' Jesus replied, 'Yes, I do. Have you never read,
"From the mouths of little children and infants,
you have created praise"?'"**
(Matthew 21:14-16).

Did you catch that? Kids were shouting just outside of church!
They were so excited to see the Savior that they couldn't stop
jumping and yelling that the Savior was here—finally!

When the older church leaders heard that, they were angry.
They had made all sorts of rules for people to follow, but Jesus
told them, "I am the way. The rules aren't the way. I came to take
away your sin. You don't have to follow a bunch of rules to earn
forgiveness."

God says praise starts with children; he commands it from
children. You worship the exact same Jesus that those children
two thousand years ago were shouting about. Maybe you don't get
to see Jesus performing miracles, but you hear about them in the
Bible. With the joy you show in worship, you get to pass along the
same excitement that those young kids did all those years ago.

The children in the temple courtyard—the children who shouted
their praises—were God's children, just like you are.

Chomp on this!

List some ways that *you* can show praise to God in your
everyday life.

The Holy Spirit

Sometimes your moods are confusing. You know what it's like when you feel blah or sad or mad, but you can't figure out why. When your mom asks what's going on, you start to ramble because it doesn't make sense in your head. Finding the words to explain it to her makes it sound even worse.

It helps, then, when your mom reads your mind and knows what you need, even when you don't. She knows your stomach hurts because you are nervous about the band concert. She knows you yelled at her because you miss your friends. She knows when you are tired from too much activity and you need time alone.

The Holy Spirit knows you even better than your mom does. He reads your mind and knows what you need, even when you don't. **"In the same way, the Spirit helps us in our weakness. We do not know what we ought to pray for, but the Spirit himself intercedes for us through wordless groans"** (Romans 8:26 NIV).

When you can't figure out what words to pray, the Holy Spirit talks to the Father for you. When you say, "Dear God, I don't know what's wrong," the Holy Spirit says, "Dear Father, he is really missing the friend that moved away. He'd really like you to send him someone to hang out with."

When you say, "Dear God, my stomach hurts," the Holy Spirit says, "Dear Father, she is scared because her parents are fighting and she'd like you to remind her that you always see her and love her."

When you don't have the words, the Holy Spirit does.

Holy Spirit,

thank you for praying for me, even when I don't know what to say. Thank you for knowing me better than I even know myself and for asking the Father to protect me, to watch over me, and to work in my life. Amen.

God can shut lions' mouths

In more than 50 countries around the world, it is dangerous for children your age to believe in Jesus. In some of those countries it is against the law to be a Christian, and Christians can be put to death. In other countries, believers are beaten up, their homes burned, and parents are thrown into prison. Still, these Christians believe in Jesus because the alternative—being on Satan's team—is not an option to them.

Six hundred years before Jesus was born, the same thing happened to a believer named Daniel. A bunch of men wanted to get Daniel into trouble. So they convinced King Darius to pass a law. **"The decree should state that for the next 30 days whoever asks for anything from any god or person except you, Your Majesty, will be thrown into a lions' den"** (Daniel 6:7).

King Darius signed the law, not realizing it would end up hurting his friend Daniel. Daniel, who knew he couldn't follow a fake god, continued to pray to the real God, and the men turned him in. **"So the king gave the order, and Daniel was brought to him and thrown into the lions' den. The king told Daniel, 'May your God, whom you always worship, save you!' At dawn, as soon as it was light, the king got up and quickly went to the lions' den. As he came near the den where Daniel was, the king called to Daniel with anguish in his voice, 'Daniel, servant of the living God! Was God, whom you always worship, able to save you from the lions?' Daniel said to the king, 'Your Majesty, may you live forever! My God sent his angel and shut the lions' mouths so that they couldn't hurt me. He did this because he considered me innocent'"** (verses 16, 19-22).

Your God can close hungry lions' mouths, so you know he can do amazing things for the people who are persecuted for believing in him today. He also can protect you when you have to make the hard choices to follow him or follow your friends, Satan, or your own sinful mind.

Liar, liar, pants on fire

> "The devil was a murderer from the beginning.
> He has never been truthful.
> He doesn't know what the truth is.
> Whenever he tells a lie,
> he's doing what comes naturally to him.
> He's a liar and the father of lies"
> (John 8:44).

In 1810 William Blake wrote a poem titled "The Liar." This is how it begins:

> ### Deceiver, dissembler
> ### Your trousers are alight ...

That might sound kind of old-fashioned, but I bet you've used this phrase too, although you've probably said, "Liar, liar, pants on fire." That's right; we are still using a phrase that was written over two hundred years ago.

Satan's pants have been on fire for more than two hundred years, for more than two thousand years. Because not only is he a liar, liar, but the Bible tells us that he is the father of lies. When he tells you that you aren't valuable or worth loving, Satan's a big, fat liar. He wants you to pass along the lies too. He wants you to be sneaky, to scheme, to lie, to put people down, and to hurt others. Satan is messed up, and he wants you to be just as full of lies as he is.

When the lies get old and wear you down, remember that Satan is only free to work for a little while. God isn't ignoring him; he is simply waiting until the right time to act. **"God didn't spare angels who sinned. He threw them into hell, where he has secured them with chains of darkness and is holding them for judgment"** (2 Peter 2:4).

Life lessons

John Wooden was the first person to ever be inducted into the Basketball Hall of Fame both as a player and as a coach. He won ten NCAA championships in 12 years. He received the Presidential Medal of Freedom, which is given to those who have made significant contributions to the United States. All his accomplishments might have led him to be arrogant. Instead, John Wooden, in one of his most famous quotes, shares the wisdom he had:

Talent is God-given. Be humble.
Fame is man-given. Be grateful.
Conceit is self-given. Be careful.

Those same ideas are throughout God's Word:

Talent is God-given. Be humble.
"A person's pride will humiliate him, but a humble spirit gains honor" (Proverbs 29:23).

"Brothers and sisters, in view of all we have just shared about God's compassion, I encourage you to offer your bodies as living sacrifices, dedicated to God and pleasing to him" (Romans 12:1).

Fame is man-given. Be grateful.
"The person who is greatest among you will be your servant. Whoever honors himself will be humbled, and whoever humbles himself will be honored" (Matthew 23:11,12).

Conceit is self-given. Be careful.
"A conceited look and an arrogant attitude, which are the lamps of wicked people, are sins" (Proverbs 21:4).

"Don't act out of selfish ambition or be conceited. Instead, humbly think of others as being better than yourselves" (Philippians 2:3).

As you dream big about the ways God might use you, be humble, be grateful, be careful.

You are an alien

What do aliens look like?

In *Monsters vs. Aliens*, Gallaxhar has a big egg-shaped head, four eyes, and octopuslike legs.

In the movie *E.T.*, the extraterrestrial alien is a small wrinkly creature with a light on the end of his finger.

God tells you that if you want to know what an alien looks like, you should look in the mirror.

Really? You bet.

The night before Jesus died, he was eating dinner with his disciples. He looked to heaven and prayed, **"I have given them your word and the world has hated them, for they are not of the world any more than I am of the world. My prayer is not that you take them out of the world but that you protect them from the evil one. They are not of the world, even as I am not of it. Sanctify them by the truth; your word is truth"** (John 17:14-17 NIV).

When Jesus prayed, "They are not of the world," he was saying that even though you are living here for a while, you are not really from here. You are part of God's kingdom. Your time on earth is just a visit; you are waiting for God to take you back to your real home.

When Jesus asks God to sanctify you, he is asking God to set you apart, to make you look different. When you stop bullies from picking on someone, when you refuse to get involved in drama at school, when you choose not to pass along a rumor, you look different. You look like an alien. That is exactly what you are.

The Sky declares God's glory

In the middle of winter, Fairbanks, Alaska, only has about 3 hours and 40 minutes of daylight. The sun rises just before 11:00 A.M. and sets around 2:40 P.M. The positive side of that is the sheer amount of darkness makes for spectacular night skies.

When you're far away from the lights of the town, you see as many stars as God showed to Abraham in Genesis. You also get to see *aurora borealis*. Known as the Northern Lights, electrically charged particles from the sun enter the earth's atmosphere and create a light show one thousand times more impressive than any fireworks display. Green, pink, red, yellow, blue, and violet colors dance around the sky.

What's in the sky where you live? Do you have the stunning sunsets of North Dakota or the clear blue skies of southern California? Do you watch the sunrise over the ocean in Florida or see the clouds rolling across the Midwest? No matter where you live, the sky is just one more reminder of the power of your God.

"The heavens declare the glory of God, and the sky displays what his hands have made" (Psalm 19:1). When he made the sky on the second day of creation and all the lights in the sky on the fourth day, he showed just how powerful he is. He used that power to give you a beautiful world. Now, when you look up at the sky, you see just how creative your Creator is. Like the sky, you get to declare the glory of God.

Dear God,

you created the countless numbers of beautiful stars in our sky. We are amazed at your glory! Amen.

The Great Artist

When you are painting, your picture never says, "I think you should add a little more blue." The modeling clay doesn't say, "Are you sure you know what you're doing? That side seems a little crooked; maybe you should straighten it out."

Obviously that doesn't happen because that would be ridiculous. An art project doesn't get to decide what it becomes; that's the artist's job.

God is a Great Artist too—and you are his masterpiece. Each of us is tempted, though, to ask God if he really knows what he's doing. "Why did he put me in *this* family?" "Why can't I be more like the popular kids?" "Why can't I be smarter?" God thinks your questions are, well, a bit ridiculous too. **"How horrible it will be for the one who quarrels with his maker. He is pottery among other earthenware pots. Does the clay ask the one who shapes it, 'What are you making?' Does your work say to you, 'There are no handles'?"** (Isaiah 45:9).

When God looks at you, he sees the finished masterpiece, even while he's building you, shaping you, molding you into the person he wants you to be. As you live and serve him, you don't question how he made you. You simply marvel at the unique, amazing way he created you.

Chomp on this!

Share what makes you unique. Talk about how you can use those qualities to glorify God.

Give up your life

Elsa's curse accidentally hit Anna—a second time. Now Anna was slowly freezing to death from the inside out. Only an act of true love could save her. (If you haven't seen the movie *Frozen*, I'm about to spoil it for you. Sorry.)

In Anna's last moment, as she is at her weakest, she sees that her former fiancé is about to murder her sister. Anna runs, leaps in front of the sword, and saves her sister's life. That act of love, though it killed Anna, was the act of love that actually brought her back to life. Now both Anna and Elsa would live.

In real life, Jesus calls that "the greatest love."

As Jesus was talking about how to love, he told his disciples, **"Love each other as I have loved you. This is what I'm commanding you to do. The greatest love you can show is to give your life for your friends. You are my friends if you obey my commandments"** (John 15:12-14).

Is Jesus asking us to give up our lives? Yes, maybe. Mainly, though, we remember that Jesus is our friend. He showed us the greatest act of love when he gave up his own life for us. He came back from the dead, and now we all get to live together in heaven.

Dear Jesus,

thank you for calling us your friends. You ran in front of us and took the punishment we deserved. Thank you for your greatest act of love. Amen.

Betrayed!

Young ladies, you expect your BFF to keep your secret about which boy you have a crush on. How would you feel if she went and told the other kids in the class? Heaven forbid she tells *The Boy*! (There goes the *forever* part of BFF!)

Young gentlemen, at recess you expect your best friend to pick you first for his kickball team. How would you feel if he kept choosing other people before you, telling you that you just weren't good enough? (You would be desperate to kick a home run just to rub it in his face!)

Your heart tightens and you get sick to your stomach just imaging it, don't you? That's because you have already experienced it. Whether your friends have hurt you on purpose or accidentally, even in your young life you have felt the sting of betrayal.

Jesus was a human being—just like you—and he knows exactly how much it hurts to be betrayed. **"Even my closest friend whom I trusted, the one who ate my bread, has lifted his heel against me"** (Psalm 41:9).

For three years Judas was one of Jesus' 12 BFFs. They had walked from city to city—together. They had eaten hundreds of meals—together. They had spread the news that the Messiah was here—together. Yet for 30 pieces of silver, Judas kissed Jesus on the cheek and handed him over to his enemies. Betrayed!

When you are hurt, Jesus understands exactly what you are going through because his friend hurt him too. Here's something important to keep in mind, though: Judas' betrayal led to Jesus' death. Jesus' innocent death paid for the times you hurt your friends—and the times they hurt you. You are all forgiven and can then forgive each other.

The Lord's voice

When you are sick, nothing soothes you like the sound of your mom's voice. Her gentle words make you feel better. When you're healthy, though, you don't always hear her or you tune out what she says. (That doesn't make it right, so don't use that as an excuse.)

There's something about your dad's voice, however, that you just can't ignore. It's deeper, louder, and gets your attention. When he calls for you, you know you'd better come quickly.

For as loud as your dad's voice might be, have you ever thought about what your heavenly Father's voice can do?

Psalm 29 tells you, **"The voice of the Lord rolls over the water. The God of glory thunders. The Lord shouts over raging water. The voice of the Lord is powerful. The voice of the Lord is majestic. The voice of the Lord splits the oaks and strips the trees of the forests bare. Everyone in his temple is saying, 'Glory!'"** (verses 3,4,9).

Wow! Your God's voice booms, crashes, and can rip the leaves and bark right off of trees. His voice makes everything and everyone fall before him because of his glory.

You know what's amazing about this? Your God never uses his powerful voice to yell at you. Because Jesus lived and died for you, God uses his powerful voice to help you. **"The Lord will give power to his people. The Lord will bless his people with peace"** (verse 11).

The Lord, whose voice thunders louder than your dad's, also has a voice that soothes you like your mom's.

Who's the greatest?

Kids have definite opinions about which superhero is the greatest. Spider-Man is cool because he can spin a web that's any size. Batman has an awesome bat car and bat cave. Wonder Woman has an invisible plane and bracelets that deflect bullets. Let's not forget Superman because, let's be honest, the dude can fly.

Jesus' disciples had definite ideas about greatness too, and they wanted to know what Jesus thought. **"At that time the disciples came to Jesus and asked, 'Who is greatest in the kingdom of heaven?'"** (Matthew 18:1).

Secretly, you know they each wanted to be picked. (Wouldn't you?) Instead, Jesus completely surprised them: **"He called a little child and had him stand among them. Then he said to them, 'I can guarantee this truth: Unless you change and become like little children, you will never enter the kingdom of heaven. Whoever becomes like this little child is the greatest in the kingdom of heaven'"** (verses 2-4).

For Jesus, there's no debate. You know who he says is the greatest? You. That's right; you're the greatest. Not because you have superpowers, but because you trust in the One who can quiet the waves, heal the sick, and raise the dead. You trust that Jesus, who is all-powerful, used that power to rescue you from Satan and from hell.

You're the greatest.

Dear Jesus,

I don't always feel like the greatest. I feel too young to be important, like I have to be grown up to really matter. Thanks for telling me today that you think kids are cool too, that adults should have a faith more like mine. Thanks, Jesus, for giving me faith, for saving me, for making me the greatest. Amen.

God will use your problems

Nobody likes to get sick. When nothing good is going on at school, staying home and watching movies seems fun for a bit. You'd be really bummed, though, if you missed the field trip to the children's theater. Still, you know that in a few days you'll feel better.

What about when you find out you have something more serious going on? Maybe you found out you have ADHD or dyslexia. Some kids get cancer or need heart transplants. It can be scary when you have no idea if you'll get better or not. How can God possibly make even these things work for your good?

Jesus had a friend who was so sick that he was about to die, and everyone was worried. Jesus said, **"This sickness will bring glory to God so that the Son of God will receive glory through it"** (John 11:4).

How can your problems bring God glory? Sometimes you'll see how God works—right away. If you're in the hospital, you get to tell your doctors and nurses about Jesus. The other kids in the hospital with you are probably scared too. Let them know that God promises to be with them and watch over them, the same way he is with you.

Maybe you'll see how God works—in the future. If you have a tough time focusing because of ADHD now, maybe you will grow up and tutor kids who have the same struggles. Because you know what they are going through, you can set an example for them.

No matter when or how God uses your problems to make you into the person he wants you to be, you give him the glory when you say, "God helped me. He wants to help you too."

God plans your picture*

Go grab some partners, a piece of paper, and a pen or pencil. For five seconds draw something. When your time is up, pass it to the next person. That person will add on to your picture for five seconds and then pass it to the next person. Keep going for two or three rounds. We'll wait for you. . . . Ready? Draw!

Now that you're finished, could you see what the picture was in the beginning? Did it turn out the way you expected? Probably not. You didn't understand until the picture was finished. Our life is like that too. Proverbs 16:9 says, "**A person may plan his own journey but the LORD directs his steps.**"

God has a plan for each of us. You may not realize what God is doing, but the Lord knows what he will do with your life. You have a small picture of what he's doing. Bad times, good parts—those are all part of God's final picture of you. The picture is a good one too. Jeremiah 29:11 states, "**'I know the plans I have for you,' declares the LORD. 'They are plans for peace and not disaster, plans to give you a future filled with hope.'**"

All we can do is wait for the final picture to turn out. Meanwhile, tell others about God's final plan for them too.

Chomp on this!

Did you ever wonder what God was doing with your life or think that you have your entire life planned out? Discuss with your family how this devotion changed your thinking on how your life will turn out.

Dear Lord,

thank you for having remarkable plans for my life. I want to praise you by obeying your commands. Amen.

*This devotion was written by Lydia, a kid just like you.

God isn't forced to love you

You know what it's like to be forced to be nice to people or to show them love simply because that's what is expected of you. Maybe it's that one relative who doesn't smell so good, but you have to hug her anyway so you can get your birthday present. Or sometimes there's a kid who's kind of mean at school, but because your parents are friends, you have to spend time with him on the weekends.

In your heart you know you don't actually like these people at all, and you're just faking it to be nice.

So when we think about our God's love, it's even more amazing. The Bible tells us, **"Christ died for us while we were still sinners. This demonstrates God's love for us"** (Romans 5:8). God wasn't nice to us because we brought him a present. He wasn't nice to us because he was forced to. Instead, he chose to like us even when deep down we didn't like him. While we were still stinky sinners and still mean by nature, God came up with a plan to show us how much he loves us. Even while we were enemies, he sent Jesus for us.

Now because of what he has done for us, we get to love him back. He doesn't force us. Instead, **"we love because God loved us first"** (1 John 4:19).

Dear Father,

thank you for loving me even though my sin made me unlovable. Because of what Jesus did for me, my sins are forgiven and I am your child. Amen.

You need the Spirit

Think of all the things you don't like about yourself.

I bet you came up with at least three things in three seconds. Maybe you think you get angry too quickly or you don't like being so quiet. Maybe you think you're stupid, or maybe you don't like your ears.

If you were left on your own, you would truly believe the bad things you tell yourself. That, right there, is the whole reason you have the Holy Spirit, the reason you need the Holy Spirit. You can't believe God's message without him.

When you were baptized, the Holy Spirit stamped God's name on your heart. **"Now, we didn't receive the spirit that belongs to the world. Instead, we received the Spirit who comes from God so that we could know the things which God has freely given us"** (1 Corinthians 2:12).

Thanks to the message of the Bible, the Holy Spirit whispers that God freely paid an exorbitant price, the life and death of Jesus, for you—all because he absolutely loves you. Heaven's Coach encourages you to see that Jesus has paid for the times you got angry too soon—and he loves you. He tells you that he designed you exactly the way he wants you to be. He tells you that you are wise. And he tells you that no matter what the world tells you, you know you have a God who loves and forgives you—all because he chose you to be in his family.

Chomp on this!

Take turns sharing some positive qualities that God has blessed you with.

You are hyper

Have you been feeling beaten up lately? Maybe literally? Sometimes kids get in actual fights and come out with real bumps and bruises. Or maybe you're just tired from all the things you have going on: keeping up with tests at school, trying to make a sports team, trouble with friends, lack of money, going hungry, moving back and forth from dad's house to mom's house.

When you're feeling run down, you need to be reminded of this: **"Who shall separate us from the love of Christ? Shall trouble or hardship or persecution or famine or nakedness or danger or sword? No, in all these things we are more than conquerors through him who loved us"** (Romans 8:35,37 NIV).

In Greek, the word for "more than" is *hyper*. You know what it means to be hyper, right? If someone tells you that you are hyper, it means you are extra-crazy or have extra energy. So when God tells you that you can overcome all the problems you have, he tells you that you won't just eke out a win; you are going to hyper-conquer. You are going to extra-win. Jesus came to hyper-defeat death, and now your biggest worry is gone. That victory gives you the strength to face your temptations, worries, and fears. Through the strength of Jesus who loves you, you can do anything. You don't have to cross your fingers and hope you might make it. Not one single physical problem, not one single trouble can stop God from loving you. You can—and will—hyper-conquer!

Dear Jesus,

you've given me your victory and tell me that I am not just an almost-conqueror. I'm a hyper-conqueror. I am going to smoke everything this world throws at me because nothing can stop you from loving me. That's awesome. Thanks! Amen.

What God wants you to know

Today God wants you to remember this:
**"It is by grace you have been saved,
through faith—and this is not from yourselves,
it is the gift of God—not by works,
so that no one can boast"**
(Ephesians 2:8,9 NIV).

To get your allowance, you have to do chores. So I don't blame you if you think that you might have to earn God's love. God loves you because he is good, not because you are good. It's by grace.

Satan tries to make you think that you are such a loser that Jesus couldn't possibly love you and want to be with you. But Jesus does love you, and he died for you. You believe that he is the only way to heaven. You have been saved, through faith.

You can't choose God, just the same way that dead people can't choose to come alive. God chose to create faith in you because he loves you and loves to give you good gifts. This is not from yourselves; it is the gift of God.

You can't work for your salvation; you can't earn it by doing good things for other people. If you could, you might be tempted to take credit for it. God gets the glory. Not you. You've been saved, not by works, so you can't brag that you earned anything. Instead, you can brag that God loves you!

Dear Lord,

thank you for doing everything for me so I can be in heaven with you. Help me give you glory in all that I do. Amen.

Celebrities are humans too

Kids—and adults too—tend to gobble up information about celebrities. You follow your favorite stars on the Internet, news, TV, and magazines. You imitate them, dress like them, and do your hair the same way. You'll gladly buy whatever shoes or clothes they advertise and whatever music they make.

It's okay to have role models, if you choose the right ones. The problem comes when you choose to spend your money to imitate celebrities who flaunt their bad behavior—getting drunk, crashing their cars, being obnoxious, and treating other people poorly.

God has an opinion on that. **"Dear friend, never imitate evil, but imitate good. The person who does good is from God. The person who does evil has never seen God"** (3 John 1:11).

Celebrities don't, and probably never will, know who you are. Be careful how much influence you let them have in your life. Imitate those who are kind, who serve others, who treat people well, who use their fame to tell the story of Jesus. Don't waste your time on those who set a bad example for you, tempting you to do evil.

As this psalm reminds us, **"Do not trust influential people, mortals who cannot help you. When they breathe their last breath, they return to the ground. On that day their plans come to an end"** (Psalm 146:3,4).

 ## Chomp on this!

Which celebrities do you like? What have you heard or seen about their behavior?

How do you pick role models?

Don't bow down

King Nebuchadnezzar made a statue 90 feet tall. Three of Daniel's friends wouldn't bow down and worship this powerless hunk of gold—and Nebuchadnezzar was furious, so furious that he ordered Shadrach, Meshach, and Abednego to die in a fiery furnace.

Not even that threat would get them to change their minds. They told the king, **"If our God, whom we honor, can save us from a blazing furnace and from your power, he will, Your Majesty. But if he doesn't, you should know, Your Majesty, we'll never honor your gods or worship the gold statue that you set up"** (Daniel 3:17, 18).

They knew their God was the one true God and that he could rescue them. If he didn't, well, they'd be in heaven.

The men were tied up and thrown into the furnace. **"Then Nebuchadnezzar was startled. He sprang to his feet. He asked his advisers, 'Didn't we throw three men into the fire?' 'That's true, Your Majesty,' they answered. The king replied, 'But look, I see four men. They're untied, walking in the middle of the fire, and unharmed. The fourth one looks like a son of the gods'"** (verses 24, 25).

Our God gives courage to people whose lives are threatened for believing in him. He also gives you the strength to not give in when others want you to break God's commandments. You are given the same conviction as the men in the furnace.

Shadrach, Meshach, and Abednego—young men who wouldn't dishonor God—were God's children, just like you are.

 ## Chomp on this!
Read the whole story in Daniel chapter 3.

Salvation is God's gift

*Today let's **Dig In!** Read this section of Scripture, and then use the questions to talk about what God has to say in his Word.*

You were once dead because of your failures and sins. You followed the ways of this present world and its spiritual ruler. This ruler continues to work in people who refuse to obey God. All of us once lived among these people, and followed the desires of our corrupt nature. We did what our corrupt desires and thoughts wanted us to do. So, because of our nature, we deserved God's anger just like everyone else.

But God is rich in mercy because of his great love for us. We were dead because of our failures, but he made us alive together with Christ. (It is God's kindness that saved you.) God has brought us back to life together with Christ Jesus and has given us a position in heaven with him. He did this through Christ Jesus out of his generosity to us in order to show his extremely rich kindness in the world to come. God saved you through faith as an act of kindness. You had nothing to do with it. Being saved is a gift from God. It's not the result of anything you've done, so no one can brag about it. God has made us what we are. He has created us in Christ Jesus to live lives filled with good works that he has prepared for us to do. (Ephesians 2:1-10)

Chomp on this!

What does God teach you in this passage?

What makes you say, "Thank you, Jesus"?

What makes you say, "I'm sorry, Jesus"?

Based on this reading, what would you like to ask God for?

Jesus purifies us

Around the world 800 million people do not have access to clean water. Because their drinking water is contaminated with bacteria, one child dies every 21 seconds from water-related diseases. To help save these little children, a number of organizations provide water purification tablets. These little pills get put into the water to kill all the germs, to make water safe for drinking so the children can live.

Around the world, seven billion people are contaminated with sin. Because sin brings death, every single person is in danger. To save his people, God sent his Son as his world purification tablet. When Jesus came to earth, he lived the perfect life for you. He obeyed every single thing his parents told him to do. He obeyed every single rule his heavenly Father gave. When Jesus was on the cross, God punished him for the sins you have done. The apostle John tells us, **"The blood of Jesus, his Son, purifies us from all sin"** (1 John 1:7 NIV).

When Jesus rose from the dead, he declared that you are no longer eternally contaminated. You are a new creation. Jesus did this so God's children, his brothers and sisters—that's you—can live.

Dear Father,

we pray for children around the world who drink contaminated water. Thank you for the people who work to give them clean water so they can live. We also pray for the people who do not know that they are eternally contaminated because of sin. Use us to tell them about Jesus, who purifies us all. Amen.

Don't be ashamed*

Have you ever felt ashamed? Maybe you got caught spreading rumors about a friend. Or you completely disobeyed your parents, and they were disappointed. Or are you ashamed because of how your family acts? Sometimes you might even be ashamed of God. I mean, it's embarrassing to be different from others, to make choices that make God happy even if they make your friends mad, to believe things that other people think are old-fashioned.

So when a friend asks, "Why do you believe in this stuff?" have you been ashamed that you believe in God or have you been proud of Jesus?

In our minds we know what's right, so why is it so hard? Usually it's because we are afraid that talking about God's Word will ruin our reputations. Or because Satan wants us to keep quiet so more people don't hear the good news.

Paul wasn't worried about that at all. He wrote, **"I'm not ashamed of the Good News. It is God's power to save everyone who believes"** (Romans 1:16). The gospel—the Good News that Jesus loved and died for the world—is how God uses his power to save all believers. That is amazing news! We share it not because we have to, but because we can't wait to.

Dear Lord,

we know we should never be ashamed of the gospel. Please help us spread your Word boldly with all people and not be ashamed of it. In your name we pray. Amen.

This devotion was written by Lizzy, a kid just like you.

February

No more waiting

Being a kid means always having to wait. Waiting to get your ears pierced. Waiting until you're old enough to be on the A-team for basketball. Waiting to watch PG-13 movies. Waiting until you're old enough to stay home by yourself. Waiting. Waiting. Waiting.

I think one of the best things about God is that he tells you that you don't have to wait to be in his army. You're in it—right now! The devil isn't waiting until you're older to tempt, deceive, or attack, so God says you're old enough to wear his battle gear.

"For this reason, take up all the armor that God supplies. Then you will be able to take a stand during these evil days. Once you have overcome all obstacles, you will be able to stand your ground.

"So then, take your stand! Fasten truth around your waist like a belt. Put on God's approval as your breastplate. Put on your shoes so that you are ready to spread the Good News that gives peace. In addition to all these, take the Christian faith as your shield. With it you can put out all the flaming arrows of the evil one. Also take salvation as your helmet and the word of God as the sword that the Spirit supplies.

"Pray in the Spirit in every situation. Use every kind of prayer and request there is. For the same reason be alert. Use every kind of effort and make every kind of request for all of God's people" (Ephesians 6:13-18).

These next few days, as we learn more about the armor you get to wear, remember that this isn't about when you get older; this is about your life—right now!

Dear Jesus,

you won the ultimate war for me. Thank you for being on my side, on my team, as I fight battles each day. Give me all the armor I need to fight so I can defeat all my enemies. Amen.

Keep your pants up!

I think having your pants fall down at school ranks pretty high on the list of most embarrassing things that could ever happen in the whole entire world, right? That's why you wear a belt—not because belts are comfortable, but to keep your pants up.

Back in Bible times, a belt wasn't to protect someone from dying from embarrassment; a belt could actually help stop him from dying for real. It not only kept his armor in place, but it was also nice and wide to cover his vital organs, to protect him in battle.

God's truth protects us today from the lies we are constantly told. Satan tells you, "You don't really need to believe in Jesus." God says, **"I am the way, the truth, and the life. No one goes to the Father except through me"** (John 14:6).

Through TV, movies, and magazines, the world tells you, "You aren't enough—smart enough, strong enough, or loved enough." God says, "I have loved you with an everlasting love."

You tell yourself, "I can't be happy unless I have …" God tells you, "I will supply all your needs."

The thing is, the truth isn't always comfortable. Sometimes you won't be popular because of it; sometimes others will make fun of you. But you wear the belt because you need it. Keep your spiritual pants up.

Chomp on this!

Talk about or write down some lies that Satan tries to tell you. Now list God's truths.

Dear Jesus,

everything you say is the truth. Help me wear the belt of truth so that I stick to what you say. Let your truth wrap around me and protect me when I am tempted to listen to the father of lies. Amen.

Jesus is your bulletproof vest

Why do soldiers wear bulletproof vests? (Take time to answer that.)

Getting shot in the arm or leg still hurts—really hurts—but it doesn't kill you. You need to protect your heart, though, because that wound could be fatal. There weren't guns back in Bible times, but the soldiers then knew they had to protect their hearts and lungs too. That's why they wore breastplates.

In our battle against Satan, it's just as important to protect our hearts. That's why today we **"put on God's approval as [our] breastplate"** (Ephesians 6:14). There's a churchy word for "God's approval"; we call it *righteousness*. It means that you are now right with God. You are worthy to be with Jesus—all because Jesus lived for you and took your punishment.

This approval is your bulletproof vest. In Psalm 5:12 David tells us the truth about God: **"You bless *righteous* people, O LORD. Like a large shield, you surround them with your favor."**

Satan's lies can't pierce your heart because you know the truth. God loves you. God likes you. God looks at you and smiles. His approval covers and protects your heart.

 ## Chomp on this!

What arrows or bullets does Satan use to try to get to your heart?

Dear Lord,

every day is filled with so many choices, so many spiritual struggles. You have given me a bulletproof vest by buying me with your blood. You cover my heart with righteousness. Give me the power and courage to do the things you want me to do. I love you because you loved me first. Amen.

Shoes of peace

Nobody shovels in flip-flops. (Well, usually not.) For sure, though, I've never seen anyone ski with swim fins or garden in high heels or do ballet in army boots.

You have to wear the right shoes for the right job. When you wear God's armor, you might expect to be told to wear big heavy combat boots—after all, you're a Christian soldier. So today's clothes might surprise you. God tells you to **"put on your shoes so that you are ready to spread the Good News that gives peace"** (Ephesians 6:15).

You know that God has already won the battle. Jesus is your substitute, and your salvation is guaranteed. This means you aren't an angry soldier with a quick temper. Instead, you are confident. You live in peace with others because you are at peace with God.

God tells you to walk around, always ready to share that peace with others. You don't yell at them; you don't fight with them. Instead, **"as much as it is possible, live in peace with everyone"** (Romans 12:18).

Get your shoes on. There's a whole world of people who need the peace that you have.

 ## Chomp on this!

What happened to you today that made it hard for you to walk in peace?

Do you know people who need to hear about the peace that Jesus gives? How can you share Jesus with them?

Dear Lord,

I'm sorry for the times I walk with the wrong shoes, when I'm angry or mean or jealous. Let me walk around with your shoes of peace today. Walk with me so that wherever I go I carry your message of love and forgiveness and peace through Jesus. Let me stand strong against Satan's attacks. Amen.

Your faith Shield

In a Nerf gun battle, the best way to protect yourself is to hide behind a wall. Or maybe a couch. Or a table. The last thing you would do is run into the middle of the room with nothing to protect you from those foam bullets. That would be dumb, right?

On a real battlefield, soldiers are often out in the open—and there's no way to carry furniture into a fight. So, they need some kind of protection that's light enough to carry but strong enough to protect them. That's why they need shields.

In your battle with Satan, you don't usually run into him when you're in the safety of your church walls. You often meet when you're out in the open—at school, at sports games, when you're hanging out with your friends. So you carry your faith with you. You **"take the Christian faith as your shield. With it you can put out all the flaming arrows of the evil one"** (Ephesians 6:16).

The shield is armor that Christ gives you. It protects you wherever Satan shoots at you. Is it doubt that you are loved? Is it worrying about if you fit in? Is it telling you that fighting is the way to handle your problems or that cheating will help you get what you want? Each one of those lies is a flaming arrow. The faith that God gives you helps you dodge those bullets and keeps you safe.

Remember, though, that the strength in your shield doesn't come from you. It comes from God. **"The Lord is faithful and will strengthen you and protect you against the evil one"** (2 Thessalonians 3:3).

 ## Chomp on this!

What are the ways God makes your shield—your faith—stronger?

How can you encourage the people around you to strengthen their shields too?

Salvation helmet

When a baseball player is up to bat, he or she wears a helmet. It might not be comfortable, but it's way better than being hit in the head with a 95-miles-per-hour fastball.

A hardball going that fast will, at best, leave you with a huge lump on your head and a nasty bruise. Through Major League baseball history, though, some players have gotten hurt far worse. Batters have needed stitches, suffered from concussions, and broken their bones. Way back in 1920, a player died after being hit in the head with a pitch.

No one jokes about taking shots to the head. That's why God tells you to **"also take salvation as your helmet"** (Ephesians 6:17). The fact that God has saved you protects your head—it protects your thinking. When Satan tells you that you are worthless, God tells you that you are worthy. When the world tells you that you aren't strong or powerful enough, God tells you that he is strong and powerful enough for you. When you start thinking that no one loves you, God's thinking tells you that you are so valuable that he gave up his own Son so you could spend forever with him.

The Bible helps you know the things God wants you to think. There you read about your salvation. There you read what God wants you to know. **"Since you were brought back to life with Christ, focus on the things that are above—where Christ holds the highest position. Keep your mind on things above, not on worldly things"** (Colossians 3:1,2).

Dear Lord,
help me put your helmet on. Protect my mind and imagination with the helmet of salvation. Keep me thinking about your love, your power, and the salvation you gave me. Amen.

God's Word is a Sword

When God tells you that you get to be in his army, don't you think the first thing you would do is get a weapon? Nope. God gives you a list of five things you need to wear to protect yourself. Not until the end of the list, when he makes sure you are good and covered, does he say, "Oh, and you need a weapon too."

But this is no typical weapon; he says you will use **"the word of God as the sword that the Spirit supplies"** (Ephesians 6:17). When Jesus was tempted in the desert by Satan, he didn't wrestle or fight. Instead, when Satan tempted him, he fought back with God's Word. Satan does the same thing today. He'll try to tempt you to sin too.

But . . . using God's Word sounds, well, kind of boring. How can a book that is thousands of years old be powerful? Because the God who gave it to us is still alive. The Bible is still how he gets his message to us today. God's Word is your personal way of knowing what is right and wrong. It gives you strength to stand up to Satan.

Hebrews 4:12 tells us, **"God's word is living and active. It is sharper than any two-edged sword and cuts as deep as the place where soul and spirit meet, the place where joints and marrow meet. God's word judges a person's thoughts and intentions."**

Only the word of a living God can still judge, still be powerful, still help you fight the battles you face today.

Chomp on this!

What are some of the lies you hear or see on TV?

What are lies that you sometimes believe about yourself?

What passages have you used or can you use to fight back, to poke holes in those lies?

Don't forget to pray

The whole time we've been talking about God's armor you've been picturing yourself all alone, haven't you? The part about being a soldier is that you aren't alone. You are part of an entire army that believes that no one gets left behind.

What's different about this army is that you get to talk to the Commander of the entire army anytime you want about anything you want. God invites you to **"pray in the Spirit in every situation. Use every kind of prayer and request there is. For the same reason be alert. Use every kind of effort and make every kind of request for all of God's people"** (Ephesians 6:18).

So now that you are fully dressed for battle, remember to be part of the army of Christ. You are attached to them. The God of the entire universe is the power source for his army. Talk to him. Use the power of God who answers prayer to protect yourself and others and to praise him.

It doesn't matter how you pray. You can whisper or shout, you can sing or talk, you can keep your eyes open or closed, you can fold your hands or hold someone else's hand or raise your hands to heaven, or you can sit or stand or lie down.

You can pray long prayers or quick ones, morning or night. It doesn't matter. Just pray, trusting that God loves to hear your prayers and is excited to answer them.

Today, make up your own prayer. Here are some ideas:

- Thank God that the Holy Spirit lives in you, encouraging you to pray.

- Pray for God's strength to be alert.

- Talk to God about the people in your life who need his strength, encouragement, or peace.

Call for your Dad

Most kids are afraid of the dark at some time. Or of the boogeyman. Or of a spider. Usually, the first thing they do is call for their dads—especially if there's a spider. Dads use their bigger size to protect you from the things that scare you—real or imagined.

As you get older, maybe you feel silly about your toddler fears. As you get bigger, though, your fears get bigger and more serious too. Maybe you fear bullies or your grandparents dying or if you'll make new friends at your new school.

God tells you that even though you are older, when you are afraid, you still call for your dad, your earthly one, and also your heavenly one. He calls himself your *Abba*, your Daddy. **"You haven't received the spirit of slaves that leads you into fear again. Instead, you have received the spirit of God's adopted children by which we call out, 'Abba! Father!'"** (Romans 8:15).

It's true that just because God loves you doesn't mean you'll never have anything bad happen ever—after all, we still live in a sinful world. However, your Abba doesn't want you to hide from your fears by yourself. Thanks to Jesus' life and death, you have the right to call for him. Go to him with your fears—and leave them with him.

Thanks, Dad!

Chomp on this!

What fears have you been keeping to yourself? (Be sure to talk about those in your prayers.)

Dear Daddy,

you are our big, strong, protective Father. Thank you for letting us call you our Abba and for promising to protect us when we are afraid. You're the best! Amen.

Tell your enemies

"Naaman, the commander of the Aramean king's army,
was respected and highly honored by his master.
The Lord had given Aram a victory through Naaman.
This man was a good soldier, but he had a skin disease.
Once, when the Arameans went on raids,
they had brought back a little girl from Israel.
She became the servant of Naaman's wife.
The girl told her mistress,
'If only my master were with the prophet in Samaria.
Then the prophet could cure him of his skin disease'"
(2 Kings 5:1-3).

This young girl, who was probably only 8 to 10 years old, is the hero in this story. She ended up in the home of a man who led the army that killed her parents and took her siblings as slaves. How did she not hate him?

Instead, she knew where her captor could find healing—and she told him. She could have kept quiet, but instead she shared the good news of a great God.

Jesus was separated from his Father too. He could have been resentful and angry at us. Instead he was a servant to the people responsible for his suffering. He tells us how to be healed.

You do the same thing too when you act with compassion on those you consider to be your enemies. When you forgive, love, and tell them where to find healing, you are sharing the news of a great God.

The little girl—the slave who had compassion on her enemy—was God's child, just like you are.

 ## Chomp on this!

Read the rest of Naaman's story in 2 Kings chapter 5.

Don't be part of the drama

"A friend always loves"
(Proverbs 17:17).

At your age, there can be so much drama, can't there? You know what I'm talking about. Meghan won't play with you because you were talking to Sophia, who is hanging out with Maria lately. Or maybe you don't want to play on the swings with Jadyn and Katie, so they tell you that they don't want to be around you anyway. By the end of the day, when you get in the backseat of your car, you just start crying. It's just so hard!

I'm not sure it makes you feel better, but adults can get caught up in drama too. The apostle Paul ended up writing a letter to people who lived in a town called Thessalonica because the drama there was so bad. **"We hear that some of you are not living disciplined lives. You're not working, so you go around interfering in other people's lives. We order and encourage such people by the Lord Jesus Christ to pay attention to their own work so they can support themselves. Brothers and sisters, we can't allow ourselves to get tired of doing what is right"** (2 Thessalonians 3:11-13).

Drama simply means you are interfering in other people's lives and stirring up trouble. Your whole life there will always be people who don't mind stirring up trouble. So this is a great time to practice how to handle it. Be disciplined. Stay focused on your homework, on reading a good book, on becoming a better artist.

Look for a friend and be a friend who does what is right, who always loves.

What's your foundation?

Have you seen a picture of the *Torre di Pisa*? You probably know it better by its more popular name: the Leaning Tower of Pisa, which is a bell tower for the cathedral in the city of Pisa, Italy.

Construction started on the bell tower in 1173, but the ground was too soft and the foundation wasn't strong enough. (The foundation is at the bottom of a building and needs to hold up all of the top part.) The building started to lean almost right away. Five years later, construction stopped. Off and on for 199 years people kept building, sometimes trying to correct the lean, sometimes not. Modern technology has helped stop the tilt, but the bell tower still isn't straight.

This tower is famous only because the builders made a pretty big mistake, one that causes the tower to be well-known a thousand years later.

God wants you to get your personal foundation right. If you don't have something strong holding you up, your life tilts and leans. Your omnipotent God, which is a big churchy word that means "all-powerful," tells you that **"he will be the foundation of your future. The riches of salvation are wisdom and knowledge. The fear of the LORD is your treasure"** (Isaiah 33:6).

When you build on God and his promises, he is the foundation of your future. He gives you the wisdom and knowledge to build strong and straight.

A humble attitude like Christ

*Today let's **Dig In!** Read this section of Scripture, and then use the questions to talk about what God has to say in his Word.*

So then, as Christians, do you have any encouragement? Do you have any comfort from love? Do you have any spiritual relationships? Do you have any sympathy and compassion? Then fill me with joy by having the same attitude and the same love, living in harmony, and keeping one purpose in mind. Don't act out of selfish ambition or be conceited. Instead, humbly think of others as being better than yourselves. Don't be concerned only about your own interests, but also be concerned about the interests of others. Have the same attitude that Christ Jesus had.

Although he was in the form of God and equal with God, he did not take advantage of this equality. Instead, he emptied himself by taking on the form of a servant, by becoming like other humans, by having a human appearance. He humbled himself by becoming obedient to the point of death, death on a cross. (Philippians 2:1-8)

Chomp on this!

What does God teach you in this passage?

What makes you say, "Thank you, Jesus"?

What makes you say, "I'm sorry, Jesus"?

Based on this reading, what would you like to ask God for?

You need an Organ transplant

What is today? I bet you said Valentine's Day. You're right, but today is also National Organ Donor Day. It might sound a little strange, but it kind of fits. On the day when we talk about exchanging love, people want you to consider giving part of yourself to help someone who is very sick.

This might also sound a little strange, but did you know that you've already had an organ transplant?

In Ezekial 36:26, God tells you that he's already performed an operation on you: **"I will give you a new heart and put a new spirit in you; I will remove from you your heart of stone and give you a heart of flesh"** (NIV).

At your baptism, God took your original heart—the one that didn't love him, the one that loved doing bad stuff—and gave you a new heart. Your new heart loves what God loves. It wants to learn more about him. With your new spirit, you get excited to tell others about Jesus.

Happy National Organ Donor Day! And thank you, God, for giving me a new heart.

Dear God,

my old heart was cold and hard and full of sin. You knew that, and you knew I couldn't change it on my own. Thank you for sending Jesus—the best Valentine—to live in my place so that I could have a new heart that loves you. I love my new heart and my new spirit. Thank you! Amen.

Real love

Happy day after Valentine's Day! Are you still feeling the love that came from the notes that got handed out in your classroom? Or are you feeling kind of sick because you ate too much of the candy that came with them?

The problem with love here on earth is that it comes and goes. Sometimes it's great—and some days you can't tell if it's here at all. Real love is not found on those little pieces of paper or in the candy you got. (Those things are fun and yummy, though!) God, who is love, gives you a definition of what real love is:

"Love is patient. Love is kind. Love isn't jealous. It doesn't sing its own praises. It isn't arrogant. It isn't rude. It doesn't think about itself. It isn't irritable. It doesn't keep track of wrongs. It isn't happy when injustice is done, but it is happy with the truth. Love never stops being patient, never stops believing, never stops hoping, never gives up" (1 Corinthians 13:4-7).

This is the kind of love he wants you to share. And you can do it every single day of the year. Can you think of some ways that you can do this?

Chomp on this!

Read the passage again, this time saying God instead of the word love.

Read the passage another time. This time say your name in place of love. Remember that because you get credit for the life Jesus lived, you have a new person inside of you. You are all these things.

National Do a Grouch a Favor Day

Think back to your preschool days. Do you remember Oscar the Grouch from *Sesame Street*? Always cranky, he lives in a trash can and declares that he doesn't like anybody or anything that is nice. (Except sometimes he admits that he likes kids.)

Do you know a grouch? Sometimes it's the man across the street. Sometimes it's a stranger at the store. These people don't live in trash cans, but grouchiness can make them seem as if they are living in filthy emotions—short tempers, crankiness, mean words, and grumpy faces.

Proverbs tells us that it's not necessarily the outside of them that's a problem but the inside: **"As a face is reflected in water, so a person is reflected by his heart"** (27:19).

Sometimes a grouch might simply be a person who is lonely or hurting on the inside and needs a kind word. Sometimes grouches don't know Jesus and just don't know how to be kind. Today, if you meet a grouch, do that person a favor. Say hello, smile, help with his or her groceries if allowed. Follow God's advice to always do good.

"'If your enemy is hungry, feed him. If he is thirsty, give him a drink. If you do this, you will make him feel guilty and ashamed.' Don't let evil conquer you, but conquer evil with good" (Romans 12:20,21).

Dear Lord,

help me always be kind to people, even when they are grouchy. I pray that your love will shine through me to them—brightening their day. Amen.

God is the Judge

Olympic figure skating judges have a reputation for not judging fairly. Time and time again, judges are accused of giving higher scores to people who haven't earned them. They do this to help give the gold medal to someone who doesn't necessarily deserve it.

You've seen this in your life too. Any human judge or referee or umpire will never be able to judge 100 percent accurately. It's simply impossible to see every play or hear every note correctly.

The only one who can see all and hear all is God. **"He alone judges the world with righteousness. He judges its people fairly"** (Psalm 9:8). God is our judge, and he will hold everyone accountable for every single thought, word, and action that he or she has done—or hasn't done.

The thing is, in figure skating it's considered cheating to help out those on the ice. In God's world, however, it makes perfect sense. The way God works is that he doesn't take our performance and add a few points to it, making us good enough to win. We can't earn our place in heaven. Instead, he looks at Jesus' performance and gives us his perfect score. You, the one who doesn't deserve it, get the gold.

Chomp on this!

Explain in your own words what it means to get the gold because of Jesus.

In the Olympics only one person wins a gold medal in an event. Is that true for our prize of heaven? Who wins through Jesus?

Speak up for Others

During recess, have you seen (or been) the kid picked last? In the classroom, do you see kids picking on the one they don't think is cool? As much as you like kids your age, you also know that kids can be cruel. They choose words that hurt. Or they roll their eyes in such a way you'd almost rather they used words. Sometimes you might even be the one picking on kids, rolling your eyes, being super sarcastic, putting down a kid so another person will think you're cool.

In Jesus' family, though, kids are different. They treat each other differently. In his family, kids get to **"speak out for the one who cannot speak"** (Proverbs 31:8). In his family, *you* get to speak up.

With the Holy Spirit inside of you, you get up the courage to stand up for those who cannot seem to speak up for themselves because they are scared or hurt or embarrassed or shy. When you defend others, when you protect those who are getting picked on, you show what it means to be a true friend. You show them that what Jesus thinks about you is more important to you than staying quiet so you can be popular. You get to speak up and show that because Jesus loves everybody, you do too. You get to be their hero—and a hero for Jesus.

Chomp on this!

With your family, brainstorm some of the things you could say when you stand up for other kids. Or when you stand up for yourself.

You are Special*

Do you ever feel that you aren't very special? Maybe you don't get the best grades in class or have the fastest mile time or create the best paintings. Maybe you can't play piano that well, or you think that the freckles on your face look weird.

You might feel sad and disappointed for a while because you think you aren't as good as everybody else. Here's some news you should hear: **"I will give thanks to you because I have been so amazingly and miraculously made. Your works are miraculous, and my soul is fully aware of this"** (Psalm 139:14).

God made you special. He gave you specific gifts for reasons you may not see now. He made you exactly the way he wants you to be, down to the last freckle or toe. You probably haven't thought about that. Everything about you was designed by God before the world began. How cool is that?

Chomp on this!

List five things that are unique about you and the gifts God has given you. Then thank him for his miraculous work of making you.

Dear God,

sometimes my brain forgets that you made me so amazingly, especially when I see kids who do things better than I do. Thank you for the Holy Spirit who lives inside of me and reminds me that every single one of your creations—including me—is miraculous. Amen.

This devotion was written by Abby, a kid just like you.

God controls nature

Do your parents keep the news on when you're in the room? If so, it can seem like the weather is out of control. You hear reporters talking about "Mother Nature" and her devastating tornadoes, earthquakes, terrible snowstorms, hurricanes, tsunamis, and mudslides.

In the Bible, we learn that when Adam and Eve sinned, the world started to break down. Trees and water and plants and winds were affected too. **"Creation was subjected to frustration but not by its own choice. The one who subjected it to frustration did so in the hope that it would also be set free from slavery to decay in order to share the glorious freedom that the children of God will have"** (Romans 8:20,21).

Even the created world knows that the way things are is not the way they were meant to be. These signs are reminders that God is going to come back and both we and the world will someday be set free. Until then, we remember that we have a God who created the world and sent his Son who calmed a storm just by saying, "Be still!" He will calm your heart when the frustrated world and weather scares you too.

Dear Father,

sometimes the weather scares me. Thunderstorms, winds, hail, lightning, and floods hurt people and damage the world you made. When I'm scared, remind me that you created the world and it is still in your control. I'm also thankful, Lord, that you will give us a new earth when you come back, one that will never scare us again. Amen.

You make God happy

"The LORD your God is with you.
He is a hero who saves you.
He happily rejoices over you,
renews you with his love,
and celebrates over you with shouts of joy"
(Zephaniah 3:17).

At some point in almost every day, I bet you feel like a failure. You didn't study enough, so you didn't do well on the test. Fail! You struck out when the bases were loaded. Fail! You dropped the dishes, and they broke all over the floor. Fail! You got grounded for fighting. Fail!

Stop that right now. When you call yourself a failure, you are calling God a liar. You act as if Jesus didn't actually win. Do you make mistakes? Absolutely. Did Jesus cover all of that when he died on a cross? He sure did. Because of Jesus' success, every day you get to know that God—your hero—saved you from eternal failure. Not only do you get to live in heaven forever with him, but he is happy because he gets to spend eternity with you! He loves you, he likes you, and he thinks you rock. You make him so happy that he wants to throw a party.

That's what you need to know today. Believe it. It's true.

Dear God,

sometimes I forget that I make you happy. You tell me that I do, though, and I know you don't lie. Thank you for being my hero, for making me special. Help me remember every day that you are with me, love me, and shout for joy because I'm yours. Amen.

Under attack

Before you start, get a piece of paper and write the word peirasthes *on it. It's pronounced like this:*

pie (as in rhubarb or pumpkin)

ras (rhymes with gas)

thas (rhymes with base)

"Watch yourself so that you also are not tempted"
(Galatians 6:1).

Pretending to be a pirate is fun. You can walk with a "peg leg"; say, "Argh, matey"; or wear an eye patch. Real pirates are terrifying, though. Throughout history, pirates have attacked boats, stolen treasure, and killed people. That's why boats had crow's nests; sailors used them as lookout points. Today pirates still sail the seas, taking what isn't theirs and holding people hostage. Nowadays ships pay armed guards to protect them from attacking pirates.

In today's passage, the Greek word for "tempt" is pronounced *peirasthes,* the word you wrote down. Now cross out the first e and the s, h, and other s.

What word is left? *Pirate.*

That's right, God is telling you to be careful so you aren't pirated. Pirates don't send you an e-mail, letting you know they are coming. You have to keep a lookout, spotting them while they are still a ways off. Temptation doesn't announce itself either. It sneaks up on you. Temptation leads to sin. Sin takes you hostage and hurts you.

Today, keep a lookout. Go into the crow's nest to watch. Patrol your life so you aren't pirated. Use the power of God to prevent an attack.

Chomp on this!

How can we keep a lookout for temptation?

How can we help each other watch out for attack?

Praying for Just enough

Do you dream of being rich—really, really rich? Who doesn't want a limousine and a mansion and a cook and a maid? Wouldn't the best part of life be to live in an awesome house with people who clean your room and make your food and drive you places?

A smart man named Agur, who lived about three thousand years ago, knew that being rich maybe wasn't the best idea in the world. In Proverbs 30:8, he wrote, **"Keep falsehood and lies far from me; give me neither poverty nor riches, but give me only my daily bread."**

Okay, first, don't we all understand the part where he prays, "God, please don't let me be poor"? Agur didn't want to break the Seventh Commandment and dishonor God. That we can all understand. I bet you pray that too.

Yet Agur also prayed not to be rich. That doesn't make sense. Why would he pray for only exactly what he needs each day? Well, he has a pretty good reason for that too: **"Otherwise, I may have too much and disown you and say, 'Who is the LORD?'"** (verse 9 NIV).

Having too much can distract you, and you forget to keep God at the center of your life. You start to think you have earned it or deserved it and forget that every single thing you have comes from God.

Dear God,

please help me tell the truth. Don't make me too poor; don't make me too rich. Give me only what I need so I remember that everything I have is a gift from you. Amen.

You wear Jesus' Jersey

"Clearly, all of you who were baptized in Christ's name have clothed yourselves with Christ" (Galatians 3:27).

For Spirit Week at school, everyone loves Team Day. That's the day you get to proudly declare which team is your favorite. Some kids choose jerseys from their favorite NBA teams, the ones with their favorite players' names on the back. Other kids wear their own soccer team's jerseys, the ones with their own names on the back.

The day you were baptized, you got your personalized heavenly jersey—with Jesus' name on the back. Maybe you can't see it, but God can. He sees Jesus' holiness that covers you completely. He sees your jersey and says, "That's my child!"

Other people see Jesus' jersey on you too. You let them know you're on his team by the words you choose, the attitude you have, and the kindness on your face. When you talk to them about the Brother who loved you so much that he was willing to die for you, you proudly declare whose team you're on.

Every week is Spirit Week when you're on Jesus' team.

 ## Chomp on this!

Have you been baptized? Ask your parents to tell you about it!

Dear Jesus,

thank you for making me part of your team and for giving me your jersey to wear. When you died for me, you set the standard for how teammates should act. Help me love and serve everyone on your team the way you love and serve me. Amen.

3, 2, 1...

The team is down by one point. There are 3.7 seconds left on the clock. The crowd holds its breath. The inbounds pass goes to the best shooter. The clock counts down—3, 2, 1...SWISH! A buzzer beater! The team runs onto the court to celebrate its victory. The stands clear as fans swarm the team.

What if you miss that shot, though? When the buzzer sounds and the ball bounces off the backboard but not through the net, your team loses. You don't get three more seconds to try again.

God says there is a clock running on your life too, but you don't know how much time is left. He tells you to **"seek the LORD while he may be found. Call on him while he is near. Let wicked people abandon their ways. Let evil people abandon their thoughts. Let them return to the LORD, and he will show compassion to them. Let them return to our God, because he will freely forgive them"** (Isaiah 55:6,7).

No one—not adults, not kids—knows, though, how much time is left on his or her personal board. Maybe it's 70 more years, but it could be just 70 more days. That's why—right now—God wants you to read his Word, trust in his forgiveness, and share the good news with the people around you. Do you have a friend or cousin who could use God's good news—right now? The clock is counting down. When the buzzer sounds, we'll swarm heaven's court and celebrate!

Dear Lord,

there are many people in the world who don't know about Jesus and what he has done for them. Use me to share Jesus' love with those around me. Amen.

Words do hurt

"Sticks and stones may break my bones, but words will never hurt me." Way back in 1862, this first appeared as a children's rhyme. That's right; over 150 years ago, kids were saying mean things to each other and the one being picked on tried to come up with a way to let the others know that it wasn't going to bug him.

When I was a kid (not 140 years ago), we'd bust out the phrase, "I'm rubber; you're glue. Whatever you say bounces off of me and sticks to you."

Each of those phrases is wrong, isn't it? Words do hurt. We just pretend they don't. Nobody likes to hear, "Nobody likes a know-it-all." Or "We don't want you to play with us at recess."

God knows that your heart will hurt because of other people. So he wants you to be part of a group that makes a difference. **"Don't say anything that would hurt another person. Instead, speak only what is good so that you can give help wherever it is needed. That way, what you say will help those who hear you"** (Ephesians 4:29).

You can practice building people up now: "Thanks for being a great friend." "Would you like some help with your homework?" "Hey, are you okay? Want to talk?" "That was really nice. Thanks!"

Dear Jesus,

sometimes I say things that aren't very nice or helpful. Please forgive me for those times and help me encourage others instead. Amen.

LOST all he had

King Nebuchadnezzar attacked Jerusalem. Not only did he kill people, but he robbed the temple and put the real God's things in the temple of a fake god in Babylon. But that wasn't enough for him.

"The king told Ashpenaz, the chief-of-staff, to bring some of the Israelites, the royal family, and the nobility. They were to be young men who were healthy, good-looking, knowledgeable in all subjects, well-informed, intelligent, and able to serve in the king's palace. They were to be taught the language and literature of the Babylonians" (Daniel 1:3,4).

These weren't just any random kids. They had to be the smartest in the class, the strongest, the ones willing to work hard, and they had to come from rich families. These were kids who had it all, until Nebuchadnezzar took them from their homes.

Daniel was one of the captives, along with his friends Hananiah, Mishael, and Azariah. Even though Daniel was offered the royal food, he knew that it was first offered up to false gods. He wouldn't go against his God's commands, even though the food was incredibly yummy. Instead, he asked for water and vegetables. (Can you even imagine?)

God saw their faithfulness and **"gave these four men knowledge, wisdom, and the ability to understand all kinds of literature. Daniel could also understand all kinds of visions and dreams"** (verse 17).

You will never be taken captive and carted off to be a servant in Babylon, but that doesn't mean you and Daniel have nothing in common. You know that no matter what you face, God will give you the wisdom to handle it—and to give him all the glory. Daniel—a kid who stayed faithful to God even when it was hard— was God's child, just like you are.

Don't worry; be happy

*Today let's **Dig In!** Read this section of Scripture, and then use the questions to talk about what God has to say in his Word.*

Always be joyful in the Lord! I'll say it again: Be joyful! Let everyone know how considerate you are. The Lord is near. Never worry about anything. But in every situation let God know what you need in prayers and requests while giving thanks. Then God's peace, which goes beyond anything we can imagine, will guard your thoughts and emotions through Christ Jesus.

Finally, brothers and sisters, keep your thoughts on whatever is right or deserves praise: things that are true, honorable, fair, pure, acceptable, or commendable. Practice what you've learned and received from me, what you heard and saw me do. Then the God who gives this peace will be with you. (Philippians 4:4-9)

Chomp on this!

What does God teach you in this passage?

What makes you say, "Thank you, Jesus"?

What makes you say, "I'm sorry, Jesus"?

Based on this reading, what would you like to ask God for?

March

Talking donkeys

Everybody loves Donkey from the movie *Shrek*. He's goofy, happy, and kind to Princess Fiona. The problem is that Donkey never stops talking! He talks so much it drives Shrek bananas, especially when he's trying to tell Shrek the truth.

Most people think talking donkeys are only in animated movies. Did you know that the Bible has a story of a real talking donkey? It sure does.

In Numbers chapter 22, the Bible tells of a prophet named Balaam who could be bribed to say just about anything, so a prince sent him to curse the Israelites. As Balaam traveled on his donkey, God was angry—nobody gets to curse his people—and sent a "Messenger of the LORD" to stop Balaam. The donkey could see the Messenger and refused to keep walking. This happened three times, and each time Balaam hit the donkey to get it to move.

"Then the LORD made the donkey speak, and it asked Balaam, 'What have I done to make you hit me three times?' Balaam answered, 'You've made a fool of me! If I had a sword in my hand, I'd kill you right now.' The donkey said to Balaam, 'I'm your own donkey. You've always ridden me. Have I ever done this to you before?' 'No,' he answered. Then the LORD let Balaam see the Messenger of the LORD who was standing in the road with his sword drawn. So Balaam knelt, bowing with his face touching the ground" (verses 28-31).

That's when God told Balaam, "Speak only what I tell you." And Balaam listened.

God's message is so important that he will do whatever it takes to make sure people understand—even once using a talking donkey to get a prophet to listen. You won't ever see a talking donkey (unless it's on TV, that is), but God is still serious about making sure people tell the truth about him and his Word.

I don't understand God

When you're learning a new concept in math, it can be so overwhelming. I mean, come on, dividing with remainders? Is that even a real thing? Sometimes, no matter how hard you try, it doesn't make sense. You want to scream, "I don't get it!"

Sometimes we want to yell "I don't get it!" when we're talking about God too. Paul, one of God's most famous pastors of all time, didn't always understand either. As he was writing to some believers who lived in Rome, he reminded them, **"God's riches, wisdom, and knowledge are so deep that it is impossible to explain his decisions or to understand his ways. 'Who knows how the Lord thinks? Who can become his adviser?' Who gave the Lord something which the Lord must pay back? Everything is from him and by him and for him. Glory belongs to him forever! Amen!"** (Romans 11:33-36).

When you look at God, it's okay to say, "I don't get it." How could God send his Son to die for me? How can his Son also be God? Why do I get the credit? How can God live in heaven but his Holy Spirit also lives inside of me?

Even when you know the answers, things still don't always make sense. That's why we trust that God has it all under control. His way of working is so much more awesome than our minds can even fathom. So we just trust and give him the glory.

Sometimes we still have questions. Our God has all the answers.

(You'll still have to figure out the math problem, though.)

Chomp on this!

What about God doesn't make sense to you?

Serve each other

**"If any one of you thinks you're important
when you're really not, you're only fooling yourself"**
(Galatians 6:3).

Over 250 years ago, during the Revolutionary War, three men were trying to lift a log into place. It was too heavy for them to lift, but instead of pitching in, their boss just kept telling them to try again. That's when a man rode in on his horse and said, "Why aren't you helping them." The boss said, "I am a corporal."

The man got off his horse and helped the men lift the log. The man, it turned out, was George Washington, the commander-in-chief, the boss of the whole army. The corporal was fooling himself. Washington, even though he was in charge of everyone, didn't think he was so important that he couldn't help out people "beneath" him.

This would be like three first graders trying to lift something as a fourth grader watches and tells them to simply try harder. He thinks he's too cool to help the little kids. All of a sudden the principal walks by and simply pitches in. The principal knows that even though he's in charge, he also gets to pitch in and help. The fourth grader is fooling himself.

If you think like the corporal or the fourth grader, you're fooling yourself too. Jesus simply loves every single person. People who love Jesus look around for ways to serve others. Help a classmate who dropped her books, volunteer to do the dishes, or pick up someone else's trash. Just as Jesus came to serve, we get to serve too.

God's command

Today is the only day of the whole year that has a command: March 4th. Get it, march . . . forth?

Did you groan? I don't blame you; that was a pretty dumb joke.

You do have a command for today, though, and this one might sound familiar: **"Jesus answered him, 'Love the Lord your God with all your heart, with all your soul, and with all your mind.' This is the greatest and most important commandment. The second is like it: 'Love your neighbor as you love yourself'"** (Matthew 22:37-39).

Some days when you're wondering how to live your life, Jesus has a pretty simple list:

1. Love God.
2. Love other people the way you care for yourself.

Those aren't dumb commands like my joke. In fact, Jesus' list is pretty awesome and pretty easy. It doesn't have to be confusing or hard. Today—and every day—God's command for us is to march forth . . . and love.

Chomp on this!

We love God because he loved us first. What characteristics of God did you love and appreciate most today—maybe his compassion or justice, his peace or his joy, his strength or his power?

Create your own prayer. Thank God for his love. Tell him what you love about him. Ask him for strength to love more people.

Tempted Just like you

**"We have a chief priest who is able to
sympathize with our weaknesses.
He was tempted in every way that we are,
but he didn't sin"**
(Hebrews 4:15).

"No one's looking, just take it."

"Who cares if your mom said no? She won't find out."

"Just hit him; he deserves it!"

Because Jesus was perfect, it doesn't seem like he had a hard time following God's rules. But he did. He was tempted in every way— just like you are.

His friends tried to get him to disobey Mary and Joseph. His brothers and sisters teased him. Satan came and talked to him personally, trying to get him to take up his power.

The only way his life was different is that he didn't give in. He didn't sin.

Jesus loves you so much that he was willing to be picked on, called names, and tempted. Knowing how hard is it to be tempted and still make the right choices means that Jesus is willing to help you face yours. **"Because Jesus experienced temptation when he suffered, he is able to help others when they are tempted"** (Hebrews 2:18).

Did you catch that? Jesus *suffered* when he was tempted. It wasn't easy for him to say no. Yet he did it anyway so that he could take your place on the cross. He knows what you're going through, and he is ready to help.

Chomp on this!

What temptations are you facing now?

Which one of your weaknesses do you need Jesus' help with?

Bigger than the Grand Canyon?

The Grand Canyon isn't just grand. It's ridiculously enormous. The national park covers 1.2 million acres, which probably doesn't mean anything to you, but that would be 19,200,000 tennis courts. Your mind can't even picture that can it? If you rode a raft down the Colorado River, which runs through the base of the Grand Canyon, it would take you two weeks to get through.

At its deepest point, the canyon is 6,000 feet to the top. That's over a mile. To get to the bottom and back takes two days.

How wide is it? At one point it is 18 miles across. You still can't really picture that, can you? A one-way trip from the North Rim to the South Rim would take you three days on foot.

Even describing how big it is still doesn't help you picture it, right? Our minds just can't comprehend something that big until we see it. Sounds a lot like God's love. You can't know or fathom God's love on your own. But when Christ lives in you, when you see God's love in a person, then you start to get it.

Ephesians 3:17-19 describes it: **"Then Christ will live in you through faith. I also pray that love may be the ground into which you sink your roots and on which you have your foundation. This way, with all of God's people you will be able to understand how wide, long, high, and deep his love is. You will know Christ's love, which goes far beyond any knowledge. I am praying this so that you may be completely filled with God."**

You have a Grand God.

He means YOU!

It's time for a grammar lesson. (Did I just hear you groan?) One of the earliest lessons you learn in English or language arts classes is the difference between singular and plural. Singular is one. Plural is more than one.

The confusion comes when the singular and plural word can be the same. Like the word *you*. If your teacher scans the entire room and says, "You need to take out your books," she means plural, everybody.

However, if you chose to ignore her command, she will look at you directly and say, "You need to take out your book." She means you, singular—and you know she means it.

When God told Moses to bless the Israelites, he used grammar very carefully.

He knew that if it looked like Moses was talking to the whole crowd, they might not pay quite as close of attention. That's why God told Moses to use the singular form of *you*. He wanted every single person in that crowd to know that God was looking into his or her eyes and speaking directly to that person.

"This is how you will bless the Israelites. Say to them: 'The Lord will bless you and watch over you. The Lord will smile on you and be kind to you. The Lord will look on you with favor and give you peace'" (Numbers 6:23-26).

When you hear these words, you know the Lord is looking into your eyes and talking to you. He wants you to know that he blesses *you*. He watches over *you*! He smiles on *you*! He is kind to *you*! He looks on *you*! He gives peace to *you*!

Let me hear you say, "Amen!"

Chomp on this!

Read the Bible passage out loud. Hear God saying these words directly to you.

Mistake free

**"Then [the Lord] will strengthen you to be holy.
Then you will be blameless in the presence of
our God and Father when our Lord Jesus comes
with all God's holy people"**
(1 Thessalonians 3:13).

Most kids think the worst part of writing workshop at school is editing and rewriting. Really, you just finished writing a paper and you think you're all done. Then the teacher tells you to edit it. You use a red pen to mark the spelling errors, use more descriptive words, and rewrite it. Okay, done. What? No? Now you need to proofread it and give it one last look to make sure it's perfect.

Believe it or not, some people actually think proofreading is fun. They like making sure that spelling and grammar are perfect before their work is finished. For some people, that's their entire job—making sure newspapers, magazines, and websites are perfect before they get published.

Just like spelling errors and grammar mistakes on your papers, sin leaves us with mistakes and errors in our lives. Unlike our papers, we can't correct the mistakes on our own. That's why Jesus came, to live perfectly for us. Now, even though we are sinful, when God looks at us, he only sees Jesus' perfect grade.

You are now blameless—mistake free—to God.

Dear Lord,

you give me the strength to be holy. Thank you for giving me the credit, for making me mistake free, for giving me Jesus' grade. Thank you that when it's my turn to go to heaven, you'll give me a perfect grade on my life. Amen.

Trying hard or hardly trying?*

When Michael Jordan was in high school, he tried out for the varsity basketball team his sophomore year. The coach felt he was too short, so he didn't make the team. Having to play junior varsity while another sophomore played varsity motivated him. He studied and trained hard to become the star on his team, giving it his all. Michael kept that attitude through college and made a game-winning jump shot for his team to win the championship. Then he made it into the NBA and is considered to be one of the best basketball players of all time.

When I was in fifth grade, I didn't try my hardest at school for the first part of the year. I didn't even care about my grades. Then something dawned on me. I changed my attitude to be more like 1 Corinthians 10:31: **"So, whether you eat or drink, or whatever you do, do everything to the glory of God."** I tried harder and used my God-given gifts to the fullest. I succeeded. My grades rose dramatically, and I realized how important it is to try my best in everything I do.

God doesn't care if you are the best, but he wants you to *do* your best. Use God's gifts to the best of your ability and give him all the credit, give him all the glory.

Chomp on this!

When have you not always given your best effort?

How does doing your best bring God glory?

Dear Lord,

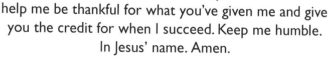

help me be thankful for what you've given me and give you the credit for when I succeed. Keep me humble. In Jesus' name. Amen.

This devotion was written by Calvin, a kid just like you.

God Just Is

God had an important job for Moses—to be the leader of God's plan to rescue the Israelites from slavery.

"Then Moses replied to God, 'Suppose I go to the people of Israel and say to them, "The God of your ancestors has sent me to you," and they ask me, "What is his name?" What should I tell them?' God answered Moses, 'I Am Who I Am. This is what you must say to the people of Israel: "I Am has sent me to you."' Again God said to Moses, 'This is what you must say to the people of Israel: The LORD God of your ancestors, the God of Abraham, Isaac, and Jacob, has sent me to you. This is my name forever. This is my title throughout every generation'" (Exodus 3:13-15).

Your God, who existed before he created the world, is the God who talked to Moses.

He is the same God who protected Noah and his family. He is the same God who protected Shadrach, Meshach, and Abednego in a fiery furnace. He is the Lord of your parents and grandparents. He is the same God who turned his back on Jesus on the cross so that he could turn his face to you. This is the I Am who watches over you. He works in your life to bring you closer to him. He will be the I Am when you grow up and have kids and teach them about I Am. He is the same I Am who will live with you forever in heaven.

You get to say with the angels, **"Holy, holy, holy is the Lord God Almighty, who was, who is, and who is coming"** (Revelation 4:8).

God is I Am.

Your Jesus is holy

Jesus was standing in an olive grove when a group of people came to arrest him.

"Jesus knew everything that was going to happen to him. So he went to meet them and asked, 'Who are you looking for?' They answered him, 'Jesus from Nazareth.' Jesus told them, 'I am he.' Judas, who betrayed him, was standing with the crowd. When Jesus told them, 'I am he,' the crowd backed away and fell to the ground" (John 18:4-6).

Yesterday we heard about the living God, whose name is I Am. Today we hear his Son, Jesus, say, "I am he."

The same Jesus who wanted little kids to run to him and hug him is the same Jesus whose words literally knocked people to the ground. He is holy and his voice, which is calm and soothing to you, is scary to those who fight against him. When the crowd came face-to-face with the real, living, holy, powerful Jesus, it knocked them off their feet. Yet they still refused to admit who he really is.

The next time Jesus is on this earth everyone is going to fall down, but there will be a different outcome. **"At the name of Jesus everyone in heaven, on earth, and in the world below will kneel and confess that Jesus Christ is Lord to the glory of God the Father"** (Philippians 2:10,11).

Dear Jesus,

you are all-powerful. Help me remember that you are always with me, watching over me. Amen.

Hosanna!

When Hurricane Katrina hit Louisiana in 2005, people who were trapped in their homes wrote "Help!" on their roofs. They wanted to be saved from the flooding. As soon as they saw the Coast Guard helicopters coming for them, they still yelled and waved. But this time, they yelled "Help! Help is here!" with a different tone. They could see their rescuers coming. They knew they were saved.

Back in the Old Testament days, the Israelites shouted, "Help!" The Hebrew word for it was *Ho-shi-ya na*. (Today we simply say, "Hosanna!") In Psalm 118, the Israelites shouted, **"We beg you, O Lord, save us!"** and then they recognized the source of their help: **"Blessed is the one who comes in the name of the Lord"** (verses 25, 26). They knew they needed saving from their enemies, and they also knew that they were saved because God delivered them.

Hoshiya na started off as a cry for help, but—just like those people who were trapped because of the hurricane saw the helicopters— the meaning changed: "Help is here! We're saved!" These were the same words that people shouted when Jesus rode into Jerusalem on a donkey. They knew they needed a Savior, and they saw that salvation had arrived.

You know you are sinful and need help. When you say *Hosanna*, you are telling Jesus, "Save me!" You also know, "Help is here! We're saved!"

 ## Chomp on this!
How has God helped you when you were feeling trapped?

Dear Jesus,
thank you for coming to *hoshiya na*, for coming to save us. We look at you and know that help has arrived. You are our salvation. Hosanna! Amen.

It's not a joke!

In a little while it's going to be time for Easter egg hunts. Wouldn't it be a cruel joke if every plastic egg you found was empty? I mean, you're expecting to find candy or money or something— anything!—and they give you NOTHING!

You'd start crying and asking your parents, "Where's my candy?"

If they said, "Surprise! We're going to Disney World!" you would stop crying immediately. That would be the best news to hear! You are smart enough to know that a trip there is way better than a chocolate bunny.

On Easter morning, Mary thought someone had played a cruel joke on her. She went to Jesus' tomb and found it was empty.

"She turned around and saw Jesus standing there. However, she didn't know that it was Jesus. Jesus asked her, 'Why are you crying? Who are you looking for?' Mary thought it was the gardener speaking to her. So she said to him, 'Sir, if you carried him away, tell me where you have put him, and I'll remove him.' Jesus said to her, 'Mary!' Mary turned around and said to him in Hebrew, 'Rabboni!' (This word means 'teacher.')" (John 20:14-16).

Mary's Jesus was alive. Your Jesus is alive. As you get ready for Easter, tell your friends and family about it. Tell them about Jesus' empty tomb. It's not a cruel joke. It's the best news you'll ever hear.

You're a new person!

*Today let's **Dig In!** Read this section of Scripture, and then use the questions to talk about what God has to say in his Word.*

Since you were brought back to life with Christ, focus on the things that are above—where Christ holds the highest position. Keep your mind on things above, not on worldly things. You have died, and your life is hidden with Christ in God. Christ is your life. When he appears, then you, too, will appear with him in glory.

Therefore, put to death whatever is worldly in you. . . . It is because of these sins that God's anger comes on those who refuse to obey him. You used to live that kind of sinful life. Also get rid of your anger, hot tempers, hatred, cursing, obscene language, and all similar sins. Don't lie to each other. You've gotten rid of the person you used to be and the life you used to live, and you've become a new person. This new person is continually renewed in knowledge to be like its Creator. (Colossians 3:1-10)

Chomp on this!

What does God teach you in this passage?

What makes you say, "Thank you, Jesus"?

What makes you say, "I'm sorry, Jesus"?

Based on this reading, what would you like to ask God for?

Decode the message

Tomorrow is John 3:16 Day—because it's 3-16. Have you ever seen people at football games holding up signs with John 3:16 written on them in big, bold letters? Tim Tebow, who played in the NFL, used to put John 3:16 in his eye black.

People who believe in Jesus and read the Bible know that reference really well, but what about two-thirds of the people in the world who are not Christians? Too many times believers speak a foreign language and the message we try to share sounds like blah, blah, blah to others.

Instead of making it a code for people to decipher, what if tomorrow we shared not only the numbers but also the actual message that **"God so loved the world that he gave his one and only Son, that whoever believes in him shall not perish but have eternal life"** (NIV)?

Tomorrow you could invite someone to go with you to church or Sunday school. You could share some of your favorite Christian music with your neighbor. E-mail or text your friends the Bible passage. Wish them a happy John 3:16 Day, and tell them what it's all about.

Chomp on this!

Make a list of other ways you can talk to people about Jesus and his love for them.

Dear God,

thank you for loving us so much that you were willing to give up Jesus, your Son, for us. Because of this love, we won't be separated from you forever. Instead, we get to go to heaven, where we'll be with you, in person, every day . . . forever. Amen.

No complaining!

Have you ever taken the No Complaining Challenge? For 24 hours you don't complain at all. Not even once. (You aren't even allowed to complain about not being able to complain.)

It's not easy. Our human nature loves to grumble. When the complaining gets too loud in my house, I often share what I Corinthians 10:10 says, **"And do not grumble, as some of them did—and were killed by the destroying angel"** (NIV). Did you even know that was in the Bible? It sure is. Let's be honest, though, keeping your mouth shut because you're terrified of a fierce angel isn't exactly why God wants you to not complain.

He gives you a better reason, the real reason, in Philippians 2:14-16: **"Do everything without complaining or arguing. Then you will be blameless and innocent. You will be God's children without any faults among people who are crooked and corrupt. You will shine like stars among them in the world as you hold firmly to the word of life."**

When you choose to be grateful, when you choose to live at peace with other people, you make a difference in this world. You shine like stars in the darkness. You let others know that being a Christian sets you apart from other people. It makes them want the same kind of joy that you have.

Your No Complaining Challenge starts today. Are you ready?

Dear Lord,

sometimes I forget just how blessed I am by you. It's then that I find myself complaining instead of being thankful. Help me remember that you promise to provide all that I need. Amen.

Establishing a new tradition

Today is St. Patrick's Day. It's the day when people who aren't Irish wish they were. Some people wear green. Others eat Irish food—including corned beef and cabbage and green Jell-O. Maybe you cut out little shamrocks for decorating. Those are super fun, even if they don't mean a whole lot.

The apostle Paul has a great suggestion for a meaningful tradition today: **"Brothers and sisters, imitate me, and pay attention to those who live by the example we have given you"** (Philippians 3:17). Today you can take note of Patrick, who, like green Jell-O, isn't actually Irish. Instead, he was a slave who escaped and eventually returned to Ireland as a missionary.

He once wrote, "After I arrived in Ireland, I tended sheep every day, and I prayed frequently during the day. More and more the love of God increased, and my sense of awe before God. Faith grew, and my spirit was moved, so that in one day I would pray up to one hundred times, and at night perhaps the same. I even remained in the woods and on the mountain, and I would rise to pray before dawn in snow and ice and rain."

This year, a great St. Patrick's Day tradition would be to imitate Patrick, to **"always be joyful. Never stop praying. Whatever happens, give thanks, because it is God's will in Christ Jesus that you do this"** (1 Thessalonians 5:16-18).

Chomp on this!

Make up your own prayer. Pray for the people whom God has put in your life, maybe who are hurting, lonely, or tired; people who are blessings to you or those who hurt you. Pray for courage to share your faith. Pray about the things that scare you or make you happy.

Build God's kingdom*

Do you play Minecraft? If you do, you know that it's all about breaking blocks and building things. When the game first came out, people built to protect themselves against nighttime monsters, but then people started using their imaginations to work together to build things. My favorite is Creative, where you get as much stuff as you need. You can fly, and you are never hungry or sick.

In God's version of Minecraft, he wants you to work together, not to build mansions, houses, or gardens, but to build his kingdom. Really! **"As a skilled and experienced builder, I used the gift that God gave me to lay the foundation for that building. However, someone else is building on it. Each person must be careful how he builds on it"** (1 Corinthians 3:10).

You might think it's a big job, but it really isn't. Just like in Creative, God gives us the stuff we need—even unlimited courage and joy—to spread his Word and build his kingdom.

While we build here, remember that Jesus is building a home in heaven for us where we will have everything we need. We will never be hungry or sick again.... We just won't be able to fly.

Chomp on this!

How old do you think you have to be to build God's kingdom?

How can you be creative and build God's kingdom with other people?

Dear Lord,

bless us as we build your kingdom. Amen.

*This devotion was written by Ben, a kid just like you.

Alive in Jesus

What are signs of spring where you live? In Northern California, spring means it stops raining. In North Dakota, the snow melts. In Arizona, baseball teams (and their fans) flock there for spring training. While everyone else is celebrating a fresh start during spring, Christians are thinking about death.

During Lent, believers spend a little more time realizing how huge of a deal their salvation is. Jesus lived. Jesus suffered. Jesus died. Did you know that during spring you could think about the part of you that is dead too?

"We know that our old self was crucified with him so that the body ruled by sin might be done away with, that we should no longer be slaves to sin—because anyone who has died has been set free from sin" (Romans 6:6,7 NIV).

When Jesus died on a cross, you were crucified too. All of your angry thoughts, sarcastic comments, hurtful words, and vicious actions were hung on that cross with him. Your old self, your body of sin, died and was buried with Jesus.

When Jesus rose from the dead, the new you came with him. True, while you are still alive, you will still sin, but it's no longer your identity. You now have eternal life. You are free.

Chomp on this!

Parents: Explain how a tulip bulb that stays dormant in the winter and then blooms into a new flower in spring is sort of like how we who were dead in sin became new and beautiful to God because of Jesus.

God and Frozen*

In the Disney movie *Frozen,* Elsa has magical ice powers that she keeps secret from her little sister, Anna. On Coronation Day, Elsa exposes her powers in front of everyone, sets off an eternal winter, and runs away to the mountains in fear that she might be a danger to everyone she loves. Anna, a courageous and determined girl, chases after her older sister to try and find her. She endures freezing snow, a giant ice monster, wolves, and a boyfriend who tries to kill her, but Anna never lets anything get in the way of finding her sister.

In some ways, Anna's love for Elsa is like God's love for us. God will never ever let anything come between us. Now that he sent Jesus in our place, we are part of God's royal family. In Romans 8:38,39, there's a long list of things that will never separate us from the love of God: **"I am convinced that neither death nor life, neither angels nor demons, neither the present nor future, nor any powers, neither height nor depth, nor anything else in all creation, will be able to separate us from the love of God that is in Christ Jesus"** (NIV).

God loves us with all our flaws, just like Anna still loved Elsa even though she ran away. God turned our frozen, sinful hearts into warm, loving hearts that want to serve and praise him. Now nothing will ever keep us from his love. No matter what.

Dear God,

we know you will never leave us nor forsake us. Please help us always remember this so we know we never walk alone. In Jesus' name we pray. Amen.

*This devotion was written by Claire, a kid just like you.

You Stink!

I bet you didn't know that today is National Fragrance Day. Yep, there's actually a day that celebrates your sense of smell. Immediately, I bet you thought of the good smells: flowers, apple pie, and bacon. Nobody wants to think about smelling the stinky stuff—skunks, garbage, and brussels sprouts.

Believers have a fragrance too. **"But I thank God, who always leads us in victory because of Christ. Wherever we go, God uses us to make clear what it means to know Christ. It's like a fragrance that fills the air. To God we are the aroma of Christ among those who are saved and among those who are dying. To some people we are a deadly fragrance, while to others we are a life-giving fragrance"** (2 Corinthians 2:14-16).

To other believers, you smell great. Just like the smell of pizza makes you happy, as part of God's family, your presence cheers up the people around you. Your encouragement and joy are all around.

However, you are as stinky as a skunk to people who don't believe in Jesus. Now, nobody wants to be the stinky kid, but the truth is that Jesus' teachings offend them. They want to hold their noses. Because you believe what Jesus said, you are just as smelly.

Today, go celebrate your stinkiness in Christ!

 ## Chomp on this!

How can you spread the life-giving smell to the people you know?

What are some ways you can handle it if people are offended by your faith? If they think you stink?

Serving God no matter what

Joseph was 17.

He let his dad know when his brothers made bad choices. (How do you feel when someone tattles on you?) Then he had a dream that his brothers bowed down to him. (Now imagine bowing down to *your* brother?) The brothers wanted to kill him, but instead they sold him to slave traders who took him 500 miles away to Egypt.

"The Lord was with Joseph, so he became a successful man. He worked in the house of his Egyptian master. Joseph's master saw that the Lord was with him and that the Lord made everything he did successful. Potiphar liked Joseph so much that he made him his trusted servant. He put him in charge of his household and everything he owned" (Genesis 39:2-4).

Isn't that passage a surprise? I might have expected to read, "Joseph was crabby. He complained about how unfair it was that he had been the favorite son but was sold by his brothers and now was a slave." Instead, he had the character to do his best. The Lord was with him and blessed him. And not only did he bless Joseph; he blessed Potiphar's house too. No matter where you are, you too can work with the same dedication, knowing that God is always with you and blesses you.

Joseph—who had the Lord on his side—was God's child, just like you are.

 ## Chomp on this!

Read the whole story of Joseph being sold in Genesis chapter 37.

It's Just a Costume

When you watch *Scooby-Doo*, don't you wonder how Fred, Daphne, Velma, Shaggy, and Scooby never ever catch on that the bad guy is always, always the caretaker who seems to look like a good guy? Seriously, you almost want to scream at the TV, "Pay attention! It's just a costume! He's trying to fool you!" Every single episode we can see who the bad guy is, but the crime-fighting friends can't. You'd think they'd learn.

About two thousand years ago, the apostle Paul warned people in the church to be careful of false prophets, of evil caretakers, of Satan himself. Some people were teaching things that weren't in the Bible. They were fooling people and leading them away from God, instead of bringing them closer to him. **"They are dishonest workers, since they disguise themselves as Christ's apostles. And no wonder, even Satan disguises himself as an angel of light. So it's not surprising if his servants also disguise themselves as servants who have God's approval. In the end they will get what they deserve"** (2 Corinthians 11:13-15).

Satan and those who follow him will do whatever it takes to make sure that you are fooled. They will sometimes appear to be kind and helpful, when really they are lying to you. So pay attention. Read your Bible. Know what God's Word says so that you can tell the difference between God's light and Satan's darkness in a light costume. Hang out with friends who will encourage you to make good choices, who when you're thinking of giving in to Satan's nice-sounding lies will tell you, "Pay attention! He's trying to fool you!"

Only nine months til Christmas!

"The angel went to a virgin promised in marriage
to a descendant of David named Joseph.
The virgin's name was Mary.
When the angel entered her home,
he greeted her and said,
'You are favored by the Lord! The Lord is with you.'
She was startled by what the angel said and tried
to figure out what this greeting meant.
The angel told her, 'Don't be afraid, Mary.
You have found favor with God.
You will become pregnant, give birth to a son,
and name him Jesus. He will be a great man
and will be called the Son of the Most High.
The Lord God will give him the throne of his ancestor
David. Your son will be king of Jacob's people forever,
and his kingdom will never end'"
(Luke 1:27-33).

Why are we talking about Christmas in March? Well, because nine months from today is Christmas Eve. Nine months before Jesus was born, the angel Gabriel appeared to Mary to tell her that she was going to have a baby, not just any baby. Her baby would be the Son of God and the King for forever.

That's why today is a good day to remember that not only did Jesus come once, but also when the time is right, he is coming again. This time to take you home to heaven.

"Look, I am coming soon! My reward is with me, and I will give to each person according to what they have done. I am the Alpha and the Omega, the First and the Last, the Beginning and the End. Blessed are those who wash their robes, that they may have the right to the tree of life and may go through the gates into the city" (Revelation 22:12-14 NIV).

You win!

Almost everybody knows the sign for "Loser." You make the letter L with your left thumb and index finger and then stick the back of your hand against your forehead.

Satan is constantly hissing at you, "Loser! Loser! Loser!"

You miss a basket. Loser!

You failed the science test. Loser!

You don't dress like all the other kids. Loser!

Stop it! Stop it! Stop it!

You are a winner! **"Everyone who has been born from God has won the victory over the world. Our faith is what wins the victory over the world. Who wins the victory over the world? Isn't it the person who believes that Jesus is the Son of God?"** (1 John 5:4,5).

When Jesus defeated death, you were declared—once and for all—a winner. You get to take Jesus' victory and make it your own.

Whenever you hear someone hissing, "Loser!" remember that Jesus has shouted, "Winner!"

Listen to what John has to say: **"I've written to you, young people, because you are strong and God's word lives in you. You have won the victory over the evil one"** (1 John 2:14).

Winner! Winner! Winner!

Dear Jesus,

thank you for making me a winner because of what you did for me. This world is temporary, and your victory lasts forever. When Satan tries to tell me that I'm a loser, remind me that you make me strong and that your Father's Word lives in me. I win. Satan loses. Thank you! Amen.

The clothes you wear

What name is on your clothes? Some kids want to wear designer clothes because they believe it makes them cool. They believe that having a specific name that's prominently displayed across the front (or the back) of you, makes you more valuable. Designers don't mind because putting their names all over their clothes means you are a walking billboard for them. Not only did you pay for that shirt, but you now tell others about them. No matter what, though, those clothes aren't going to last. You are going to either grow out of them, get tired of them and give them away, or wear them so thin that they will need to be thrown out.

God has clothes that last. He wants you to put them on and be a walking billboard for him. **"Therefore, as God's chosen people, holy and dearly loved, clothe yourselves with compassion, kindness, humility, gentleness and patience"** (Colossians 3:12 NIV).

You have been chosen by your Designer. His love is what makes you holy, makes you "cool" in his eyes. You begin to care more about his clothes on the inside and care less about what you wear on the outside. Your actions—controlling your temper, resisting the urge to be sarcastic, saying "Yes, Dad" when he asks for help—make it obvious that you are wearing Jesus' clothes. When you live like this, you won't even need "Jesus" written on your shirt. People will simply know.

Chomp on this!

Think of some examples of how you can be a walking billboard for Jesus at school, at home, at sports practice, and on the playground.

I believe, but I don't believe

"A man in the crowd answered,
'Teacher, I brought you my son.
He is possessed by a spirit that won't let him talk.
Whenever the spirit brings on a seizure,
it throws him to the ground. Then he foams at the mouth,
grinds his teeth, and becomes exhausted.' ...
Jesus asked his father, 'How long has he been like this?'
The father replied, 'He has been this way since
he was a child. The demon has often thrown him into fire
or into water to destroy him. If it's possible
for you, put yourself in our place, and help us!'
Jesus said to him, 'As far as possibilities go,
everything is possible for the person who believes.'
The child's father cried out at once, 'I believe!
Help my lack of faith'"
(Mark 9:17,18,21-24).

Those last couple of sentences are confusing, aren't they? The dad said, "I believe." Then he immediately added, "But I have a lack of faith." How could he believe and not believe all at the same time?

Wait, aren't we kind of like that dad? When you think about your faith, I bet you believe and have a lack of faith all at the same time too.

You believe God is real, yet because you can't see him, you wonder if he's really there. You believe that Jesus took away your sins, yet you still don't feel loved. You know the Holy Spirit lives inside of you, but you are afraid to share your faith because you don't want people to think you're a dork.

How does Jesus help you overcome your lack of faith? Read your Bible to see what your Jesus has done for you. Read it again and again. Pray for a stronger faith, for wisdom to believe God's plan, and for courage to stand against Satan—who wants you to not believe at all.

On the mat

When you walk onto a wrestling mat, your whole goal is to put the other person on his back and hold him there—to pin him. To make it a fair fight, you are matched up against an opponent who is about your age, about the same experience level, or who weighs the same as you. Still, on the mat, it's just you against the other person.

That's great for wrestling. How often, though, do we go into the world thinking we are up against other people? Maybe it's the kids you don't get along with at school. Maybe it's the kid on the other basketball team who seems to be cheating and getting away with it. Maybe it's someone in your own family.

Our God has a different idea. He tells us that **"this is not a wrestling match against a human opponent. We are wrestling with rulers, authorities, the powers who govern this world of darkness, and spiritual forces that control evil in the heavenly world"** (Ephesians 6:12).

We minimize Satan's existence. We aren't comfortable talking about evil spirits or demons, so we pretend they don't exist. We blame our earthly struggles on the people around us. We forget that the devil is the mastermind, the father of lies, the enemy.

Today, as you step onto the mat, remember who your real enemy is. Remember too that you've already won. Not because of what you've done, but because God **"stripped the rulers and authorities of their power and made a public spectacle of them as he celebrated his victory in Christ"** (Colossians 2:15).

God's strange memory

Without thinking too hard, I bet you can remember a time when you were insulted. Maybe someone called you stupid or ugly or a know-it-all or four eyes. It takes a little more effort to remember a time when someone was kind—and you believed it. The bad stuff gets burned into our minds, and we forget all the compliments. That's how human memory works.

That's why I'm glad God's memory works the exact opposite of ours. King David asked, **"Remember, O LORD, your compassionate and merciful deeds. They have existed from eternity. Do not remember the sins of my youth or my rebellious ways. Remember me, O LORD, in keeping with your mercy and your goodness"** (Psalm 25:7).

Because he sees all of our sins and can even see inside our sinful hearts, you'd think those memories would be burned into God's mind. Instead, because he sent Jesus to pay for the times you break his laws, God chooses to say, "Sins? What sins? I don't see any sins."

Thanks to Jesus, God cannot forget who he is and what he has done for his people. He cannot forget that he is kind and compassionate.

Dear God,

you have always been compassionate and merciful. When you look at me every day, remember what Jesus has done for me and look at me with your favor. Also, please forget my sins, the ones I do when I am foolish and rebellious. You are God and you know everything, so thank you for choosing to not make me pay for my sins. Amen.

Live God's way

*Today let's **Dig In!** Read this section of Scripture, and then use the questions to talk about what God has to say in his Word.*

As holy people whom God has chosen and loved, be sympathetic, kind, humble, gentle, and patient. Put up with each other, and forgive each other if anyone has a complaint. Forgive as the Lord forgave you. Above all, be loving. This ties everything together perfectly. Also, let Christ's peace control you. God has called you into this peace by bringing you into one body. Be thankful. Let Christ's word with all its wisdom and richness live in you. Use psalms, hymns, and spiritual songs to teach and instruct yourselves about God's kindness. Sing to God in your hearts. Everything you say or do should be done in the name of the Lord Jesus, giving thanks to God the Father through him. (Colossians 3:12-17)

Chomp on this!

What does God teach you in this passage?

What makes you say, "Thank you, Jesus"?

What makes you say, "I'm sorry, Jesus"?

Based on this reading, what would you like to ask God for?

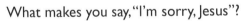

God runs to you

You really messed up big time. (You know what I'm talking about.) You actually were sick to your stomach because you felt so guilty. About then, all you wanted to do was hide in your room to avoid the shame.

There's a kid in the Bible who knows what that's like. He's known as the prodigal son. (I don't think God told us his real name so we could all put our names in the story.) He had completely offended his dad, insulted him, and left home. When he was done being foolish, he realized just how awful he had acted and was sick-to-his-stomach guilty.

"So he went at once to his father. While he was still at a distance, his father saw him and felt sorry for him. He ran to his son, put his arms around him, and kissed him. Then his son said to him, 'Father, I've sinned against heaven and you. I don't deserve to be called your son anymore'" (Luke 15:20,21).

Did the dad say, "You're right. It's good to see you, but you need to leave now"? Nope. He threw a party! His lost child had come home.

That's how forgiveness with God is. Don't hide in your room with your guilt. (God can see you in there anyway, you know.) As you go to him to tell him how sorry you are, you'll see him feel compassion for you. He'll come running to hug you and welcome you back.

Chomp on this!

Read the whole story of the prodigal son in Luke 15:11-32.

Dear God,

it amazes me that when I come to you sad, guilty, and embarrassed because of my sin, you don't yell at me. Thanks to Jesus putting me at peace with you, you have been looking for me, you run to me, hug me, and tell me how happy you are that I am back. Thank you. Amen.

April Fools' Day

Your shoelace is untied.

There's a spider on you!

Let me get the "sugar" for you.

Today is all sorts of fun for kids—and adults—who like to pull pranks. It can be super fun to trick someone and then shout, "April Fools'!"

People who study history have found that April Fools' pranks were already a tradition in Europe over three hundred years ago.

One day of fun is, well, fun. Living your whole life as a fool is, well, foolish. King Solomon, the wisest man who ever lived, tells you how to *not* be a fool: **"The fear of the LORD is the beginning of knowledge. Stubborn fools despise wisdom and discipline. My son, listen to your father's discipline, and do not neglect your mother's teachings, because discipline and teachings are a graceful garland on your head and a golden chain around your neck"** (Proverbs 1:7-9).

Start by learning how to obey God and listen to your parents. When you turn away from them, **"the parent of a *fool* has grief, and the father of a godless *fool* has no joy"** (Proverbs 17:21). That is no joke.

 Chomp on this!

Do you like April Fools' Day? What is your favorite trick? If you don't like it, tell us why.

What are some of the foolish ways we live? How do we act like fools to God?

Never alone*

My fifth-grade class read *Hatchet*. When Brian Robeson, a 13-year-old boy, gets stranded in the Canadian wilderness with nothing but his hatchet, he feels completely alone. The pilot that was supposed to take him to visit his dad was killed in a plane crash. Brian was injured by a porcupine, attacked by a moose, hit by a tornado, and missed the rescue plane that was supposed to take him to safety. Brian felt completely alone.

There are times in life when you may feel like you have crashed and are left alone, when you think there is nobody there to listen to you or talk to you. When you feel injured by your friends, attacked by Satan, hit by troubles, and there is no rescue plane in sight, you feel very alone.

In Psalm 23:4, God reminds us that **"even though** [we] **walk through the dark valley of death, because you are with** [us], [we] **fear no harm. Your rod and your staff give** [us] **courage."** Just like Brian always had his hatchet, we need to remember that God is always with us—even when we feel alone.

Chomp on this!

When have you felt alone?

How can you use today's passage to help you when you feel alone in the future? Maybe write it on a mirror with a dry erase marker or keep it on a note in your lunch bag.

Dear God,

thank you for always being with us so that we don't need to feel alone. In your name we pray. Amen.

This devotion was written by Emma, a kid just like you.

Becoming poor

So far the largest lottery ever won was for $656 million. What in the world would you do with $656 million? Would you get a limo? buy a mansion? buy all the candy in the world? get a huge pool and throw a party for your entire school?

What if you decided to give it all away? If all that money is yours and you say, "No thank you. I'll give it to someone else." Every. Single. Penny. Oh, and on top of that, you give away everything else you had before you won too. Does that sound too extreme?

That's what Jesus did. **"You know about the kindness of our Lord Jesus Christ. He was rich, yet for your sake he became poor in order to make you rich through his poverty"** (2 Corinthians 8:9).

Jesus had everything, all the glory in heaven with the Father. He was willing to give that all away because you are that important to him. He couldn't stand the thought that you would be separated from him forever in hell, so he lived for you, suffered for you, and rose again for you. You have now won the biggest spiritual lottery ever.

Jesus became poor so you would become rich. Thank you, Jesus!

Dear Jesus,

when we read the Bible, over and over we see your kindness. You were willing to give up all the riches in heaven so you could be treated miserably and horribly for us. You gave us your winning lottery ticket—the entrance to heaven. There aren't enough words to tell you just how thankful we are. Amen.

Rooted in God's love

"This is the reason I kneel in the presence of the Father from whom all the family in heaven and on earth receives its name. I'm asking God to give you a gift from the wealth of his glory. I pray that he would give you inner strength and power through his Spirit. Then Christ will live in you through faith. I also pray that love may be the ground into which you sink your roots and on which you have your foundation" (Ephesians 3:14-17).

When we lived in California, we planted some trees in the fall. They were small, and the roots hadn't really gotten established. The first time the winter rains and wind came, the trees started to fall over. We ran outside in the middle of a downpour to tie the trees to stakes and fences to help them stand up tall and straight.

You are still small too, and God wants you to be planted in his love. Putting your roots in his love helps you grow up tall and strong. Then when temptation and troubles and sadness come, you won't fall over. Instead, you can weather any storm because you are rooted in him.

Dear God,

I kneel before you as your child. You have so much glory and power and strength that you gladly share it with us—because you always have more. With the Holy Spirit living inside of us, please give us his strength and power to live lives of faith, to always show that we believe in Jesus. Help us plant ourselves firmly in your love so we aren't weak and fall over when problems come. Amen.

Do not worry!*

Do you worry? If you worry, I am very much like you. I worry about simple things, like what I look like. I worry about high school and how many friends I will have or if I will make the volleyball team. I also worry about bigger things like my faith. Will others judge me for my faith? Or what if someone asks me to defend my faith, will I mess up and not know what to do? The list could go on forever!

In Matthew 6:31-34 God reminds me not to worry: **"Don't ever worry and say, 'What are we going to eat?' or 'What are we going to drink?' or 'What are we going to wear?' Everyone is concerned about these things, and your heavenly Father certainly knows you need all of them. But first, be concerned about his kingdom and what has his approval. Then all these things will be provided for you. So don't ever worry about tomorrow. After all, tomorrow will worry about itself. Each day has enough trouble of its own."**

He says we should not worry about little things such as what we will wear, what we will eat, or what we will drink. We also don't need to worry about where we will spend eternity. And he will give us the words we need to tell others about our faith too. Share the good news so other people don't have to worry either.

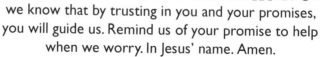

Dear wonderful Father in heaven,
we know that by trusting in you and your promises, you will guide us. Remind us of your promise to help when we worry. In Jesus' name. Amen.

This devotion was written by Kamryn, a kid just like you.

Stay on the path

At Yellowstone National Park's West Thumb Geyser Basin, you'll see all sorts of hot springs, geysers, and pools. With names like Blue Funnel, Abyss, Perforated Pool, and Percolating Spring, these pools are bright blue with rainbow edges.

As much as you'd like to explore these up close, signs everywhere warn you to stay on the boardwalk. That's because throughout Yellowstone, people have died because they left the path.

The pools look so warm that you want to jump in for a swim, but the temperature can get so hot that the water is almost boiling. You'd suffer horrible burns or even die just by falling in there. Walking to the pool could hurt you too. Though the ground may look solid, it is simply a crust. If you step on it, you could break through and be burned by the scalding hot water underneath. That's why they have the walkway. It saves lives.

Sin works the same way as those inviting pools. Sometimes it looks warm, like it would be fun to dip your toe in and take a swim. It feels good to give in to your anger and hit someone. Sometimes it feels good to put others down. Maybe it feels good to get an A, even though you got it by cheating. But sin should actually make you afraid. **"Blessed is the one who is always fearful of sin, but whoever is hard-hearted falls into disaster"** (Proverbs 28:14).

That's why God tells you to stay on his walkway, follow his guidance. He will get you safely through the dangerous areas of life. **"You will hear a voice behind you saying, 'This is the way. Follow it, whether it turns to the right or to the left'"** (Isaiah 30:21).

Stay on the path.

April 7

Help Others and Don't Give Up

*Today let's **Dig In!** Read this section of Scripture, and then use the questions to talk about what God has to say in his Word.*

Brothers and sisters, if a person gets trapped by wrongdoing, those of you who are spiritual should help that person turn away from doing wrong. Do it in a gentle way. At the same time watch yourself so that you also are not tempted. Help carry each other's burdens. In this way you will follow Christ's teachings. So if any one of you thinks you're important when you're really not, you're only fooling yourself.

Make no mistake about this: You can never make a fool out of God. Whatever you plant is what you'll harvest. If you plant in the soil of your corrupt nature, you will harvest destruction. But if you plant in the soil of your spiritual nature, you will harvest everlasting life. We can't allow ourselves to get tired of living the right way. Certainly, each of us will receive everlasting life at the proper time, if we don't give up. Whenever we have the opportunity, we have to do what is good for everyone, especially for the family of believers. (Galatians 6:1-3,7-10)

 ## Chomp On this!

What does God teach you in this passage?

What makes you say, "Thank you, Jesus"?

What makes you say, "I'm sorry, Jesus"?

Based on this reading, what would you like to ask God for?

Your archnemesis

Every good story tells of the battle of good versus evil. Every hero has to face an archnemesis. In *The Lion, the Witch and the Wardrobe*, Peter, Susan, Edmund, and Lucy Pevensie face off against the White Witch. Batman fights against the Joker. The whole family of Incredibles teams up to handle Syndrome. Gru and his minions battle Vector.

In real life you face an archenemy too. Our God tells you that **"our struggle is not against flesh and blood, but against the rulers, against the authorities, against the powers of this dark world and against the spiritual forces of evil in the heavenly realms"** (Ephesians 6:12 NIV).

It's you versus Satan and his whole team of evil minions. Sometimes we pretend like Satan, evil spirits, and demons don't exist. We blame our earthly struggles on the kid who calls us fat or on the teachers who treat us unfairly or on our parents for making our lives so miserable or on the neighbors who hate kids. We forget that the devil is the mastermind, the father of lies, the enemy.

Every good story also ends with good winning over evil, of every hero defeating the villain. The only difference in your story is that Jesus fought the battle in your place. Jesus won when he **"stripped the rulers and authorities of their power and made a public spectacle of them as he celebrated his victory in Christ"** (Colossians 2:15).

Thanks to Jesus, good wins. God wins.

For Such a time as this

Esther's parents were both dead, and she had been adopted by her cousin Mordecai.

When King Xerxes wanted to pick a new queen, he ordered that young women from all over the kingdom be brought to him. Esther was young and beautiful and didn't have a choice; she had to go.

The King loved Esther and made her queen, but he didn't know she was a Jew. Not too much later, one of Xerxes' servants, Haman, tricked him into declaring that all Jews should be killed.

"Mordecai sent this answer back to Esther, 'Do not imagine that just because you are in the king's palace you will be any safer than all the rest of the Jews. The fact is, even if you remain silent now, someone else will help and rescue the Jews, but you and your relatives will die. And who knows, you may have gained your royal position for a time like this'" (Esther 4:13,14).

Mordecai was right. Esther used her position as queen to plead for her people—and they lived. No one could have seen that coming. First an orphan, then a captive—and yet God made her royalty.

If you've had a rough beginning in life, God has plans for you. He'll use you to accomplish great things for him.

Esther—an orphan who was used by God to save his people—was God's child, just like you are.

God works for you

"I don't know why my dad lost his job."

"I don't know why I have ADHD."

"I don't know why we had to move again."

"I don't know why our house got robbed."

There's so much you don't know. There's so much adults don't know either. There is one thing you do know, for absolute certain: **"We know that all things work together for the good of those who love God—those whom he has called according to his plan"** (Romans 8:28).

You know . . . in all things God cares. He pays attention to every little thing, to every big thing, *to every single thing.*

You know . . . God works. He is active in your life. He's not just watching from above; he is busy making things happen.

You know . . . it's for your good. He uses the happy times and the sad times to help your faith grow.

You know . . . you are called. He chose you, he handpicked you, and he absolutely wants you in his family.

You know . . . he has a plan. He saved you, he brings you closer to Jesus, you live for him, and you bring him glory. You spend forever in heaven with him. That's the plan.

Even as you wonder about all the things you don't know, isn't it awesome to realize just how much you *do* know?

Redeemed

You have your eye on that giant prize behind the counter—and you will do whatever it takes to get it. You run around playing arcade games and gathering fistfuls of tickets because you know just how much it takes for that prize to be yours. When you're done, you start looking for the giant ticket chomper that says, "Redeem tickets here!" You have to turn in your tickets to take the huge prize behind the counter home.

Jesus had his eye on you and was determined to do whatever it took to get you. So **"when the set time had fully come, God sent his Son, born of a woman, born under the law, to redeem those under the law"** (Galatians 4:4,5 NIV).

Jesus became a human and followed every single one of God's rules—the law—so that he could redeem you. When he died on a cross for you, he defeated death. He pointed to you saying, "I want that one. That's the prize I've been living for." He turned in his life so he could take you home.

Now you get to say, **"I know that my redeemer lives, and that in the end he will stand on the earth"** (Job 19:25 NIV).

Dear Jesus,

thank you for redeeming me. You kept your eye on me the whole time you were following God's rules. You lived the life I couldn't and took the punishment that I deserved. Thank you for wanting me to go home to heaven with you. Amen.

Love your grandparents

Grandparents make it easy to love them. Grandpas have all the time in the world to take you fishing or to ball games. Grandmas happily sneak you a fourth chocolate chip cookie when your mom isn't looking. When they spoil you the way they never even dreamed to spoil your parents, it's easy to follow God's command to **"show respect to the elderly, and honor older people. In this way you show respect for your God. I am the LORD"** (Leviticus 19:32).

The problem comes when you say, "You're the best!" only because they do nice things for you. What about when grandparents have to tell you, "No, I won't buy that for you" or "You may not talk to me with that tone of voice"? What about when grandparents get older and they start forgetting things, maybe even forgetting your name?

God doesn't say, "Show respect only when it's easy." He says, "Show respect." When you put down your iPod and talk to them, when you sing for them in the nursing home, when you ask them about their childhoods, you honor them. When you honor them, you show that you honor your God.

 Chomp on this!

What are some ways that you can honor your grandparents?

What are ways we can show respect to elderly people, even to people we don't know?

Dear God,

thanks for my grandparents. Forgive me when I think I'm cooler or better than they are. Forgive me when I don't make time to talk to them. Help me show respect, ask questions, and love them even more. Amen.

You are God's minion

In *Despicable Me 2*, the evil El Macho keeps kidnapping Gru's minions. These hilarious yellow minions turn into evil purple mutants when they get the PX-41 serum. They become wild, destructive, indestructible, and terrifying monsters. They are doomed. There is no escape. Until their boss, Gru, comes on a rescue mission with the antidote.

When God created Adam and Eve, they were his yellow minions. When Satan, the ultimate El Macho, tempted Adam and Eve to sin, they became his evil purple mutants. Every human since then has PX-41 serum in his or her blood. We are wild, aggressive, and sinful. In Psalm 51:5, David wrote, **"Indeed, I was born guilty. I was a sinner when my mother conceived me."**

The same way the minions couldn't stop being evil on their own, there was nothing you could do to rescue yourself. So God, your boss, sent Jesus on a rescue mission. His blood on the cross is your antidote.

"At the same time we can expect what we hope for—the appearance of the glory of our great God and Savior, Jesus Christ. He gave himself for us to set us free from every sin and to cleanse us so that we can be his special people who are enthusiastic about doing good things" (Titus 2:13,14).

You are not under El Macho's control. You are no longer a purple minion. Jesus came and set you free. You have hope. You are free to be God's minion.

Jesus erased our sins

Joseph Priestley had a lot of jobs. He was a pastor, teacher, politician, philosopher, and chemist. I'm fairly certain you have never heard of him; however, almost every day you use something he invented.

In 1770 Joseph Priestley invented a vegetable gum, called it "rubber," and used it to remove pencil marks. That's right, almost 250 years ago, the eraser was invented. Tomorrow is National Rubber Eraser Day, a holiday that celebrates the invention that allows you to correct your math homework.

Every single day we get to remember that Jesus is our eraser, who wiped our sins away. Two thousand years ago Jesus died for us and came back to life. By doing that he took the punishment we should have gotten. Now we know that **"as far as the east is from the west—that is how far he has removed our rebellious acts from himself"** (Psalm 103:12). He erased our punishment and the record of every single one of our sins.

That's not it, though. What's cool is that we also get the prize we didn't earn. And this one involves NOT erasing anything. **"Everyone who wins the victory this way will wear white clothes. I will never erase their names from the Book of Life. I will acknowledge them in the presence of my Father and his angels"** (Revelation 3:5).

Your sins have been erased, but your name never will be. I love how our God works!

Dear God,

thank you that because Jesus erased my sins, you won't erase my name from the list of people in your family, from the book that gives me my ticket into heaven. Amen.

A new view on taxes

My sweet child was ready to walk up to the register, a crumpled bill clutched in a still-chubby fist and a pack of gum proudly held in the other. That's when I had to break the news: "You don't actually have enough money."

"It says $1, and I have $1," the preschooler replied.

"I know," I said sympathetically, "but you don't have enough for tax."

Today, in the United States, is the day that taxes are due. Maybe you've heard your parents talking about it. Jesus talked to the Pharisees about taxes too. Some of them had come to him asking if people should pay taxes, that's when **"Jesus said to them, 'Give the emperor what belongs to the emperor, and give God what belongs to God'"** (Mark 12:17).

Taxes are the way that we pay for our city, state, and nation's services. If your house is on fire, you'd be thankful for the fire truck that races to help. We drive to friends' homes safely because of the roads our government maintains. You don't have to buy books because you can go to the library and read books that taxes already paid for. Taxes also pay for the soldiers who serve to keep your family safe.

Today, as you hear about taxes, remember to pray for our leaders, that they serve our community well and use money wisely. Pray also that we remember that the money in our pockets is a gift from God. Pray that we use his money wisely and serve his people well too.

A dangerous job

As you think about being an adult, what jobs sound cool? Some kids dream of being fighter pilots. Others love math so much that they want to be engineers or scientists. Maybe you dream of being an artist—even though artists rarely make much money. It seems that at some point every kid considers being a veterinarian, mainly because puppies and kittens are so cute. As you hear people talk about those jobs, they all sound amazing.

When Jesus picked 72 people to do a job for him, he said, **"Go! I'm sending you out like lambs among wolves"** (Luke 10:3). Do you think they said, "Um, Jesus, thanks for the offer, but being weak and defenseless when people try to tear us apart sounds pretty dangerous. We're going to go home and be professional ice cream tasters." Nope. They went from town to town and did what Jesus said.

As you grow up, no matter what job you decide to do, your main career is to be a disciple, a student, of Jesus. You will learn from him and then go tell everyone you meet about him. Satan and his demons are going to do everything they can to make you keep quiet—they'll have people make fun of you, they'll get you to focus more on what others think of you than what God thinks of you, and they'll whisper to you that maybe the whole Jesus story isn't true. You will be like an innocent lamb among hungry wolves.

The good news is that you have the Good Shepherd on your side. Don't be afraid. Just go!

Go ask the teacher

As students try to work through an assignment, they start working their way up to the teacher's desk. The comments sound something like this: "I don't get it!" or "I don't understand this question!" or "How am I supposed to do this?" or "What do I do now?"

They know that the teacher has the manual, which has all the answers. They know she can help them figure out their problems.

As you walk through this world, you have some questions too. Should I tell on my friend who stole his sister's money? Does God hate me if I don't like going to church? How do I talk to my friends who are picking on my classmate? Why do I feel so lonely?

God, the smartest teacher of all time, wants you to come to his desk. The Bible is his manual and has the answers you need.

Through his Word, God takes your hand and guides you as you go through your day. He gives you promises that he will be with you. The stories you read remind you of how powerful he is. When you just can't understand why things are happening, he gives you encouragement to face your tough questions.

Go to the Teacher. He has the answers.

Then, like King David, you get to say, **"Your word is a lamp for my feet and a light for my path"** (Psalm 119:105).

Chomp on this!

What are some ways that you can "go to the Teacher"?

God says you can take anything to him in prayer. When does he say we can pray?

Free! Not free!

Nothing gets your attention like the word *free*. At baseball games they give away free bobbleheads, county fairs offer you free balloons, and your dad's company picnic encourages you to head over for free face painting and ice cream. Here's the deal. Bobbleheads, balloons, face painting, and ice cream might be free to you, but they are not free. Someone had to pay for them, whether the baseball team's marketing department, the people working the booth at the fair, or your dad's company.

In the Bible, God tells you that you can come to him, through Jesus, for free. You don't have to pay for anything. For Jesus, however, it was incredibly expensive. He had to obey every single one of God's rules every single day of his life. (It's hard to obey your parents for just one day, isn't it?) Then, he let people spit on him, whip him, and hang him on a cross. He stood in front of you and told his father, "Punish me instead."

"Realize that you weren't set free from the worthless life handed down to you from your ancestors by a payment of silver or gold which can be destroyed. Rather, the payment that freed you was the precious blood of Christ, the lamb with no defects or imperfections" (1 Peter 1:18,19).

Dear Jesus,

thank you for thinking that I was so valuable that you were willing to pay with your whole life and death so that I could go to heaven for free. You have saved me from guilt, from sin, and from an eternity of torture in hell. Thank you. Amen.

Get Out of the Swamp

**"Get rid of your bitterness, hot tempers, anger,
loud quarreling, cursing, and hatred.
Be kind to each other, sympathetic,
forgiving each other
as God has forgiven you through Christ"**
(Ephesians 4:31,32).

During the Civil War, 620,000 soldiers died. Two-thirds of them didn't die from wounds; they died from disease. Because many battlefields were near swamps, wounded soldiers had to walk through nasty, mucky, muddy, bacteria-filled water to get help. The bacteria worked its way into them, and they got life-threatening infections. Without running water and clean bathrooms at their camps, diseases spread quickly from one person to the next. All the bacteria and germs and bugs got into the soldiers' bodies and killed them.

God thinks that holding a grudge against someone, having a quick temper, and fighting are signs that you are walking around in a swamp. Yelling, hating others, and using "bad" words lets others know that you are walking around in nasty, mucky garbage.

Because Jesus lived and died for you, you can crawl out of the filth. You no longer enjoy living that way. Jesus has washed you clean.

Dear Jesus,

thank you for washing me clean. You have taken away all the filth from my life. I'm sorry, though, because sometimes I still like to be angry, to fight, and to hate others. Thank you for washing me clean every single day, for giving me another opportunity to live for you. Amen.

No more guilt

After hurting someone's feelings, Kylie and her mom had a conversation. This is how it ended:

Did you apologize to Jesus? *Yes.*

Did Jesus forgive you? *Yes.*

So, are you forgiven? *Yes.*

Do you still feel guilty? *Yes.*

Should you? *Yes . . . wait . . . I mean no.*

I bet you know what that's like. Even when you apologize, you still feel guilty, ashamed, and embarrassed about your sin.

God has something to tell us about our sins, our forgiveness, and our sometimes guilty consciences. **"Godly sorrow brings repentance that leads to salvation and leaves no regret, but worldly sorrow brings death. See what this godly sorrow has produced in you: what earnestness, what eagerness to clear yourselves, what indignation, what alarm, what longing, what concern, what readiness to see justice done"** (2 Corinthians 7:10,11 NIV).

After you've hurt someone's feelings, Satan wants you to feel guilty, to hide, to pretend it didn't happen. God tells you that godly sorrow—being sorry because you broke his laws, not simply being sorry because you got caught—means you admit your sins, go to Jesus, and ask for forgiveness. Hearing that Jesus took that sin and washed it away means you don't carry the guilty feeling around.

That doesn't mean you pretend it never happened. Godly sorrow means you learn from your mistakes. You become more concerned about other people's feelings, care about making sure it doesn't happen again, and pass along forgiveness when someone hurts you.

Should you be sorry for your sins? Absolutely. Should you feel guilty? Absolutely not!

Your God is not dead

**"If Christ hasn't come back to life,
your faith is worthless and sin still has you in its power.
Then those who have died as believers in Christ
no longer exist. If Christ is our hope in this life only,
we deserve more pity than any other people.
But now Christ has come back from the dead"**
(1 Corinthians 15:17-20).

Throughout the history of the world, people have looked for a religious figure—a god—to believe in.

The Egyptians believed that their pharaohs were gods. When a pharaoh died, the people believed that he would lead them in the afterlife. Ramesses II, also known as Ramesses the Great, died in 1213 B.C. The Egyptians' god is dead.

Islam was founded by Muḥammad. While he was praying in a cave, he said the angel Gabriel visited him and gave him the verses for a new holy book called the Quran. He died in 632. The Muslims' prophet is dead.

Joseph Smith, who was born and raised in the United States, claimed to have a vision from the angel Moroni. He said that he received ancient metal plates that he translated into the Book of Mormon. Smith declared that "a man would get nearer to God by abiding by its precepts, than by any other book." He died in 1844. The Mormons' prophet is dead.

There's one God, only one God, to believe in.

Jesus Christ came to earth. He died to take the punishment for your sins. If your Jesus had not risen, he would be just another religious leader—and people would pity you. But Christ has indeed been raised from the dead. He came back to life because he *is the life*—death couldn't hold him.

Because he lives, you also will live. Your God is not dead. He lives!

Put your worries in the basket*

Have you ever been scared about a test at school? When I have tests, I get really worried—worried that I don't know all the stuff I need to know, worried that I'll get an F.

When I get up in the morning before a big test, I usually tell my mom that I'm scared. But she says that I will do just fine and that God is watching over me. I say, "I'm going to get an F!" But my mom says, "You'll do great! **'Cast all your anxiety on him because he cares for you'"** (1 Peter 5:7 NIV).

That passage really helps me get over my fears. When I hear it, I think of a basket that says my name. I throw my worries in the basket, and God takes it away and says, "Give me your worries. You will do amazing!"

How about you? Do you get scared or have worries? Just remember to throw them in the basket! God will help you when you have troubles too.

Chomp on this!

What sorts of things do you worry about?

Can you think of some hymns or songs that you can sing with your family to remind you that God takes care of your worries?

Dear Lord,

thank you for your help when we have troubles, especially when we are sad or worried or maybe need help with a friend. In the name of our Father in heaven. Amen.

*This devotion was written by Sam, a kid just like you.

God knew you first

*Today let's **Dig In!** Read this section of Scripture, and then use the questions to talk about what God has to say in his Word.*

Praise the God and Father of our Lord Jesus Christ! Through Christ, God has blessed us with every spiritual blessing that heaven has to offer. Before the creation of the world, he chose us through Christ to be holy and perfect in his presence. Because of his love he had already decided to adopt us through Jesus Christ. He freely chose to do this so that the kindness he had given us in his dear Son would be praised and given glory.

Through the blood of his Son, we are set free from our sins. God forgives our failures because of his overflowing kindness. He poured out his kindness by giving us every kind of wisdom and insight when he revealed the mystery of his plan to us. He had decided to do this through Christ. He planned to bring all of history to its goal in Christ. Then Christ would be the head of everything in heaven and on earth. God also decided ahead of time to choose us through Christ according to his plan, which makes everything work the way he intends. He planned all of this so that we who had already focused our hope on Christ would praise him and give him glory. (Ephesians 1:3-12)

Chomp on this!

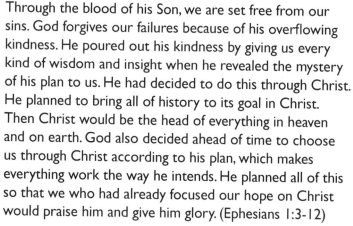

What does God teach you in this passage?

What makes you say, "Thank you, Jesus"?

What makes you say, "I'm sorry, Jesus"?

Based on this reading, what would you like to ask God for?

Dessert is coming

Which of these things is different?

A. Ice cream.

B. Cake.

C. Cookies.

D. Pie.

E. Candy.

F. God's Word.

That was a trick question. The correct answer is G. All of the above.

In Psalm 119:103, we hear that God's Word is just as yummy as any dessert: **"How sweet the taste of your promise is! It tastes sweeter than honey."** Think about dessert for a minute. (Yum!) Your parents won't let you have dessert first, will they? Nope. You need to eat your protein, your vegetables (blech!), and the other stuff your mom says is healthy before you get to have the yummy stuff. So you get through the whole meal because you know the best part is waiting for you at the end.

This earth is full of things you don't necessarily like either. Feeling lonely, fighting with friends, having trouble at school are all things you have to deal with. You get through those because you know that God has good things waiting for you: peace, joy, and living forever in heaven.

As you deal with the problems you face here on earth, remember that dessert is coming. God's promises are sweet.

Dear Father,

sometimes I'm just so sad in this world. Thank you for giving me your promises to be with me, to help me, to work things out for my good, to take me to heaven. Your promises are so sweet; they are better than dessert. Thank you also for giving us actual food that is delicious too. We know that all things—even dessert—are gifts from you. Amen.

Picked last

Two months before the end-of-the-school-year kickball game, my son was already worrying, "I hope I don't get picked last."

I bet you know that fear, don't you? Nothing seems as mortifying to a kid as standing by yourself with everyone else who has already been chosen looking at you. You'd rather the earth open up and swallow you. I've got some bad news.... At some point in your life, you are going to know and feel the deep hurt that comes from standing last, from being all alone.

This is why knowing that God picked you first is even sweeter. **"Before I formed you in the womb, I knew you. Before you were born, I set you apart"** (Jeremiah 1:5).

Before you were even born, God said, "I want you on my team." He set you apart; he picked you, because you are so valuable to him. He actually abandoned his Son, Jesus—left him hanging alone on a cross—because he didn't want you to stand alone in front of him on judgment day.

No matter what you face in this world, you get to walk around your whole life knowing that, thanks to Jesus, you are now and forever on God's team.

Dear Father,

thanks for picking me first. Thank you for forming me, knowing me, setting me apart. Even if I'm the last one people choose, I know that you have picked me. Every day when I wake up, I never worry because I know that you handpicked me. Thank you for putting me on your team. I love you, Lord. Amen.

Love the Lord

Raise your hand if you love God. Keep it up if you're eight years old. Keep it up if you're a king.

No one's hand is still up, unless of course you're being silly. I mean, really, what eight-year-old gets to be king—of anything? Well, Josiah did.

"Josiah was 8 years old when he began to rule, and he was king for 31 years in Jerusalem.... Josiah did what the Lord considered right" (2 Kings 22:1,2).

Josiah had inherited a mess. His dad was an evil king and had made a mess of the country of Judah. While Josiah ruled, he had workers rebuild the temple—and the Book of the Promise was found. (You know the country wasn't doing well when God's words were lost in the temple in the first place.)

Josiah knew that the Israelites needed to know God's words, so he called them to the temple. **"Josiah read everything written in the Book of the Promise found in the Lord's temple so that they could hear it. The king stood beside the pillar and made a promise to the Lord that he would follow the Lord and obey his commands, instructions, and laws with all his heart and soul"** (2 Kings 23:2,3).

Maybe you think that because you're 8 (or 5 or 15) you can't accomplish much. Well, you're wrong. Kids who are 8 follow God. They grow up into adults who follow God.

Josiah—the young boy who followed God his whole life—was God's child, just like you are.

Chomp on this!

Read the whole story in 2 King chapters 22 and 23 or 2 Chronicles chapter 34.

Tell your Story

Jesus went for a boat ride, and when he got out of the boat, a man came up to him. The man was naked and possessed by demons.

"When he saw Jesus, he shouted, fell in front of him, and said in a loud voice, 'Why are you bothering me, Jesus, Son of the Most High God? I beg you not to torture me!' Jesus ordered the evil spirit to come out of the man" (Luke 8:28,29).

When Jesus was about to leave that area, **"The man from whom the demons had gone out begged him, 'Let me go with you.' But Jesus sent the man away and told him, 'Go home to your family, and tell them how much God has done for you.' So the man left. He went through the whole city and told people how much Jesus had done for him"** (verses 38,39).

Today is National Tell a Story Day, a day that was created for people to tell all kinds of stories. For that once demon-possessed man, every day of his life after that was Tell a Story Day. He went all through the whole city, telling everyone about Jesus, the one who was powerful enough to order the demon to leave.

Every day is Tell a Story Day for you too. Jesus has done great things for you. Your stories will be the same—Jesus rescued you from the power of Satan, the head of demons. Your story will be different, though. You can tell others what Jesus means to you, when he has comforted you, and how you've seen his love in your life.

 ## Chomp on this!

Read the whole story in Luke 8:26-39.

Is Jesus for real?

**"When John was in prison,
he heard about the things Christ had done.
So he sent his disciples to ask Jesus,
'Are you the one who is coming,
or should we look for someone else?'"**
(Matthew 11:2,3).

John the Baptizer was born to tell people about his cousin Jesus. He lived in the desert and told people to repent, be baptized, and prepare for the Lord. He made the Pharisees mad and King Herod even madder, which landed him in jail with no hope. This was not exactly how he planned for his life to go after telling people the truth that the Savior was coming. You might not blame him for wondering, "Is Jesus really the guy?"

Sometimes we wonder if Jesus is for real too. We can't see him. Or we tell people the truth and they get mad at us and God doesn't "fix" it. Some nights, praying feels like talking to a big empty space in the sky.

When John wondered, Jesus said, **"Go back, and tell John what you hear and see: Blind people see again, lame people are walking, those with skin diseases are made clean, deaf people hear again, dead people are brought back to life, and poor people hear the Good News"** (verses 4,5).

When you wonder, open your Bible and see what Jesus did. He healed real people; he raised real people from death. He is the Savior. He is coming back for you. For real.

Dear Lord,

forgive me for the times when I doubt that you are real. I know that your Word tells me about all that you have done for me. Please strengthen my faith through that Word. Amen.

Waiting is the hardest part

The sleepy-eyed child walked into the kitchen and asked for scrambled eggs. There was a bacon, apple, and cheddar frittata in the oven, and it would be ready in 15 minutes. The famished child just could ... not ... wait.

After arguing and begging, he cried, "You're not my real mom. If you were, you'd care about me." What part of *bacon* with the eggs didn't the child fully grasp? The 15 minutes took an eternity, but eventually he ate and even went back for a second piece.

That's a true story, and maybe this sounds silly to you. But have you ever complained and whined because God isn't giving you want you want—right now—not realizing that God has something even better waiting for you?

Maybe you think that God must not care for you because your plan, which often includes only being comfortable and happy right now, doesn't seem to be his plan, which often includes waiting.

Whether we see it or not, God works in every situation. Isaiah 64:3,4 reminds us, **"When you did awesome things that we did not expect, you came down, and the mountains trembled before you. Since ancient times no one has heard, no ear has perceived, no eye has seen any God besides you, who acts on behalf of those who wait for him"** (NIV).

God does awesome things that we don't expect, and he acts in your behalf—in his time.

You're part of the band

I was at a band concert and started thinking how a band is a lot like the band of people who call themselves Christians ...

The band is one unit and yet has many parts. As all the parts form one band, so it is with Christ. By one Spirit we were all baptized into one body. Whether we are Jewish or Greek, slave or free, God gave all of us one Spirit to drink.

As you know, the band is not made up of only one part, but of many parts. Suppose a tuba says, "I'm not a flute, so I'm not part of the band!" Would that mean it's no longer part of the band? Or suppose a saxophone says, "I'm not a clarinet, so I'm not a part of the band!" Would that mean it's no longer part of the band? If the whole band were the cymbals, how would you hear the melody? If the whole band were a violin, how could you feel the tympani? So God put each and every part of the band together as he wanted it. How could it be a band if it only had one part? (That's a solo!) So there are many instruments but one band.

A French horn can't say to the bells, "I don't need you!" Or again, the snare drum can't say to the trombone, "I don't need you!" ... God's purpose was that the band should not be divided but rather that all of the instruments should feel the same concern for each other. ... You are Christ's band and each of you is an individual part of it.

What instrument are you? Be thankful for all the instruments around you.

Taken from I Corinthians 12:12-21,25,27.
You can read the actual Scripture in I Corinthians chapter 12.

Never tired

"Even young people grow tired and become weary,
and young men will stumble and fall.
Yet, the strength of those who wait
with hope in the LORD will be renewed.
They will soar on wings like eagles.
They will run and won't become weary.
They will walk and won't grow tired"
(Isaiah 40:30,31).

You leave early in the morning to be first in line at the amusement park. You know exactly which roller coaster you will do first. You're hoping the park is empty so you can ride your favorite one five times in row. Maybe you're so excited you even forget to eat. By the end of the day, though, your enthusiasm fades, you walk slower, and you're kind of ready to go home. You're tired, which is rare for kids with so much energy.

As you go through life, you start off with tons of energy too. Long days of activities, troubles with friends, and your guilty heart start to tire you out. The world tells you that you need to be an "army of one," but you know you can't make it through this world on your own. You need help.

The God who made the world has so much energy and strength that he loves to share it with you. He says that when you hope in him, you get a fresh batch of energy every day. You get through the trouble you face because you are waiting with hope. You serve him without getting tired because you're using his strength. You love the people around you without getting tired because it's his love you're sharing.

Talk to your very best friend

In the United States during the first week of May or so, you might hear about people observing a National Day of Prayer. Some get together for prayer breakfasts; others pray by themselves.

When you are invited to pray, do you sometimes wonder what to say? In Matthew chapter 6, Jesus reminds you that you don't have to make a big show of it or use big churchy words. Instead, he says you can pray in private, using your own words, and you can keep it simple. After all, prayer is simply talking to your very best friend, who also happens to be the God of the universe.

If you don't know what you should say, Jesus gives you the words:

"Our Father in heaven,

let your name be kept holy.

Let your kingdom come.

Let your will be done on earth

as it is done in heaven.

Give us our daily bread today.

Forgive us as we forgive others.

Don't allow us to be tempted.

Instead, rescue us from the evil one"

(Matthew 6:9-13).

Chomp on this!

What is your favorite time to pray?

When do you have a hard time praying?

Pray the prayer from our reading today.

Be a team player

When my son plays basketball in our driveway, I can always hear him counting down: "three … two … one" and then he shoots. He practices that game-winning shot over and over again.

I bet you do too. Don't you dream of that glory-filled moment when the game is on the line and you win it for the team? Of course you do, because that's an awesome feeling.

I have never heard of a kid who dreams of being the one who passes to the player who makes the game-winning buzzer-beater shot. Wanting to get more assists than points does not come naturally. You have to learn that winning is not about you; it's about the team.

God wants us to learn that attitude, and Jesus says the best way to do that is to look at his example. **"Whoever wants to become great among you must be your servant. Whoever wants to be most important among you will be your slave. It's the same way with the Son of Man. He didn't come so that others could serve him. He came to serve and to give his life as a ransom for many people"** (Matthew 20:26-28).

Today, look around you. Look for ways to help others, to serve them, to love them the way Jesus loves you. That's what makes you a great team player.

Dear Jesus,

please give me opportunities to serve others every day.
And when I get those opportunities, help me to serve gladly and willingly. Amen.

Don't be a guilty dog

Everybody knows what a guilty dog looks like. When you walk in the door, you see the dog hiding in the corner with its tail between its legs. As you walk around the corner, you see that it chewed on the rug, got into the trash, jumped up on the counter, and ate your sandwich.

Everybody knows how a guilty dog feels. When you've made fun of someone, hit somebody, screamed at your dad, or talked about your friend behind her back, sometimes you just want to hide in a corner. But hoping that you can hide and pretend it never happened doesn't actually help.

King David, the king of God's chosen people, had made some pretty big mistakes. When he tried to hide, he felt worse, so he tried something different. **"When I kept silent about my sins, my bones began to weaken because of my groaning all day long. I made my sins known to you, and I did not cover up my guilt. I decided to confess them to you, O Lord. Then you forgave all my sins"** (Psalm 32:3,5).

You, God's chosen child, have made some pretty big mistakes too. Hiding and worrying about your sins actually makes you feel worse. Admit your sins to God, admit that you cheated on the test or stole a kid's lunch. Tell him you are sorry, and hear him say, "I forgive you."

No more hiding.

Chomp on this!

When do you keep silent about your sins?

How do you feel when you pretend you aren't sinful?

What makes it hard to confess your sins?

No matter where you are

In Rio de Janeiro, Brazil, you'll find the Christ the Redeemer statue.

Located on the top of Corcovado Mountain on a pedestal that's 26 feet tall, you can't miss it. Jesus is 98 feet tall and his open arms—a symbol of peace—are 92 feet wide.

When work began in the 1920s, the plan was to show that Christ loves all people and wants them to come to him. The builders made it so big to make sure that, no matter where you were in the city, you could look up and see Jesus.

That's a pretty great reminder, isn't it? No matter where you are, you look to Jesus.

That's God's plan too. **"My Father wants all those who see the Son and believe in him to have eternal life. He wants me to bring them back to life on the last day"** (John 6:40). Jesus knew that was the whole point of coming to earth, living for us, and defeating Satan for us—so we can have peace now and forever in heaven.

By the way, not everybody can get to Brazil to see this statue. So you get to be a living Christ the Redeemer statue no matter where you live. **"God wanted his people throughout the world to know the glorious riches of this mystery—which is Christ living in you, giving you the hope of glory"** (Colossians 1:27). The way you live your life can make you a living, breathing statue. That way when people look at you, they see Jesus. The peace they see in you will make them want that kind of peace in their lives too.

 ## Chomp on this!

What things can we do to help people "see" Jesus?

From Slave to heir to Servant

"But when the right time came,
God sent his Son into the world.
A woman gave birth to him, and he came under the
control of the laws given to Moses.
God sent him to pay for the freedom
of those who were controlled by these laws
so that we would be adopted as his children.
Because you are God's children, God has sent
the Spirit of his Son into us to call out, 'Abba! Father!'
So you are no longer slaves but God's children.
Since you are God's children,
God has also made you heirs"
(Galatians 4:4-7).

Slaves are not free. They have to do whatever their owner says. They have no rights. They are trapped. Jesus said, **"Whoever lives a sinful life is a slave to sin"** (John 8:34).

God loves you so much that he was not okay with you being sin's slave for your whole life. So when the exact right time came, God put his rescue plan into place. He chose to send his Son to buy your freedom. By completing his mission, Jesus signed your adoption papers. You are no longer a slave. You are God's child. You are Jesus' brother. You are Jesus' sister. You get every single good thing that comes from being part of the family.

Sometimes, though, rich kids who know they have an inheritance coming forget to live in gratitude and actually live like spoiled brats. (You've seen those kids on TV, haven't you?) As God's heir, you actually live like a servant. You are now free to go around looking for more people to serve, telling them how Jesus has made them family too.

The Lord's Servant

God sent the angel Gabriel to Nazareth, a city in Galilee. **"The angel went to a virgin promised in marriage to a descendant of David named Joseph. The virgin's name was Mary. When the angel entered her home, he greeted her and said, 'You are favored by the Lord! The Lord is with you.' She was startled by what the angel said and tried to figure out what this greeting meant"** (Luke 1:27-29).

If an angel walked into this room during our devotion, you'd probably freak out. I mean, angels don't just suddenly show up at our house and start talking to us, do they? Well, Gabriel did. Mary was a teenager—probably just a few years older than you—when Gabriel went into her house to tell her she was going to be the Savior's mom.

You can probably understand why the Bible says Mary was "startled." Her whole life, Mary knew that God would send a Savior—someday. She had no idea that she would be the one God would use to bring Jesus into the world.

Did Mary say, "No way! Get out! That's weird! Thanks for the offer, but no"? Nope. She also didn't say, "Well, I'm pretty awesome, so of course you'd pick me." Instead, she said to the angel, **"I am the Lord's servant. Let everything you've said happen to me"** (verse 38).

God used Mary to bring the Savior into the world. Now you get to tell the world about the Savior. The Lord is with you too.

Mary—the Lord's servant—was God's child, just like you are.

Chomp on this!

Read the whole story in Luke 1:26-56.

At One with God

When adults have information they need to share, they'll ask, "Do you want the bad news first or the good news?"

Most adults choose the bad news first because they want to end with the good stuff. Because you're growing up, you're getting the bad news first.

When you were born, you were God's enemy. **"Indeed, I was born guilty. I was a sinner when my mother conceived me"** (Psalm 51:5).

Sin and guilt separated you from God, which means you were *at odds* with him. You didn't want what he wants, you didn't like what he likes, and you wouldn't have been able to hang out with him forever because of it.

That's *really* bad news, isn't it? Here comes the good stuff.

God knew that on your own, you'd never want to come to him. So he came up with a rescue plan to win you back.

"[Jesus] had to be made like them, fully human in every way . . . that he might make atonement for the sins of the people" (Hebrews 2:17 NIV).

That means Jesus became a little baby, put God inside a human body, so that he could live perfectly in your place. Then when he died on a cross, he made *atonement* for you. His death paid the price for your sins. You are now *at one* with God.

That is the best good news ever!

P.S. Go tell someone so they can be *at one* too!

Forgive them

When a group of guys laughs at you because you totally dropped the ball during the school softball game, you wish the teacher wasn't around so you could punch them in the face. If your best friend starts hanging around all the girls on the cheerleading squad and ignores you, you kind of hope she gets hurt and can't cheer anymore. Never do you pray, "Dear Father, please forgive them. They don't know just how bad they are hurting me."

That's why Jesus' prayer is astonishing. While he was nailed to a cross, spit on, and made fun of, he said, **"Father, forgive them. They don't know what they're doing"** (Luke 23:34). Obviously the people knew they were hurting Jesus. But he was asking God to forgive them because they had no idea they were crucifying the Savior. They couldn't have known just how much it hurt God the Father to watch his innocent Son take the punishment for all sins—the soldiers' sins, your friends' sins, and your sins too.

One more amazing thing. Did you know that Jesus still prays for you—even now? Because Jesus rose from the dead and went back to heaven to rule with his Father, now **"he always lives to intercede for them"** (Hebrews 7:25 NIV). (*Intercede* is a big word that means Jesus gets involved and talks to God about you and your life.) When Jesus talks to God, he asks for God to do what's best for you, to give you wisdom to handle the trouble you have with friends, for the strength to forgive others, and for the courage to let others know that Jesus has forgiven them too.

 ## Chomp on this!

Is there someone in your life right now whom you have a hard time forgiving?

Pray to God to help you forgive that person.

God "mothers" you

Little girls can mother their dolls for hours. They dress them, comb their hair, carry them around, and put them to bed. They put into practice what they have seen their moms do: kiss their owies, hug them when they cry, tuck them in at night, let them crawl into bed when storms scare them. Those aren't just things moms do, though. Dads do them too. Your heavenly Father does them too.

In Isaiah 66:13, he says, **"As a mother comforts her child, so will I comfort you."**

God didn't create this world to be full of sadness, but sin ruined that. Now you know the hurts that come from being left out, from getting into fights with friends, from people teasing you. Not only do you go to your parents, God says, **"Come to me, all who are tired from carrying heavy loads, and I will give you rest"** (Matthew 11:28).

He wants to hear from you. Tell him about your day, tell him when you are scared, tell him when you feel alone. One of his favorite things to do is to remind you that he loves you and cares about you, that he is always with you and is always there for you.

God, our Father, "mothers" you—for hours, for days, forever.

Dear God,

thank you for giving us parents who take care of us here on earth. Thank you for being our Father who mothers us and comforts us. We know that you watch over and protect us. Amen.

No more crying

If you have a baby in your family, you know how much they cry. If you don't, ask your parents how much *you* cried. You cried when you wanted to be held—and when you wanted to be put down. You cried when you were tired—and to let them know you were awake. You cried when you were hungry—and sometimes you just cried.

As you get older, you might cry less, but the stuff you cry about hurts more. Saying good-bye to friends hurts your heart. Moving from your house can make you sick to your stomach. You cry when your dog (or any pet) dies. You cry when you get into trouble.

That's why God's promise of heaven sounds so awesome. **"He will wipe every tear from their eyes. There will be no more death or mourning or crying or pain, for the old order of things has passed away"** (Revelation 21:4 NIV).

Jesus' death guaranteed that in heaven you will never cry again. You will never be betrayed by friends. You will never have family members die.

Those who don't believe in Jesus, though, are facing an eternity without God. Maybe it's your aunt. Maybe it's your best friend. Maybe it's your teacher. Their eternity will be full of death and mourning and crying and pain. Love them enough to talk to them while there is still time.

Chomp on this!

What do *you* think heaven will be like?

Make a list of the things God tells us about heaven.

Fire drill

You practice a couple of times a year. You know the drill. When the fire alarm sounds, you get out of your desk, walk quietly to the door, and file outside where it's safe. Your school does this because if a real emergency ever happens, they don't want you to panic. Instead, they want you to know your escape route.

God wants you to know that there is an escape route when you get tempted too. **"God, who faithfully keeps his promises, will not allow you to be tempted beyond your power to resist. But when you are tempted, he will also give you the ability to endure the temptation as your way of escape"** (1 Corinthians 10:13).

It's a good idea to think about your temptation escape routes now, because in the middle of temptation you sometimes panic. Come up with a list of things you can say if someone offers you drugs, alcohol, or cigarettes. Get your parents' advice on ways you can react if someone makes fun of your clothes or your hobbies. Pick a friend who shares your values and stick together; it's easier to resist temptation when you are with someone else.

Plan now because *you will be tempted.* Trust that God will help you get out safely.

Chomp on this!

What temptations do you face?

What are some "escape routes" you can take? Come up with a list of ways you can respond when you are tempted by those sins.

It's not just luck

Have you ever played Chutes and Ladders? It's the game where you flick a spinner and you are constantly either climbing up or sliding down. You're thrilled when you land on a square with a ladder because you get to climb up and skip 50 spaces! It's depressing, though, when you are about to win ... and all of a sudden you slide all the way back to the beginning. There's no skill involved. No plan. You get what you get.

In Ecclesiastes 8:7, wise King Solomon said life is kind of like Chutes and Ladders: **"They don't know what the future will bring. So who can tell them how things will turn out?"** We really don't know what will happen tomorrow. A surprise A+ on a test will leave you feeling like you're climbing up a ladder. Maybe you fall and break your wrist, making you feel like you just slid all the way back to the beginning.

This might scare you—if you didn't believe in Jesus. As a child of God, though, you know that the Almighty is watching out for you, **"that all things work together for the good of those who love God—those whom he has called according to his plan"** (Romans 8:28).

Life isn't just luck. Your God sees your life and is actively involved in making the great moments work out for your good. He is also actively involved in taking what you think are setbacks and using them to bless you even more than before. Every flick of the spinner fits into God's plan.

Chomp on this!

How have you seen God turn a setback into a blessing?

Sink into love

*Today let's **Dig In!** Read this section of Scripture, and then use the questions to talk about what God has to say in his Word.*

This is the reason I kneel in the presence of the Father from whom all the family in heaven and on earth receives its name. I'm asking God to give you a gift from the wealth of his glory. I pray that he would give you inner strength and power through his Spirit. Then Christ will live in you through faith. I also pray that love may be the ground into which you sink your roots and on which you have your foundation. This way, with all of God's people you will be able to understand how wide, long, high, and deep his love is. You will know Christ's love, which goes far beyond any knowledge. I am praying this so that you may be completely filled with God. (Ephesians 3:14-19)

Chomp on this!

What does God teach you in this passage?

What makes you say, "Thank you, Jesus"?

What makes you say, "I'm sorry, Jesus"?

Based on this reading, what would you like to ask God for?

Wear the right gear

The next time you run at a track meet, you should wear swim fins and a life vest.

What? You won't wear that? Why not? Well, first, everybody would laugh. Second, no one who wants to win would even think about wearing something so foolish. You'd take off the floppy fins and the bulky vest and put on your track shoes. That's because you need to wear the right gear for the right race.

God tells us to get rid of the wrong gear we wear every day so we can run our life race. **"We must get rid of everything that slows us down, especially sin that distracts us. We must run the race that lies ahead of us and never give up"** (Hebrews 12:1).

When you run through this life, what foolish sins slow you down? Your bad habits and hobbies or maybe even your friendships or technology can cause you to stumble. Running is no fun when you wear the wrong gear. Take it off. When you are distracted by sin, you can fall on your face. Focus on Jesus, don't give up, and run your best race.

By the way, in God's race, more than one person can win. So as you see your friends struggling with wearing the wrong gear, you can encourage them to get rid of everything that slows them down too, to get rid of the sin that trips them up. Help them run and never give up.

God is our refuge*

Camping in the wilderness can be very scary, especially if it's rainy and windy and you start hearing trees and branches creaking and falling. You start to worry and wonder if something might happen. Will it rain in the tent? Will your stuff blow away? What if a branch falls right on your tent? You wish you could be home where it's warm and dry and safe in your strong house.

Sometimes life can be very scary too. When a parent dies or a kid on your lacrosse team offers you drugs or the neighbor's house starts on fire, you wonder what's going to happen. That's when Nahum 1:7 is a good passage to keep in mind. **"The LORD is good, a refuge in times of trouble. He cares for those who trust in him"** (NIV).

No matter what happens to us, God will make it work out for the best. God is the best! He is almighty and is always protecting us. He is our refuge; our hearts and minds are safe with him when we're scared. He cares for us when we think we are alone.

Because God sent Jesus to take care of our biggest fear—being separated from him forever—we know he will take care of us no matter what happens when we are scared. God is by your side. He is your refuge. He is good!

Dear God,

we sometimes worry when we are scared. Help us remember that you love us and that you are our refuge in times of troubles. Amen.

This devotion was written by Eric, a kid just like you.

Jesus was bullied

Back in the Stone Age, you know, when your parents were in elementary school, kids used to have to write on paper to pass notes to each other. Often, the notes were filled with gossip—talking about other people behind their backs.

Today, thanks to computers, there's a whole new level of gossip—it's called cyberbullying. From the "safety" of their homes, kids who want to put people down can taunt their classmates and ruin their reputations—all with a few keystrokes.

Maybe you've even done that. For a little while, mocking others might make you feel more powerful, but that's not what true power looks like. Jesus, who has all the power of the almighty God, actually gave up his power to come to earth. He lived his whole life being mocked by others. While he was on trial, **"Herod and his soldiers treated Jesus with contempt and made fun of him"** (Luke 23:11). As he was about to be crucified, **"the soldiers finished making fun of Jesus, they took off the cape and put his own clothes back on him"** (Matthew 27:31).

Every time you use your words to hurt people, Jesus knows exactly how those kids are feeling.

Maybe right now you are feeling a little guilty. God wants you to know that when the mockers nailed him to a cross, Jesus took the punishment for the times you mock other people. Not only is your sin gone, but your guilt is gone too. When God looks at you, he sees Jesus and chooses to not even remember what you have done.

Now with true power, the real power of the Holy Spirit who lives inside of you, you can choose to use your words for good.

Your Shepherd's voice

Playgrounds make parents nervous sometimes. When there are so many other kids, parents worry that you'll get lost. That's why your dad will check on you by hollering your name. It carries all the way from the sidewalk past the monkey bars to the swings. The other kids don't even look up, but you do. All because you know his voice. When it's time to go, he'll call your name again, because he wants to make sure you get home safely.

You know another voice too. As Jesus was talking about being the Good Shepherd, he called his followers his sheep: **"My sheep respond to my voice, and I know who they are. They follow me, and I give them eternal life. They will never be lost, and no one will tear them away from me"** (John 10:27,28).

When Jesus was on the cross, he was thinking of you because he didn't want you to get lost. Because he knew you, he stayed on the cross for you. By taking your sins away, he's given you the gift of knowing his voice. Now, when your Shepherd calls for you to come, you listen to him because you know his voice. Even though you can't see him, your Shepherd is still thinking of you while he prepares your place in heaven. His love is what gives you the strength to look up when he calls and to get through all of Satan's temptations each day so when he calls for you to go home, you get there safely.

Dear Jesus,

you know me by name. You know me and you love me.
I am your child. Thank you! Amen.

Accepting instruction

Poor Joash. His dad was an evil king and died when Joash was one. His grandma, herself a special kind of crazy-evil, decided to start killing off her children and grandchildren so that she could be the queen. Fortunately, Joash's aunt came to the rescue and hid Joash in the temple for six years.

When Joash was seven, Jehoiada, the priest who had helped hide him, said it was time for Joash to be king. He told the guards, **"Surround the king. Each man should have his weapons in his hand. Kill anyone who tries to break through your ranks. Stay with the king wherever he goes"** (2 Kings 11:8).

Very few second graders need bodyguards—and if they do, it's not because their grandmas want to kill them. Very few second graders are wise enough to rule a country. So Joash needed some adult help. The Bible tells us, **"Joash did what the Lord considered right, as long as the priest Jehoiada instructed him"** (2 Kings 12:2).

You are young too. That's why God gives you adults to help you through this life. He puts people in your life to give you instruction and help you learn what he has done for you. Maybe, though, like Joash, some adults in your life don't follow what God says. God will take care of that. He loves you and will put other adults in your life to help you learn about him.

Joash—who accepted instruction—was God's child, just like you are.

 ## Chomp on this!

Read the whole story in 2 Kings chapters 11 and 12.

Three mistakes*

Chomp on this!

Read Matthew 26:69-75 before you start.

You're in a soccer game. You're about to make a pass, but you totally miss the ball. Then you run down the field with no one around you and fall. Everyone laughs. To cover up those mistakes, you decide you have to score a goal. You make the perfect run and receive the ball. You take one touch and shoot. The goalie blocks the ball, which comes back and hits you, knocking you over. You lie on the ground, feeling horrible and wishing you could start the game over.

I bet that's how Peter felt after he betrayed Jesus three times. At the moment when the rooster crowed, Peter remembered everything. He remembered how Jesus told him he would sin and how he refused to believe Jesus. After that he felt really bad. The Bible says, **"Then Peter went outside and cried bitterly"** (Matthew 26:75).

He didn't feel bad because Jesus wouldn't forgive him; he felt bad because he didn't listen to Jesus. Peter knew he would be forgiven no matter how bad of a mistake he made, but he also knew that as a disciple he had not done what God wanted. Just like Peter knew he was forgiven when he sinned because of what Jesus was about to do, we know our sins are forgiven too, no matter how big they are.

God's mercy is new every morning. You can start over each day.

Dear Lord,

when I make a mistake, please help me trust in you and be confident that my sins are forgiven because of what you did for everyone. Amen.

This devotion was written by Hannah, a kid just like you.

All your heart

Time for a little exercise. Raise your hands above your head. Not by your ears; all the way up. Put them down. Roll your shoulders; stretch a little. Now raise your arms back up. Did they go a little higher? I'm sure they did. Now ... raise them another inch.

I bet you could do it, couldn't you? That's because you weren't giving me everything you had—not the first time or the second time either. It took until that third try for you to realize I wanted you to give me everything you had. I wanted your hands *all* the way up.

God wants you to give it everything you've got, no matter what. **"Whatever you do, work at it with all your heart, as working for the Lord, not for human masters, since you know that you will receive an inheritance from the Lord as a reward. It is the Lord Christ you are serving"** (Colossians 3:23,24 NIV).

He wants you to work with *all* your heart. Squeaking by on your test or purposefully slowing down in a race you won't win or stuffing your dirty laundry under the bed isn't working with *all* your heart. That's working halfheartedly so you don't get into trouble.

You don't have to *be* the best, though, to do *your* best. If you studied and did your very best and still squeaked by on the test, you worked with your whole heart. If you ran the fastest you could and still finished last, you worked with all your heart. If the laundry you folded doesn't look like your mom's but you tried your best, that's fine too.

Whatever you do, work as if you are working for God. Because you are.

Build your faith muscles

We spent a long day hiking a mountain near Lake Tahoe, California. The next day our legs were sore, and even the kids moved a little more slowly and stiffly. You know what that's like, don't you? After a long, hard day of any physical activity, you have DOMS, delayed onset muscle soreness. Exercise puts teeny tiny tears in your muscles. When your muscles heal, they knit back together and get stronger. That sounds weird, doesn't it? Usually if you tear something, you make it weaker, but tearing your muscles makes you stronger than before.

God says the troubles that cause soreness in your heart and life actually make you stronger too. **"Consider it pure joy, my brothers and sisters, whenever you face trials of many kinds, because you know that the testing of your faith produces perseverance. Let perseverance finish its work so that you may be mature and complete, not lacking anything"** (James 1:2-4 NIV).

This explains why your life is often hard. Troubles don't come because God doesn't love you anymore. He allows little tears in your life so he can build you up and make you stronger. When you're lonely, when people tease you, when others think you're foolish for believing that God created the world in seven days, you open up the Bible and hear what God has to say. You learn to trust him more. Your faith gets stronger. The next time trouble comes, remember that God will use it to build your faith muscles.

Dear God,

I don't think to say thank you for the troubles in my life. Today, though, thank you for using the things that hurt and make me sad to make my faith stronger and bring me closer to you. Amen.

Everything is awesome

Over and over during *The Lego Movie*, you hear the song "Everything Is Awesome." All the Lego minifigures sing,

Everything is cool when you're part of a team.

Everything is awesome when we're living our dream.

Over and over in the Bible, God reminds you that everything is awesome when you're part of his team. In 1 Corinthians 12:25-27, we hear, **"God's purpose was that the body should not be divided but rather that all of its parts should feel the same concern for each other. If one part of the body suffers, all the other parts share its suffering. If one part is praised, all the others share in its happiness. You are Christ's body and each of you is an individual part of it."**

As part of God's team, his believers stick together, work together, and look forward to the party forever in heaven. You care about each other, help each other out, celebrate each other's successes, and thank God for living in harmony.

Let's sing it together: "Everything is awesome. Everything is cool when you're part of God's team."

Chomp on this!

How is your life awesome because you are on God's team?

How do you work and stick together with others?

Dear Father,

thank you for putting me on your awesome team. Help me remember that the people in my life are working side by side with me. Let me take care of them and protect them. Amen.

Real friends tell the truth

"You are awesome."

"You are right."

"You are my best friend."

Don't you love hearing those words?

"That is not a good idea."

"Don't be a jerk."

"Maybe we shouldn't . . ."

How about *those* words? Well, those don't sound all that great, do they?

The people we like best are the ones who tell us how amazing we are. We usually say or think mean things about the people who tell us no. We've got it backward. Proverbs 27:6 tells us, **"Wounds made by a friend are intended to help, but an enemy's kisses are too much to bear."**

The Bible tells us that real friends will tell you the truth, even when it's hard to hear. Friends care about you too much to let you act like an idiot. They don't want you to get hurt or to hurt others. So, even though they might be scared, they stand up to you and let you know that sometimes your choices aren't all that great. Those are the "wounds" that friends give.

Enemies, however, don't actually care about you. They don't care if you become a better person. They tell you that you are awesome when you're selfish. They tell you that the teacher totally deserved it when you talked back to her. And enemies' "kisses" may look good on the outside, but they are evil on the inside. (Does that sound familiar? I thought so. Judas betrayed Jesus with a kiss.)

As you walk through the day, notice who your real friends are.

God is protecting them

There's a figure of speech that goes like this: only the good die young. It's not true, but it's a way of making people feel better when someone they love doesn't live to be 80 or 90. Usually when we talk about dying, we talk about old people, grey-haired people, great-grandmas and grandpas. We don't think about young people dying. But the horribly sad truth is that sometimes younger people die. They get cancer, have heart attacks, or die in an accident at work. Sometimes brothers or sisters die too—from a tumor, a drive-by shooting, or car accidents.

It's horrible and tragic because death was not part of God's original design; we were made to live forever. When Adam and Eve sinned, God made sure we wouldn't have to live forever in a world that hurts and makes us feel lonely. As awful as death is, God uses it to take us out of this sad world and give us the heaven that Jesus has prepared for us. In Isaiah 57:1,2, we read, **"The righteous perish, and no one takes it to heart.... No one understands that the righteous are taken away to be spared from evil. Those who walk uprightly enter peace; they find rest as they lie in death"** (NIV).

If it weren't for Jesus, death would be the end. Instead, when Jesus defeated death, he made it possible for us to be with him forever. Now, while we wait for our turn to go to heaven, we know that the people who died young are with a living God who is caring for them and rejoicing because they were spared from even more evil. They are resting in peace. You will see them again. That's a promise—and God never lies.

Did you THINK?

We were leaving a picnic, deciding which kids would go in which car. My daughter chimed in, "I want to go with Grandma." I piped up, "Ah, but does Grandma want *you* to go with *her*?"

That's when my firstborn asked, "Mom, did you THINK about what you said?"

At some point in every family, we each get tired, have short tempers, tease a bit too much, or just want to annoy someone. So we remind each other to THINK:

Is what you say . . .

True. Do you exaggerate what someone else did? Do you "forget" to look at your part in the problem?

Helpful. Do your words support the people around you? Do they offer solutions to problems? Do you comfort others when they are sad?

Inspiring. Do your words encourage the ones around us to be their best? Or do you put down their ideas?

Necessary. Do you *have* to speak? Sometimes silence is best.

Kind. Do you cheer other people on? If you say something hard, do you say it in love? Do you intentionally put someone down?

Did you, like I did, have a rough time with this today? The good news is that God forgives the times we don't THINK. **"The reason I can still find hope is that I keep this one thing in mind: the Lord's mercy. We were not completely wiped out. His compassion is never limited. It is new every morning. His faithfulness is great"** (Lamentations 3:21-23).

Each day is another chance to THINK.

Your ticket to heaven

"Whoever believes and is baptized will be saved, but whoever does not believe will be condemned"
(Mark 16:16).

When it's time to board an airplane, you have to have a ticket to be allowed to walk through the gate. If you don't have a ticket, you don't get on the plane. It's that simple. You can beg; you can plead; you can cry; you can try to draw your own ticket; but, let's be honest, none of that will work. The airline has to give you the official ticket, or you aren't getting on. You are left outside, and you watch the plane take off without you.

You can't get through heaven's gates without the right document either. You can't ask nicely, you can't beg, you can't cry, and you can't be such a good person that you earn your way in. The only way to get a ticket is from Jesus.

When Jesus came to earth, he obeyed every single one of God's rules. Then, in your place, he accepted punishment for your sins. Finally, when he came alive again, he went to hell to let Satan know, "I've won." When you were baptized, you got a baptismal certificate. It lets you know that Jesus washed away your sins and now you are his.

Through faith in Jesus, your baptismal certificate is your ticket to your heavenly home.

Chomp on this!

Make a list of people you know who aren't baptized or don't believe in Jesus. Talk about how you can tell them so they aren't left outside of heaven.

Run away!

**"My son, if sinners lure you, do not go along.
My son, do not follow them in their way.
Do not even set foot on their path"**
(Proverbs 1:10,15).

Your parents have warned you about talking to strangers. If an adult would say, "Hey, I want to kidnap you," you'd never even go near that person because you know it's dangerous. In fact you'd run away.

Parents know, though, that you might be tempted to go by a strange car if someone offered you candy or wanted to show you puppies. After all, who doesn't love candy, and puppies are adorable. That's why your parents warn you over and over about being careful of the offers that sound awesome.

That's what King Solomon is warning you about in today's passage. He's telling you to be careful of the sins that lure you, that tempt you because they sound good. It's pretty easy to turn down obvious sins like this: "Hey, let's go beat someone up." But when you hear, "Wow, can you believe she's wearing that?" sometimes it's easy to join in. We think we won't get caught or we're afraid our friends will be mad at us if we tell them to stop.

Your parents are wise when they tell you to run away from strangers' cars. Solomon was wise when he told you to run away from temptation.

He's not late

Softball practice was over at 5:00 P.M. At 5:06 the first text came: Hey, Mom, did you forget about me?

Every child knows the panic that comes when Mom or Dad doesn't show up when they are supposed to. Only six minutes late, and you start to panic, thinking that you've been forgotten. Your mind starts racing: "Where are they? How am I going to get home? What if something bad happened?"

We also start to panic when we think God is late. "Why didn't he answer my prayer yet?" "How come I'm still having problems with my friends?" "Why are my parents and I still fighting?" "Why can't God just come back and take us all to heaven?"

"The Lord is not slow in keeping his promise, as some understand slowness. Instead he is patient with you, not wanting anyone to perish, but everyone to come to repentance" (2 Peter 3:9 NIV).

God doesn't always answer our prayers in the time we think he should. Instead, God acts when the time is right. Everything in this world is designed to strengthen you, to bring you closer to him, to give him the glory, and to reach out to those who don't yet believe.

When you're tempted to panic, remember that God's not late. He hasn't—and never will—forget about you.

Dear God,

please help me realize that you act in your time, which is the right time. Help me trust that you know what's best for me and will work all things for my good. Amen.

Christians are a bunch of chickens

Chickens love to be together. They work together to find food and keep each other warm. As they spend the day going in the coop, heading back out, scratching in the yard, looking for food, and taking dust baths, it seems they can't stand to be apart for more than a few minutes. Whatever one does, the others do. They also stick together because it's safer that way—possums, foxes, and coyotes would love to have them for dinner. At the end of the day, when the sun starts to set, they make a line and head back home for the night.

God wants his children to act like chickens. He wants them to flock together, to not willingly be apart from others who love Jesus. On your own, you are an easy target for temptation. When you flock together with other believers, they encourage you to stay strong, they remind you where to find spiritual food, they support you when you are sad, and they remind you that you aren't alone. They encourage you to get in line because it's almost time to go home.

Take the advice God gives you: **"We should not stop gathering together with other believers, as some of you are doing. Instead, we must continue to encourage each other even more as we see the day of the Lord coming"** (Hebrews 10:25).

If you see another believer who's been hanging out on his own, invite him to come back into the flock. It's an awesome place to be.

You are Set free

*Today let's **Dig In!** Read this section of Scripture, and then use the questions to talk about what God has to say in his Word.*

So I tell you and encourage you in the Lord's name not to live any longer like other people in the world. . . .

However, you were taught to have a new attitude. You were also taught to become a new person created to be like God, truly righteous and holy.

So then, get rid of lies. Speak the truth to each other, because we are all members of the same body.

Be angry without sinning. Don't go to bed angry. Don't give the devil any opportunity to work.

Thieves must quit stealing and, instead, they must work hard. They should do something good with their hands so that they'll have something to share with those in need.

Don't say anything that would hurt another person. Instead, speak only what is good so that you can give help wherever it is needed. That way, what you say will help those who hear you. Don't give God's Holy Spirit any reason to be upset with you. He has put his seal on you for the day you will be set free from the world of sin.

Get rid of your bitterness, hot tempers, anger, loud quarreling, cursing, and hatred. Be kind to each other . . . forgiving each other as God has forgiven you through Christ. (Ephesians 4:17,23-32)

Chomp on this!

What does God teach you in this passage?

What makes you say, "Thank you, Jesus"?

What makes you say, "I'm sorry, Jesus"?

Based on this reading, what would you like to ask God for?

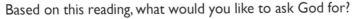

My anxious thoughts

Kids are more stressed than parents realize. Some kids worry about getting a C on a test, while other kids just hope they don't get an F. Other kids worry about striking out when the team really needs them. Other kids struggle because they don't feel like they have friends. Maybe there's even bigger stuff. Are your grandparents sick? Are your parents divorcing? What if you are moving across the country or starting a new school? Maybe you have worries so big that you haven't talked about them with anyone.

Each one of these can make you worry so much that you get a stomachache or you can't sleep. Once you talk to someone, though, you can almost feel the worries get lighter because you realize you aren't alone.

David felt a little sick to his stomach too; sometimes he couldn't even sleep at night because of all his worries. When he was king, his nation was at war and his children were out of control. So he had problems at work and at home. Still, David knew where to find his peace. **"Examine me, O God, and know my mind. Test me, and know my thoughts"** (Psalm 139:23).

David was asking God to look over him like a doctor checks you at your annual visit. Are you afraid of asking God to examine you because you're worried what he'll find? Just like talking to a friend or parent helps, talking to your God is even better. He's the God of the whole entire world, and he loves it when you talk to him. When you ask him to examine you, you are asking him to find those hidden worries—and take them away! As you read the Bible, have family devotions, and pray, you remember that the King is your Daddy, who loves to forgive your anxious thoughts and bring you peace when you worry.

Don't Say, "I'm only a kid"

How many more years until you are 20? (Go ahead, do the math.)

What do you think you'll be doing when you're 20? (Go ahead, come up with some ideas.)

When Jeremiah was about 20, he had a conversation with God. It went like this: **"The LORD spoke his word to me, 'Before I formed you in the womb, I knew you. Before you were born, I set you apart for my holy purpose. I appointed you to be a prophet to the nations.' I, Jeremiah, said, 'Almighty LORD, I do not know how to speak. I am only a boy!' But the LORD said to me, 'Don't say that you are only a boy. You will go wherever I send you. You will say whatever I command you to say. Don't be afraid of people. I am with you, and I will rescue you,' declares the LORD"** (Jeremiah 1:4-8).

Before God formed you, he knew you too. He has also set you apart for a holy purpose. Now, right now, even though you are young, you get to tell people about Jesus. Don't be afraid. He is with you.

Jeremiah—who was young when he spoke God's words—was God's child, just like you are.

Chomp on this!

There's a whole book in the Bible about Jeremiah. You can read this whole story, though, in Jeremiah chapter 1.

Dear God,

I'm "not only a kid"; I'm *your* kid. Before I was even born, you set me apart. Sometimes I'm afraid people will make fun of me for telling the truth about you. Sometimes I feel like I'm too young and don't think anyone will believe me. Give me your courage so I am not afraid of what anybody thinks. I know you sent Jesus to rescue me from Satan, so you will rescue me from any other enemy—or even friends—that I face. Amen.

What family does

**"God's purpose was that the body
should not be divided
but rather that all of its parts
should feel the same concern for each other.
If one part of the body suffers,
all the other parts share its suffering.
If one part is praised,
all the others share in its happiness"**
(1 Corinthians 12:25,26).

What if . . . your friend wins the geography bee, your classmate gets picked for select soccer, your uncle wins the lottery? You'd be jealous right?

Now, what would happen if . . . your friend trips and falls on the way back from the bee, your classmate gets kicked off the soccer team, your uncle loses all of his money? You'd probably breathe a sigh of relief and think, "I'm glad that didn't happen to me."

Everyone would understand your reaction. Well, everyone except God. In God's family we make up a body, a body that is so connected to each other that it changes how our brains work. It changes how we react. With Christ's body, when one person wins, we are thrilled for that person. We hug her, tell her how happy we are for her. When someone is hurt, we feel his pain. We hug him and support him however we can.

We don't do this, though, because we are nice people. We do it because, with the Holy Spirit living inside of us, we can't help ourselves. We love each other because we are family—and that's what family does.

He Started it!

**"We must focus on Jesus,
the source and goal of our faith"**
(Hebrews 12:2).

What's the first thing you do when your teacher catches you and your friend in the middle of something you shouldn't be doing? Be honest. You point to the other one and say, "He started it!" That's because you are quick to pass the blame.

But if the teacher comes to you and your friend and says, "I really like that project," you're quick to say, "It was my idea." That's because you are quick to take the credit.

Being a Christian changes your way of thinking. If someone asks you how you became a Christian, you don't get to say, "Well, it was my idea." You get to point to God and say, "It was his idea. He started it."

You were dead in your sins—and dead people can't choose to come alive. God sent his Holy Spirit to create faith inside of you, to help you believe that because Jesus defeated death, you will now live forever in heaven.

Now every day you get to choose to live out the faith he gave you by the way you act and how you talk to people. Still, God doesn't say, "Okay, I did my part. You're on your own." The Holy Spirit lives in you to give you the strength and love to be kind to others, to make choices that bring him glory, and to have faith your whole life through.

"[Be] confident of this, that he who began a good work in you will carry it on to completion until the day of Christ Jesus" (Philippians 1:6 NIV).

Point to God and say, "He started it—and he'll finish it!"

Focus on the finish line

**"It's not that I've already reached the goal
or have already completed the course.
But I run to win that which Jesus Christ
has already won for me.
Brothers and sisters, I can't consider myself a winner yet.
This is what I do: I don't look back, I lengthen my stride,
and I run straight toward the goal to win the prize
that God's heavenly call offers in Christ Jesus"**
(Philippians 3:12-14).

The first time my daughter ran a cross country race, she told me, "I just want to be in the top ten." When she came home with a smile on her face and the first-place trophy in her hand, she added, "Well, I really wanted to win. I just didn't want to be disappointed if I didn't."

All over the country people run to reduce stress, stay healthy, and simply because they like it. Some people, like my daughter, run because they want to win.

The apostle Paul looked at his life and his faith like it was a race. He knew Jesus had already run the race for him—and won the race for him—yet Paul didn't claim victory yet. Like a cross country runner, he stayed focused on the finish line and didn't look back. Instead, he stayed focused, wanting to hold that trophy.

You are in a race. Don't get distracted or slow down. Finish strong.

 ## Chomp on this!

What are some things that can distract you in your race?

How can you focus on the finish line of heaven?

Who holds you together?

The Great Pyramid of Giza, Egypt, is made of 2,300,000 stone blocks that weigh at least 4,000 pounds. Some blocks weigh between 60,000 to 100,000 pounds.

No one knows how the stones got to that place or how builders managed to lift them up to create the pyramid. Also, no one knows how those stones are held together. Even today, with all that we know of science and technology, no one can figure out where the mortar came from. Scientists have analyzed it, and they even know its chemical composition—what things make it up. Still, they can't reproduce it. And the thing is, the mortar is even stronger than stone. It hasn't deteriorated over the past four thousand years.

When it comes to the world, science and technology have allowed us to learn about atoms and creatures at the bottom of the sea. Yet there's still so much we don't know. What we do know, though, is who made it and how it sticks together: "[God] **created all things in heaven and on earth, visible and invisible. Whether they are kings or lords, rulers or powers— everything has been created through him and for him. He existed before everything and holds everything together**" (Colossians 1:16,17).

Everything you see in this universe and even everything you can't see was created by the Master Builder for his glory. Once he made it, he decided how it would all fit. Your God is the mortar—the One who holds everything together.

Dear God,

everything would fall apart if it weren't for you. Your goodness, your blessing, and your power keep the world going. When I get scared and confused because this world is terrifying, help me trust in you as my strong mortar. Amen.

The bigger picture

Have you ever heard the saying that a picture is worth a thousand words?

At the best part of a roller coaster, there is always a camera that captures the moment. At the end of the ride, amusement park staff then try to sell it to you for $20. That photo tells you more about how scared or excited or sick to your stomach you were than if you tried to write a thousand-word essay about it. Still, that picture doesn't tell you the whole story. What looks like a scared or angry face might just be a scream of happiness. The picture can tell me a lot, but it can't tell me all about the ride. It just tells me about that moment.

I think we do the same with our lives. If you took a snapshot of one moment, it doesn't tell the whole story. When you are feeling lonely, you might think that God doesn't care about you or that he doesn't take the time to notice little you. When you feel guilty, maybe you think God is angry and punishing you.

False! What's true is that **"the LORD, the LORD, [is] a compassionate and merciful God, patient, always faithful and ready to forgive. He continues to show his love to thousands of generations, forgiving wrongdoing, disobedience, and sin"** (Exodus 34:6,7).

When you feel scared, lonely, or guilty, God's grace reminds you that there is a bigger picture.

You get the credit

It's Saturday morning. Your parents need to run some errands, so they leave a whole list of chores for you and your sister to do. You work and work and work while your sister watches cartoons and eats candy and breaks stuff and makes a mess.

When your parents come home, they walk in the room and tell your sister what a great job she did. Would you let them praise her? No way! You would come running into the room screaming, "BUT I DID IT! She did nothing, and I did everything!" You want the credit for what you did!

On this earth, Jesus worked and worked and worked, doing every single thing his Father asked of him. Each one of us wastes, hurts people's feelings, disobeys him, and makes a mess. Still, because of Jesus' work, when God comes back to take us home, this is how it's going to sound: **"Then the king will say to those on his right, 'Come, my Father has blessed you! Inherit the kingdom prepared for you from the creation of the world'"** (Matthew 25:34).

The way it works in God's plan is that Jesus does all the work, but you get all the credit. Now you don't have to worry when it's time for you to go home. You know you get to hear, "Good job! You're a good and faithful servant! Come and share your master's happiness."

You get the credit for what Jesus did. And Jesus couldn't be happier.

Dear Jesus,
thank you for doing it all for me! Amen.

Jesus came for "that kid"

Have you earned the reputation as "that kid"? Do you spend more time in the principal's office than the classroom? Possibly you are setting a record in after-school detentions. Have you stolen money from the backpacks in the classroom? Maybe you've been kicked out of your school for throwing things at your teacher.

There's a story in Matthew chapter 9 about "that kid." Back in Bible times, nobody liked tax collectors. They made people pay more than was owed and kept the extra money for themselves. Everybody considered them to be cheaters.

"When Jesus was leaving that place, he saw a man sitting in a tax office. The man's name was Matthew. Jesus said to him, 'Follow me!' So Matthew got up and followed him. Later Jesus was having dinner at Matthew's house. Many tax collectors and sinners came to eat with Jesus and his disciples. The Pharisees saw this and asked his disciples, 'Why does your teacher eat with tax collectors and sinners?' When Jesus heard that, he said, 'Healthy people don't need a doctor; those who are sick do. Learn what this means: "I want mercy, not sacrifices." I've come to call sinners, not people who think they have God's approval'" (Matthew 9:9-13).

By telling Matthew to follow him, Jesus let everyone know that God had great plans for "that kid." Matthew the tax collector became Matthew the disciple, who then invited all his "that kid" friends to meet the One who would die on a cross for their sins.

When you feel like "that kid," remember that Jesus came for you, he lived for you, and he paid the price for your sins. Now he walks up to you and says, "Follow me." You are his disciple.

God doesn't lie

Here's what the news, your schoolbooks, and museums will tell you:

- A 4.4-billion-year-old zircon was found in Australia.

- A 66-million-year-old long-nosed "Pinocchio rex" dinosaur was discovered in China.

- Almost 14 billion years ago, the world as we know it was formed when all matter in the universe got squeezed so tightly and got so hot that it exploded all over the place.

In Genesis chapter 1, here is what God tells you:

"In the beginning God created heaven and earth."

Day 1: **"God said, 'Let there be light!' So there was light.... God named the light** *day,* **and the darkness ...** *night.***"**

Day 2: **"God made the horizon and separated the water above and below the horizon."**

Day 3: **"Then God said, 'Let the water under the sky come together in one area, and let the dry land appear.... Let the earth produce vegetation.'"**

Day 4: **"God made the two bright lights: the larger light to rule the day and the smaller light to rule the night. He also made the stars."**

Day 5: **"God created the large sea creatures, every type of creature that swims around in the water and every type of flying bird."**

Day 6: **"God made every type of ... animal, and every type of creature that crawls on the ground.... Then God said, 'Let us make humans in our image.' ... And God saw everything that he had made and that it was very good."**

When you wonder what things to believe, trust your God.

God is with you*

The end of the school year was always my favorite time. It was the end of something I'd been doing for a whole year. I had small worries about next year's teacher, or I was excited because I might meet a new kid. During the summer months, I'd miss seeing my friends every day, so when the next school year started, I would be happy to go back. What didn't occur to me until my last few weeks of middle school was that most of the people I had seen every day would no longer be in my classes in high school—or even at the same school!

I bet you know what that's like. Moving from elementary school to middle school, from grade school to high school, or moving to a completely different school in a different state is scary. We all have to do it.

Then I remembered that God will always be with me. No matter how stressful or difficult my life gets as things change, he will always be by my side. Even though I may be afraid of change, God has promised that he will never leave me. When Jesus moved from earth back to heaven, he promised the disciples, **"Remember that I am always with you until the end of time"** (Matthew 28:20).

That promise is for us too.

Dear heavenly Father,

we know that you have promised to be with us. Please help us remember your promises in every situation. In your name we pray. Amen.

*This devotion was written by Hailey, a kid just like you.

Beware the dark Side

In *Return of the Jedi*, as wise 900-year-old Yoda is dying, he passes along some important final information to Luke, "Remember, a Jedi's strength flows from the Force. But beware: anger, fear, aggression—the dark side, are they. Once you start down the dark path, forever will it dominate your destiny."

It sounds like Yoda picked up that wisdom from King Solomon. In the very first chapter of his wisdom book, Proverbs, he passed along some important information.

Remember, your strength comes from your God and his teachings.

"Listen, my son, to your father's instruction and do not forsake your mother's teaching. They are a garland to grace your head and a chain to adorn your neck" (verses 8,9 NIV).

You can't get through this life trying to be strong on your own. God's power to handle all problems is what will give you strength to face every day.

But beware of the dark path.

"My son, if sinful men entice you, do not give in to them. If they say, 'Come along with us . . .' my son, do not go along with them, do not set foot on their paths. Such are the paths of all who go after ill-gotten gain; it takes away the life of those who get it" (verses 10,11,15,19 NIV).

Cheating, hurting others to get what you want, putting down other people, fighting, holding grudges, and gossiping all hurt you more than they hurt others. By doing what Satan and his dark side want, you are following the wrong path—the path that leads to destruction.

Let God guide your destiny.

NOT MINE!

Ask your mom or dad how well you shared your toys when you were little. They can easily think of a time or two when another toddler wanted your toy, so you clutched the prized possession in your chubby little hand and screamed an ear-piercing, "MINE!"

Before you believe in Jesus, your heart is as selfish as a toddler's. You think that sharing cheats you out of the best toys, the best stuff. When you are baptized and God makes you part of his family, he gives you Jesus' heart and mind, one that knows the best part of being family means you share with each other.

The Christians who lived around the time Jesus did totally understood this. In Acts 2:44-46, we hear just how generous they were: **"All the believers kept meeting together, and they shared everything with each other. From time to time, they sold their property and other possessions and distributed the money to anyone who needed it. The believers had a single purpose and went to the temple every day. They were joyful and humble as they ate at each other's homes and shared their food."**

Isn't that awesome? Having Jesus in your heart means you share—your food, your toys, your home, your money—even without being asked. It means you gladly shout, "NOT MINE!"

Chomp on this!

What ways can you share your talents with other believers?

How can you plan to give some of your allowance back to God? to church? to charities that reach out with the love of Jesus to a hurting world? to missionaries?

God loves different

Most kids hate to be different. That's why you buy the same kinds of clothes, eat the same kinds of food, play the same sports, and listen to the same music. As hard as you try, each one of you also knows the pain that comes from being different. You get singled out and feel less important than everyone else. There are some kids who live with that feeling every single day.

In the Bible, Jesus told a story—called a parable—that teaches you how God works. All the "normal" people turned down an invitation to a party and the master said, **"Run to every street and alley in the city! Bring back the poor, the handicapped, the blind, and the lame"** (Luke 14:21).

At God's party, he makes a special point of inviting those who are "different." If you use food stamps to pay for food, if you need braces on your ankles, if you have Down syndrome, if you can only communicate through sign language or have to read with Braille, he says, "You're invited! Come to my party!" Your God, who doesn't look at the outside, doesn't actually think you're different. He simply sees you as his child, the one he gets to love, forgive, and live with forever in heaven. You're invited! Come!

Chomp on this!

If you are poor or have physical challenges on this earth, talk about the ways that God's love gives you courage.

If you don't face these challenges, talk about how you can reach out and encourage those around you who do.

Holy in every way

*Today let's **Dig In!** Read this section of Scripture, and then use the questions to talk about what God has to say in his Word.*

Brothers and sisters, we ask you to show your appreciation for those leaders who work among you and instruct you. We ask you to love them and think very highly of them because of the work they are doing. Live in peace with each other.

We encourage you, brothers and sisters, to instruct those who are not living right, cheer up those who are discouraged, help the weak, and be patient with everyone. Make sure that no one ever pays back one wrong with another wrong. Instead, always try to do what is good for each other and everyone else.

Always be joyful. Never stop praying. Whatever happens, give thanks, because it is God's will in Christ Jesus that you do this.

Don't put out the Spirit's fire. Don't despise what God has revealed. Instead, test everything. Hold on to what is good. Keep away from every kind of evil.

May the God who gives peace make you holy in every way. May he keep your whole being—spirit, soul, and body—blameless when our Lord Jesus Christ comes. The one who calls you is faithful, and he will do this. (1 Thessalonians 5:12-24)

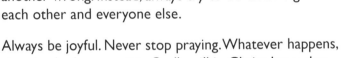
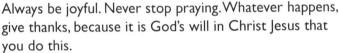

Chomp on this!

What does God teach you in this passage?

What makes you say, "Thank you, Jesus"?

What makes you say, "I'm sorry, Jesus"?

Based on this reading, what would you like to ask God for?

It's not fun!

**"We don't enjoy being disciplined.
It always seems to cause more pain than joy.
But later on, those who learn from that discipline
have peace that comes from doing what is right"**
(Hebrews 12:11).

While doing something wrong, no child in the history of all children has ever said, "I sure hope I get caught!"

After getting caught—and punished—no child in the history of all children has ever said, "Hey, thanks! I was really hoping I'd get into trouble. I sure am grateful you taught me a lesson!"

While you are getting disciplined, all you can think about are the consequences. No child wants to lose electronics for a week or do extra chores or spend four days cleaning up the graffiti he or she sprayed on another kid's house. So I bet you agree with the writer of Hebrews. We don't enjoy being disciplined. It's often, literally, painful.

I'm going to let you in on a secret. Your parents, who seem to be masters at catching you doing wrong things, don't actually enjoy having to dole out consequences. It's as painful for them to constantly have to come up with ways to help you learn how to follow the rules. They do it because they know that kids who learn how to obey their parents are kids who learn to obey their God. They stick with it because they are intensely interested in seeing you grow up to be an adult who has the peace that comes from doing what is right.

I don't expect you to really understand it now. I promise that it will make sense someday. Probably around the time you have to discipline your own kids.

Chomp on this!

Talk about a time when you've been disciplined.

Can you see now how it was actually for your good?

Not better, just different

Boys' view: Boys go to Mars to get more candy bars. Girls go to Jupiter to get more stupider.

Girls' view: Girls rule! Boys drool!

God's view: **"When God created humans, he made them in the likeness of God. He created them male and female. He blessed them and called them humans when he created them"** (Genesis 5:1,2).

Instead of making fun of each other and fighting over who is better, God thinks that having two types of people with unique differences is equally cool! Boys have an awesome energy level and fearlessness that helps show God's power and strength. Girls are great at communicating and bring a compassion that demonstrates how loving and ready-to-listen God is. When you try to make yourself seem better or more important by saying mean things about the opposite gender, you are telling God, "I'm not sure your plan was all that great." Instead of looking at each other's differences, look for the ways that you all have been blessed by God to work for him.

By the way, on the sixth day of creation—after making both males and females—**"God saw everything that he had made and that it was very good"** (Genesis 1:31).

Chomp on this!

When you watch TV, how do the kids on TV talk about boys and girls? Do they say nice things about each other or put each other down to try to get a laugh?

Dear God,

forgive me for the times I thought I was more awesome than someone else. Remind me that the way you created the world is the way you wanted it to be. Let my words be kind. Amen.

Set an example

Chomp on this!

What qualities do you look for in a role model?

In your life, which person do you look up to? What made you pick that person?

(Take some time to discuss this before starting the devotion.)

When you were picking your role model, did you pick anyone your age? Probably not. Most kids usually pick a teacher who is positive, parents who encourages them, or a coach who pushes them just enough to make them better.

The apostle Paul, however, encouraged young Timothy to be a role model—even for older people. **"Don't let anyone look down on you for being young. Instead, make your speech, behavior, love, faith, and purity an example for other believers"** (1 Timothy 4:12).

That goes for you too. Yes, you are young, but you are also a valuable part of God's family. Sometimes adults get too worried, too anxious, and too distracted by all the adult decisions they face. Your faith, your simple trust in God, the way you ask people if they know about Jesus, all of those are examples for other believers. God uses you to encourage and remind adults to have faith like a child.

Timothy—who set an example for other believers—was God's child, just like you are.

Dear Holy Spirit,

thank you for living inside of me. With your power, let me be an example for other believers. Use my words, actions, love, faith, and life to encourage others and bring them closer to you. Amen.

God hears you

Sometimes you call from your bed because you're scared.

"Mom … Mom … MOM!"

If she doesn't come right away, you yell louder. Sometimes her room feels so far away that you wonder if she will ever hear you. Then she comes through your door to let you know, "I hear you. I'm here. What do you need?"

God, who sometimes seems far away because he lives in heaven, wants you to know that he is right here too. He wants to hear what you need. **"This is the confidence we have in approaching God: that if we ask anything according to his will, he hears us"** (1 John 5:14 NIV).

When you are calling for him because you're scared of moving or because there's a tornado warning, he says, "I hear you." When you are asking him to watch over and protect you on vacation, he hears you. When you ask him to help your parents because they are fighting, he hears you. When you talk to him because your uncle is really sick, he listens. If you're super happy because there is a new baby in the family, he loves to hear about that too.

No matter where you are—school, home, in a new town, or at a sleepover—he hears you. No matter what time of day—when you wake up, at recess, before dinner, and at bedtime—he hears you. Your heavenly Dad loves to hear you calling for him. He's listening. He's ready.

Trusting in the ending

Have you seen the movie *Air Bud*? At the saddest part, when Josh (a young boy) was trying to send Buddy (the dog) away, my daughter covered her eyes. She didn't want to watch because it made her sad. Her sister reminded her, "Don't worry. It'll all work out. It's a Disney movie."

Real life isn't like a Disney movie. Sometimes there seem to be more sad parts and no happy ending. Some kids are in wheelchairs and don't miraculously start walking. Classmates get cancer and die. Friends' parents get divorced. You move to a new school and don't see your friends anymore.

King David had plenty of troubles too, and he knew where to put his trust. **"I will rejoice and be glad because of your mercy. You have seen my misery. You have known the troubles in my soul. I trust you, O Lord. I said, 'You are my God.' My future is in your hands"** (Psalm 31:7,14,15).

God sees the sadness and the worries in your heart. At the same time, you trust him because you know he will use these experiences to help you grow closer to him and to grow up to be the person he knows you will be.

So for now, while you struggle, **"Be strong, all who wait with hope for the Lord, and let your heart be courageous"** (verse 24).

Your Daddy knows how the story turns out.

What's on your list today?

Parents often leave a list of things to do for kids to help around the house. In Titus 3:1,2 God gives you a list of things to do too, but these aren't to earn points and get an allowance from God. This is simply a list you pitch in on because you are happy to be part of the family.

Remind the people to be subject to rulers and authorities,

Don't be the one encouraging kids to throw paper at the teacher or to make fun of them. Instead, respect your teachers and turn in your homework on time.

to be obedient,

Your parents make the rules. You don't get to choose which ones to obey. Someday when you're the adult, you'll have to be obedient to your boss' rules too. So practice now.

to be ready to do whatever is good,

Look for opportunities to pitch in. Hold the door open for the people behind you. Pick up trash on the street that isn't yours. Help your classmates with their homework.

to slander no one,

Don't gossip—even if it's the truth. Don't exaggerate your stories to make them sound better and to make the other person sound worse. Help your friends and your siblings have good reputations.

to be peaceable and considerate,

Open your eyes and look at other people. See how you can serve them. Is one kid being left out at recess? Invite her to play. Is there a new kid at school? Sit next to him at lunch.

and always to be gentle toward everyone (NIV).

There are plenty of kids ready to pick on others. Be different. Be the one who gets along with everyone.

You have your own angel

**"Be careful not to despise these little ones.
I can guarantee that their angels in heaven
always see the face of my Father, who is in heaven"**
(Matthew 18:10).

Sometimes when you do something really foolish—like jumping off a roof or running out into the street or any of the other dangerous things you do—adults will joke that your guardian angel is working overtime just to keep you alive.

Jesus says that's not so far off. In today's passage, Jesus tells adults to pay attention to kids, to treat them well. Then he adds this sentence: **"I can guarantee that their angels in heaven always see the face of my Father, who is in heaven."**

Just because you are a child doesn't mean you are ignored or overlooked or unimportant. In fact, you are so valuable to your God that he assigns angels to watch over you.

What do your angels do? The Bible tells us, **"What are all the angels? They are spirits sent to serve those who are going to receive salvation"** (Hebrews 1:14).

Angels get their greatest joy in carrying out God's will—and that means serving you. God's servants protect you with their power. They watch over you because they are intensely interested in making sure that Satan's lies don't work on you and that you end up in heaven forever—where you will see God's face too.

Stop being childish

"Foolishness is firmly attached to a child's heart"
(Proverbs 22:15).

Sometimes when you are in trouble and your parents are frustrated, they might yell, "What were you thinking? Act your age!" Deep down, your parents know the problem is that you are acting your age. Foolishness and silliness are just part of your heart, and sometimes you can't help yourself.

As children, you have a lot of learning to do. Your brain is still developing; you are still learning how to control your reactions and impulses. One of your parents' jobs is to help you get the foolishness out of your heart. One of your jobs is to grow up a little more every day.

You learn that there is a right time to have fun and to be silly and a time when you need to practice self-control and keep your mouth shut. There may be a time to respectfully ask your parents to change their minds and a time to simply say, "Yes, Mom. Yes, Dad."

This is a lesson that every single person has had to learn. Those that don't learn might grow up physically, but they don't grow up mentally. When they don't learn to respect authority, it is hard for them to get a job and keep a job.

Even Paul, one of God's chosen apostles, admitted that he was foolish as a child too. **"When I was a child, I spoke like a child, thought like a child, and reasoned like a child. When I became an adult, I no longer used childish ways"** (1 Corinthians 13:11).

Every day is a chance to grow up a little more.

The Sun Stands Still

"For my birthday I want to go to the playground and then go swimming. Then I want to have an obstacle course and build a fort and have ice cream. Oh, and I want to go bowling and play Legos and football," the eight-year-old boy declared.

His mom laughed and said, "There's only 24 hours in a day!"

God has given you only 24 hours in each day, and there's only so much you can do. Only one time in history was there a day with more than 24 hours. The true story is in Joshua chapter 10.

Five Amorite kings had attacked an important city called Gibeon. Joshua, the leader of the Israelite army, had promised to protect the people of Gibeon, so the army marched 20 miles at night and surprised the Amorites in the morning. But there was so much to do! Each of the five kings had their own army. How would little Israel be able to handle them all?

"Joshua spoke to the LORD while Israel was watching: 'Sun, stand still over Gibeon, and moon, stand still over the valley of Aijalon!' The sun stood still, and the moon stopped until a nation got revenge on its enemies. Isn't it recorded in the Book of Jashar? The sun stopped in the middle of the sky, and for nearly a day the sun was in no hurry to set. Never before or after this day was there anything like it. The LORD did what a man told him to do, because the LORD fought for Israel" (verses 12-14).

Your God is so powerful that he stopped the sun and the moon.

Chomp on this!

Read Hebrews 4:16 (NIV) out loud. "Let us then approach God's throne of grace with confidence, so that we may receive mercy and find grace to help us in our time of need."

How can you follow Joshua's example and use this passage to be confident when you pray?

Training is hard

Navy SEALs are some of the most elite military members in the world. They train for 18 months to 2 years to become SEALs. In their worst week of training, they spend five and a half sleepless days constantly working, cold, hungry, wet, and dirty—all while getting yelled at. They can quit at any point; they simply have to go ring a bell three times. It's such a brutal training that 70 to 80 percent drop out. (If you haven't learned percent yet in math, that means if ten people are training, only two to three finish.)

Lots of people are invited to participate in SEAL training, but not many finish. Jesus says it's the same with believers. God's Word, his invitation, goes out to everyone, but some people choose to ring the bell and quit because it is too hard.

There's a story in John chapter 6 where Jesus was teaching at a synagogue: **"When many of Jesus' disciples heard him, they said, 'What he says is hard to accept. Who wants to listen to him anymore?' Jesus' speech made many of his disciples go back to the lives they had led before they followed Jesus"** (verses 60, 66).

Those disciples thought that it was too hard to follow Jesus, that it required too much of a commitment. So they quit their training and went back home to what they thought were comfortable lives.

If only they had known that even though following Jesus can be hard, it's worth it. **"Blessed are those who endure when they are tested. When they pass the test, they will receive the crown of life that God has promised to those who love him"** (James 1:12).

Hang in there while you are tested. It will be worth it in the end.

God's plans

When adults run out of things to say to kids, they usually ask, "What do you want to be when you grow up?" The list begins: doctor, athlete, teacher, physical therapist, writer, and artist. Those are just from one kid's list of replies.

No kid ever says, "I want to become addicted to smoking and alcohol too. I don't want to have a warm place to live either. And I'm really hoping to get fired from lots of jobs."

When you're young and you have a whole long life to live yet, it's fun to hope and dream about all the ways your life can work out. You never think about the way that your life could fail. Neither does God.

In Jeremiah 29:11, he tells you, **"I know the plans that I have for you, declares the LORD. They are plans for peace and not disaster, plans to give you a future filled with hope."**

God has plans for you, good plans that have an exciting future. He created you to be his own, he sent his Son to rescue you, and he wants to be in heaven with you forever.

No matter what job you get, God has work for you to do your whole life. He has great plans for you to bring him glory and to share his good news with others.

As you grow up, follow God's plans.

Choose your friends wisely

**"Don't let anyone deceive you.
Associating with bad people will ruin decent people"**
(1 Corinthians 15:33).

Do you know why your parents want to know who your friends are? Because they care, that's why. Their most important job is to teach you everything God has done for you. God also gave them to you because he knew you'd need someone to help you learn how to make good choices, how to become a responsible member of society. (Be honest, if you could, you'd eat pizza and ice cream for almost every meal, you'd skip school, and you'd never clean your room.)

That's why they are also absolutely interested in the people who influence you. Do you spend the majority of your time with people who encourage you to follow God's laws? Or do you hang out with people who care more about themselves? Do your friends gossip about or bully other people? Or do they say, "Hey, that's not right. Don't talk that way"?

Don't be fooled. The kids you hang around with now help determine what kind of adult you'll become. Choose wisely.

(By the way, this isn't a new idea. In today's passage, the apostle Paul was quoting a poet named Menander who lived three hundred years before Jesus was born.)

 ## Chomp on this!

Have everyone name three friends.

How did they become your friends?

Do they help you make good choices or do you get into trouble when they are around?

Be a helper

"Would you please come here? I need your help," calls your mom.

"Time to help me mow the lawn," says your dad.

Don't you just feel like saying, "Mom, really? I'm playing with my dolls" or "Oh, Daaaaaaad! But we're in the middle of a game."

Whenever your parents ask for your help, it always feels like you are the only one in the whole entire world who ever has to do chores. (By the way, you're not. Every kid I know has to pitch in around the house.)

King David had no problem asking God for help—all the time. He often called out to God and said, **"Hear, O Lord, and have pity on me! O Lord, be my helper!"** (Psalm 30:10).

What's amazing is that the God who is in control of the entire universe actually loves helping. He doesn't say, "Ugh! Aww man, do I have to?" He doesn't think it's a waste of his time. He thinks being a helper is awesome, and he loves it when we ask him to help. He is interested in your life, and it makes him happy to be involved. Whatever you need help with—your friendships, your parents, your problems—talk to him. Ask him to be your helper, and don't be surprised when he says yes. Then, like King David, you get to say, **"God is my helper! The Lord is the provider for my life"** (Psalm 54:4).

 ## Chomp on this!

Do you have something in particular that you need God to help you with?

Say a prayer about it as a family right now.

You are God's goose

Duck, Duck, Goose is pretty much a universal kids' game. Everyone sits in a circle while one person walks around tapping kids on the head saying, "Duck, duck, duck, duck, duck … goose!" The goose gets up, runs around, and chases the person who is It.

The thing is, when you're It, you know who the goose is going to be, don't you? You'll walk around the circle saying, "Duck, duck, duck" … but you've got your eye on your best friend. He's the one who's going to be the goose.

It may sound silly, but God's had his eye on you. You are God's goose. **"Before the creation of the world, he chose us through Christ to be holy and perfect in his presence. Because of his love he had already decided to adopt us through Jesus Christ. He freely chose to do this"** (Ephesians 1:4,5).

Before this world even started, he knew how things were going to turn out. He knew he'd have a salvation plan; he knew he wanted you to be part of it. So before the world even started, God had you picked out. Now, because of Jesus, you are holy and perfect. Because of Jesus, you are loved. Because you are loved, you are his child.

By the way, you know how sometimes a teacher notices that the same kids are getting picked over and over so she says, "Make sure you pick someone else" and it wasn't who you really wanted to choose? God *freely* chose you. Before the world was even formed, God had his eye on you. Duck, duck—goose!

Dear God,
thank you for choosing me as your child. Amen.

Hold on tight!

*Today let's **Dig In!** Read this section of Scripture, and then use the questions to talk about what God has to say in his Word.*

We always have to thank God for you, brothers and sisters. You are loved by the Lord and we thank God that in the beginning he chose you to be saved through a life of spiritual devotion and faith in the truth. With this in mind he called you by the Good News which we told you so that you would obtain the glory of our Lord Jesus Christ.

Then, brothers and sisters, firmly hold on to the traditions we taught you either when we spoke to you or in our letter.

God our Father loved us and by his kindness gave us everlasting encouragement and good hope. Together with our Lord Jesus Christ, may he encourage and strengthen you to do and say everything that is good. (2 Thessalonians 2:13-17)

Chomp on this!

What does God teach you in this passage?

What makes you say, "Thank you, Jesus"?

What makes you say, "I'm sorry, Jesus"?

Based on this reading, what would you like to ask God for?

I don't like church

You love your best friend's house, don't you? There you can share your secrets, your problems, and you know you are safe.

Going to church, well, that's another matter. It's easy to grumble because you go to school all week and now you have to wake up early on the weekend too. That doesn't seem right. Maybe you don't like the music or you think the pastor is boring. Sometimes you wish that being a Christian wasn't so boring either—all those commandments and all those rules take the fun out of life.

Jesus is your best friend. Church is his house. This coming Sunday when you might be feeling crabby, tell yourself, "I get to go to my best friend's house."

There you get to tell him your secrets and hear him say, "I forgive you."

There you tell him your problems and hear him say, **"Come to me, all you who are weary and burdened, and I will give you rest"** (Matthew 11:28 NIV).

There you hear him tell you how much he likes being around you.

So keep going. You will hear the pastor tell you about your best friend and his love for you. Through that message, the Holy Spirit will work in your heart and someday you'll even say, **"I was glad when they said to me, 'Let's go to the house of the Lord'"** (Psalm 122:1).

 ## Chomp on this!

How can you stay focused in church this week? (Write down two things from the message that you hadn't heard before. Write down three people or things to pray for.)

For parents: How can you help the children you know stay focused on worship? How can you make the church a more welcoming place to be?

No whining!

Read this in your best whining voice: "Why won't you buy that for me?" "Why won't you help me?" "You don't understand me."

Does whining work in your house? Probably not. Whining is selfish. It means you've forgotten just how blessed you are.

The Israelites were feeling pretty whiney, having forgotten just how much their God had blessed them. So Isaiah, a prophet from God, passed along this message: **"Jacob, why do you complain? Israel, why do you say, 'My way is hidden from the Lord, and my rights are ignored by my God'? Don't you know? Haven't you heard? The eternal God, the Lord, the Creator of the ends of the earth, doesn't grow tired or become weary. His understanding is beyond reach. He gives strength to those who grow tired and increases the strength of those who are weak"** (Isaiah 40:27-29).

If you're tempted to whine today, wondering why God hasn't given you more or why God doesn't seem to be answering your prayers, hear him tell you, "<Put your name here>, why do you complain? <Put your name here>, why do you say, 'God ignores me'?"

God, who created the world out of nothing, has never once gotten tired of being your God, of being everybody's God. He has plans for you and uses everything in your life to shape you into the person he wants you to be. He is busy helping you and giving you strength to face each day.

I can't think of any good reason to whine, can you?

You reflect Jesus

As you get ready each morning, one of your jobs is to look in the mirror. Usually when people look in the mirror, they are critical. You need to make sure there's nothing in your teeth, that breakfast is all off your face, and that your hair isn't sticking out even more than normal.

Today, the people who started National Compliment Your Mirror Day want you to say nice things to the face in the mirror, to see just how awesome your God-designed face is.

The other thing about a Christian's mirror is that you don't just see you. You see Jesus. As Jesus' brothers and sisters, **"all of us reflect the Lord's glory with faces that are not covered with veils, we are being changed into his image with ever-increasing glory"** (2 Corinthians 3:18).

When Jesus came to earth, he lived his whole life *for you*. He never disobeyed his parents *for you*, never did anything wrong *for you*, and he chose to die on a cross—*for you*. Then he rose from the dead to make you part of God's family, which means you get to claim his victory as yours.

Because of your faith, the face in the mirror looks just like Jesus.

Chomp on this!

Sometimes we don't see Jesus in ourselves very well. Tell how you see Jesus in each of your family members.

Freedom at a price

On July 4, 1776, the United States declared its independence from Great Britain. That wasn't the end of this new nation's problems, however. It was actually the start.

The British did not want to give up its land without a fight. After signing the Declaration of Independence, the Revolutionary War went on for seven more years. To secure this freedom, 25,000 Americans died and another 25,000 were wounded.

When Jesus died on a cross, he was a one-man army who defeated Satan. His death secured your freedom. This isn't the end to your earthly problems, however. It's more like the start of another battle. Satan refuses to give you up without a fight. That's why he tempts you, fights against you, and tries to get you back.

But he can't have you, because **"there is now no condemnation for those who are in Christ Jesus, because through Christ Jesus the law of the Spirit who gives life has set you free from the law of sin and death"** (Romans 8:1,2 NIV).

Today, celebrate the freedom that comes only from Jesus. He won it on a cross, and he wants you to share it with the world.

Dear Jesus,

you sacrificed your life to fight for me because you love me. Thank you for securing my freedom from sin and death. Amen.

You are a Jewel

At the Coast Guard base on Kodiak Island, Alaska, there's a fun spot known as Jewel Beach. For years people have been going to this beach to collect what adults call sea glass. Kids, however, know the truth; these are "jewels."

These treasures started out as junk. Some were simply pieces of glass from trash in the water; some were shards of glass that were dragged into the ocean by a tsunami in 1964. No matter how the glass got there, these shards were tumbled around in the water. Sometimes they were battered by the waves and ocean storms; other times they got dragged back and forth along the rocks as the tide came in and out.

After years of being tossed and tumbled and banged up, the glass pieces ended up smooth and frosted, looking like jewels.

Paul, who actually suffered from beatings because of his faith in Jesus, let the people who lived in Rome know this: **"We also glory in our sufferings, because we know that suffering produces perseverance; perseverance, character; and character, hope. And hope does not put us to shame, because God's love has been poured out into our hearts through the Holy Spirit, who has been given to us"** (Romans 5:3-5 NIV).

We might think that hard times in our lives are all bad. But we each have bad habits and personal sins that are ragged in our lives. When God allows you to suffer, he smooths out those rough edges—he makes you more kind, faithful, compassionate, and courageous. He uses the rough times in your life to turn you into a jewel.

 ## Chomp on this!

What stuff in your life has made you feel like you were being tossed around in the waves?

How did God use that to smooth your rough edges?

Washed clean

**"Also get rid of your anger, hot tempers, hatred,
cursing, obscene language, and all similar sins.
Don't lie to each other.
You've gotten rid of the person you used to be
and the life you used to live,
and you've become a new person.
This new person is continually renewed in knowledge
to be like its Creator"**
(Colossians 3:8-10).

You've been outside playing in the dirt. There's mud in between
your toes, in your hair, and all over your clothes. Personally, you
don't care so much, but you know the minute you walk in the
door your mom is going to say, "You are filthy! Get in the tub!"
You also know exactly how she'd react if you put your dirty
clothes back on after your bath.

Before you were part of God's family, it was like you were playing
in the mud. Fighting, being sassy, disobeying your parents, and
whining didn't bother you. But now that you are clean, the dirt
feels, well, dirty. When you were baptized, you were washed clean
by Jesus, and now your sins feel filthy.

Every day when you wake up, remember that Jesus has forgiven
your sins. You are clean. You are new.

Dear Jesus,

thank you for washing away the dirt from all of my sins. You have
made me a clean person, a new person. You have made me to be
more like you. Thank you. Amen.

Don't go there

The Do Not Enter! sign on the street tells you not to drive that way. The yellow tape around a crime scene lets you know you aren't allowed in. The No Trespassing sign on your neighbor's house tells you that strangers aren't welcome. All these warning signs tell you where you shouldn't go.

King David used all sorts of words to describe God's law. In Psalm 19:7-11 he says, **"The *teachings* of the LORD are perfect.... The *testimony* of the LORD is dependable.... The *instructions* of the LORD are correct.... The *command* of the LORD is radiant.... The *fear* of the LORD is pure.... The *decisions* of the LORD are true.... As your servant I am warned by them. There is a great reward in following them."**

God's law, the commandments he gives you, is there as a warning sign. He put his law there to keep you safe. When he says, "Obey your parents, do not murder, do not covet, do not steal," he's saying, "I'm warning you. Don't go there." Bad things happen when you ignore the signs. (I'm sure you can think of a few times you've had to suffer the consequences for your choices.)

Jesus told the people the same thing when he talked to them: **"Whoever does and teaches what the commands say will be called great in the kingdom of heaven"** (Matthew 5:19).

That's the reward David was talking about. Pay attention to the signs God puts in front of you.

Pray for everyone

*Today let's **Dig In!** Read this section of Scripture, and then use the questions to talk about what God has to say in his Word.*

First of all, I encourage you to make petitions, prayers, intercessions, and prayers of thanks for all people, for rulers, and for everyone who has authority over us. Pray for these people so that we can have a quiet and peaceful life always lived in a godly and reverent way. This is good and pleases God our Savior. He wants all people to be saved and to learn the truth. There is one God. There is also one mediator between God and humans—a human, Christ Jesus. He sacrificed himself for all people to free them from their sins.

This message is valid for every era. I was appointed to spread this Good News and to be an apostle to teach people who are not Jewish about faith and truth. I'm telling you the truth. I'm not lying. (1 Timothy 2:1-7)

 ## Chomp on this!

What does God teach you in this passage?

What makes you say, "Thank you, Jesus"?

What makes you say, "I'm sorry, Jesus"?

Based on this reading, what would you like to ask God for?

Living water

Before you read this devotion, have someone get a glass of water and take a drink.

How long did it take you to get water? Fifteen seconds, or maybe a bit longer if you had to use a drinking fountain? Where you live, getting clean drinking water is not a big deal. Every single time you are thirsty, you grab a glass, walk to the sink, and turn on the faucet.

In countries throughout the world, people have to work much harder to get their water. Every day they walk for miles and make the same journey home carrying their heavy loads so they won't be thirsty. In Bible times, people didn't have faucets either; they had to walk to the nearest well. Without water, they would die. That's why they went every day.

One day Jesus met a woman at a well and started talking to her about water. Then he started talking about a different kind of water. He said, **"Those who drink the water that I will give them will never become thirsty again. In fact, the water I will give them will become in them a spring that gushes up to eternal life"** (John 4:14).

That sounds a little confusing, doesn't it? How can you not be thirsty ever again? When the Holy Spirit uses God's Word to help you believe that Jesus has defeated death and you get to live forever, you get Jesus' living water. You don't have to keep searching for anything else to survive. Your forgiveness, salvation, and eternal life are guaranteed. You'll never be spiritually thirsty again.

Take a big drink!

Chomp on this!

Lots of people are spiritually thirsty. They look for all sorts of ways to help them be happy or to try to get through sad times in their lives. Talk about the people you know who need to hear about Jesus and his living water. Come up with two ways that you might be able to tell them.

No-See-umS

No-see-ums are itty-bitty bugs so small that, you guessed it, they can't be seen. (That's how they get their name.) Sometimes it seems like angels are God's version of no-see-ums. Because you can't see them, you don't actually believe they are there. You forget that **"he will put his angels in charge of you to protect you in all your ways"** (Psalm 91:11).

Elisha, God's prophet, had a servant who felt like angels were no-see-ums too.

"When the servant of the man of God got up in the morning and went outside, he saw troops, horses, and chariots surrounding the city. Elisha's servant asked, 'Master, what should we do?' Elisha answered, 'Don't be afraid. We have more forces on our side than they have on theirs.' Then Elisha prayed, 'Lord, please open his eyes so that he may see.' The Lord opened the servant's eyes and let him see. The mountain around Elisha was full of fiery horses and chariots" (2 Kings 6:15-17).

Elisha was given the gift of seeing God's angels as they really are—surrounding and protecting the city from its enemies. For a brief moment his servant got to see it too.

Just because we can't see angels the way Elisha did doesn't mean they aren't there. God has said they will be all around you, protecting you no matter where you go. Even—and especially—when you can't see them.

Cheer up!

Today is National Cheer Up the Lonely Day. Here's what God says about cheerful hearts, cheering others up, and what brings real cheer.

"Every day is a terrible day for a miserable person, but a cheerful heart has a continual feast" (Proverbs 15:15).

Have you ever been grumpy for a few days in row?

How do you react to everything that happens?

Talk about how your days go when you're in a great mood.

"We encourage you, brothers and sisters, to instruct those who are not living right, cheer up those who are discouraged, help the weak, and be patient with everyone" (1 Thessalonians 5:14).

Are there any people in your life who seem discouraged lately?

How can you cheer them up?

What if they are discouraged because of something really serious, like a death in their family? How can you gently encourage them and support them?

"Jesus got into a boat, crossed the sea, and came to his own city. Some people brought him a paralyzed man on a stretcher. When Jesus saw their faith, he said to the man, 'Cheer up, friend! Your sins are forgiven'" (Matthew 9:1,2).

When you listened to that passage, what did you think would follow the words, "Cheer up, friend!"?

Was being paralyzed that man's biggest problem? If not, what was his biggest problem?

Dear Jesus,

open our eyes to see when our friends or family are sad and need encouragement. Help us remember that the most important thing that will cheer people up is telling them that you have forgiven them. Help us bring them the joy that comes from being loved by you. Amen.

Learning about Jesus

When you were two, you knew the difference between right and wrong. You knew it was wrong to hit. You'd run and hide if you did hit someone because you didn't want to get into trouble.

What you didn't know when you were two was that, even though you got a time-out from your parents, Jesus took the ultimate punishment for your sins. You aren't born knowing that. You need someone to tell you. That's why God gave you parents and grandparents.

Timothy, who ended up becoming a missionary and traveling all over his part of the world, had to learn about Jesus when he was little too.

His dad was a Greek, which meant that his dad didn't know about Jesus. His mom and grandma did, though, so they made sure he knew all about God's plan to save the world. **"I'm reminded of how sincere your faith is. That faith first lived in your grandmother Lois and your mother Eunice. I'm convinced that it also lives in you"** (2 Timothy 1:5).

Timothy—who learned about Jesus from his mom and grandma—was God's child, just like you are.

Chomp on this!

Timothy grew up to be a pastor. The apostle Paul wrote him a couple of letters to tell him how to serve people. You can read those letters in 1 and 2 Timothy.

Dear God,

thank you for giving me adults to help me learn about Jesus. Without them, I wouldn't know about you and your awesome plan to save me. For the adults in my life who don't know you, like Timothy's dad, help me to tell them. Amen.

Water into wine

You would be so embarrassed if you ran out of cake at your birthday party. I mean, that's one of the best parts of parties. You always make sure you'll have enough for your friends.

Jesus was at a wedding reception where the hosts ran out of wine. The couple would have been embarrassed to know they didn't have enough for their guests, so Jesus' mom talked to him about the problem. Jesus had a solution.

"Jesus said to the servants, 'Fill the jars with water'; so they filled them to the brim. Then he told them, 'Now draw some out and take it to the master of the banquet.' They did so, and the master of the banquet tasted the water that had been turned into wine. What Jesus did here in Cana of Galilee was the first of the signs through which he revealed his glory; and his disciples believed in him" (John 2:7-9, 11 NIV).

With just a thought, Jesus performed his first miracle, his first sign. That sign told his disciples, "Look, I have power over creation. I am God, and I am here on the earth to be with you." Watching Jesus do these signs for his friends reminds you that he loves to act in your life too, to work things for your good.

Water to wine—that's what your God can do.

Dear God,

I am amazed at the wonderful things you can do. You created the world; you turned water into wine; you make sick people well, and you sent Jesus to earth to live, die, and rise for me.
All glory to you. Amen.

You are a padawan

Luke wasn't born a Jedi. He had to spend years as an apprentice, a padawan, learning from Obi-Wan Kenobi. When you were born, you were part of the Dark Side. When you are baptized and by believing in Jesus, no matter how young you are, you are a member of God's kingdom. At the same time, you also have a lot to learn. You are a padawan too. Your parents are the Jedis whom God has put in your life. He gives them a job to do: **"Train a child in the way he should go, and even when he is old he will not turn away from it"** (Proverbs 22:6).

Your parents' most important job is to teach you what God has done for you. Every day they share how Jesus lived for you and died for you. They take you to church and pray with you. They share how Jesus has changed their lives so that you know Jesus is really alive and working in people's lives today. They also teach you how the world works and what it looks like when you live out your faith. They "make" you volunteer and do nice things for other people so you learn the good habit of serving others. They give you chores to teach you how to be responsible; they allow you to suffer consequences so you learn how to make better choices. They say, "I'm sorry" when they mess up because they model how to ask for forgiveness. They pay attention to the friends in your life because they want to help you make good decisions.

They do all of these things when you are young because they want you to become Jedis too. They want you to train your children, the next group of padawans. **"We will tell the next generation about the Lord's power and great deeds and the miraculous things he has done"** (Psalm 78:4).

Listen to your parents, you must.

Chomp on this!

Talk to the Christian adults in your life. Ask them how they learned about Jesus.

Jesus calms the storm

Storms can be terrifying. Thunder makes you run to your parents' bed. Lightning has you hiding under the covers. A tornado warning will send you straight to the basement.

Adults get scared of storms sometimes too. **"That evening, Jesus said to his disciples, 'Let's cross to the other side.' Leaving the crowd, they took Jesus along in a boat just as he was. Other boats were with him. A violent windstorm came up. The waves were breaking into the boat so that it was quickly filling up. But he was sleeping on a cushion in the back of the boat. So they woke him up and said to him, 'Teacher, don't you care that we're going to die?' Then he got up, ordered the wind to stop, and said to the sea, 'Be still, absolutely still!' The wind stopped blowing, and the sea became very calm. He asked them, 'Why are you such cowards? Don't you have any faith yet?' They were overcome with fear and asked each other, 'Who is this man? Even the wind and the sea obey him!'"** (Mark 4:35-41).

Because sin is in the world, there will always be storms. Your Jesus, however, wants you to come to him—to pray and let him know you are scared. Sometimes he might make the storm stop. Sometimes he'll use your parents to comfort you. Other times he'll say, "Be still!" to your heart and you can relax knowing that the wind and waves and storms obey your God.

Chomp on this!

Do you get anxious and worried sometimes? About what? Why can you "be still" in these situations?

Let's hear it

After your performance in the community theater play, you would be offended if the audience got up and walked out quietly. When they clap and cheer, the audience lets the cast know that they appreciate all the time and effort.

When your little league team wins its first game, does your coach look bored? No way! He cheers louder than the rest.

When you win the spelling bee or get a leadership award, your parents don't simply smile and nod. No! They clap and cheer and can't wait to take your picture so they can share their happiness with family and friends.

It's time to make some noise for your God too. Every single awesome thing in this world and in your life is because of the work he did. A brain that controls the legs that move you from place to place—his idea. Creating elbows so you could bend your arms to feed yourself—he thought of that. Giving you aunties and uncles to love you—his blessing to you. Clothes to wear and food to eat—bought by the money he provides. Stars, waves, beaches, mountains—his creative genius made those! Coming to earth to defeat sin, death, hell, and Satan—entirely his plan! Preparing a place in heaven for you—his sweet idea.

"Clap your hands, all you people. Shout to God with a loud, joyful song" (Psalm 47:1).

God gives you permission—**get loud!**

Exactly who he wants you to be

Everyone else is better than you.

At least you think so, don't you? You look at other people and wish that you were more cheerful or talented, happier or stronger, faster or smarter. Whatever it is, you compare yourself and wish you were less like you and more like them.

God wants you to stop that crazy thinking. Think of yourself the way he thinks about you.

"The body is one unit and yet has many parts. As all the parts form one body, so it is with Christ. So God put each and every part of the body together as he wanted it" (1 Corinthians 12:12,18).

God made you exactly the way he wants you to be. The people around you are exactly how God wants them to be too. No, you aren't the same, but that's the way God made it. He loves it when the people he created are unique. He loves it when you make lonely people feel part of the group. He loves the kids who are confident enough to ask random strangers if they know about Jesus. He loves when big kids willingly help little kids learn about Jesus at Sunday school. He loves when the kids who do well in school say thank you for the brain he gave them. He loves when the artist sketches a beautiful picture of the world he created. But if he gave you every single one of those gifts, you wouldn't have time to use them all. Instead, he gave you the exact gifts he wanted you to have, so you would use them fully, completely, to the best of the ability he gave you.

Today, celebrate that you are exactly how God wants you to be.

Chomp on this!

Discuss what gifts God has given you that make you unique. How can you use those gifts to serve others?

What makes you great

Girls, today's devotion is going to sound more like it's for guys. Right now, you might think boys are gross, but someday—a long time from now— you might think about marrying one of them. God thinks it's important that you know, right now, what he values. Plus, if you ever have a son, it will be your job to teach him what true strength is. So pay attention!

For boys everything is a competition. They want to know who is the best at sports, who has the biggest muscles, who has the most kills in a video game. The athletes who have the biggest egos sell the most jerseys. Gangsta and hip-hop culture is all about young men boasting that they are the best.

The disciples—grown men—were arguing about the exact same thing. Jesus silenced the fight when he told them to stop using the world's definition of greatness. **"You're not going to be that way! Rather, the greatest among you must be like the youngest, and your leader must be like a servant"** (Luke 22:26).

Jesus mastered the sea, threw tables around in the temple, and raised the dead to life. Yet he showed his greatest strength when he got on his hands and knees and washed the disciples' feet. The God who could have climbed off the cross used self-control to stay there so he could die for the people he loved.

Use your strength to serve, lead, and protect the people in your life. That's what makes you powerful. That's what makes you great.

Your Stuff doesn't matter

*Today let's **Dig In!** Read this section of Scripture, and then use the questions to talk about what God has to say in his Word.*

A godly life brings huge profits to people who are content with what they have. We didn't bring anything into the world, and we can't take anything out of it. As long as we have food and clothes, we should be satisfied.

But people who want to get rich keep falling into temptation. They are trapped by many stupid and harmful desires which drown them in destruction and ruin. Certainly, the love of money is the root of all kinds of evil. Some people who have set their hearts on getting rich have wandered away from the Christian faith and have caused themselves a lot of grief.

But you, man of God, must avoid these things. Pursue what God approves of: a godly life, faith, love, endurance, and gentleness. Fight the good fight for the Christian faith. Take hold of everlasting life to which you were called and about which you made a good testimony in front of many witnesses. (1 Timothy 6:6-12)

Chomp on this!

What does God teach you in this passage?

What makes you say, "Thank you, Jesus"?

What makes you say, "I'm sorry, Jesus"?

Based on this reading, what would you like to ask God for?

An amazing reception*

It was a hot summer afternoon and Diego and Josh were playing catch in Diego's backyard. They had been playing for over two hours and were totally exhausted. Diego threw one way over Josh's head. Josh had to jump over a chest-high bush and catch the football one handed, while getting all scratched up by the bush. It was an amazing catch, an awesome reception.

You have made an awesome reception too—although it wasn't because you were awesome on your own. In John 1:12 we hear, **"Yet to all who did receive him, to those who believed in his name, he gave the right to become children of God"** (NIV).

On our own, we are exhausted and don't even want to hear about Jesus. Through the Holy Spirit, though, we are able to believe in Jesus and receive him. Because of that awesome reception, we become children of God.

As children of God, we don't have to worry about anything. God protects us like a mother and father protect their children—but even better. When we sin, he forgives us and doesn't bring them up again. He does this not because we have done so much for him, but because he wanted to, because the Holy Spirit gave us faith.

Josh had an amazing reception; ours is even better. We receive Christ through faith.

Dear God,

thank you for giving us an awesome reception through faith in Jesus. We are your children and get all the good things that come from you. Strengthen my faith in you. In Jesus' name we pray. Amen.

This devotion was written by Adler, a kid just like you.

Does God care when your pet dies?

While Jesus talked to a big crowd of people, he reminded them just how valuable they were to God. He put in a little nugget of information that's pretty cool. He said, **"Are not two sparrows sold for a penny? Yet not one of them will fall to the ground outside your Father's care"** (Matthew 10:29 NIV).

Did you catch that? Not only is God paying attention to you and your life, he is paying attention to every animal on the face of this earth too. God notices each duck, goldfish, cat, bear, dog, giraffe, hamster, moose, and elephant. Your Father cares for them by providing food for the wild animals. If one of those animals— hopefully not the moose—is your pet, he gives you the privilege and honor of taking care of it.

So does God care when your pet dies? He absolutely does. If he notices when a little sparrow falls to the ground, he sees when you're sad that your pet died. After all, on the sixth day of creation, **"God made every type of wild animal, every type of domestic animal, and every type of creature that crawls on the ground. God saw that they were good"** (Genesis 1:25).

Animals are part of God's plan to bless you. They are good. He does care.

 ## Chomp on this!

How does God use animals to bless us?

Serving Jesus by Serving Others

How did you serve Jesus today?

Sometimes it's hard to think of something, isn't it? Maybe you're thinking, "Well, I didn't go to church. I didn't read my Bible, and I forgot to pray."

Jesus says that you serve him this way: **"I was hungry, and you gave me something to eat. I was thirsty, and you gave me something to drink. I was a stranger, and you took me into your home. I needed clothes, and you gave me something to wear. I was sick, and you took care of me. I was in prison, and you visited me."** (Matthew 25:35,36).

Umm, but I know you didn't give Jesus clothes or food, and you definitely didn't visit him in prison today. That's when Jesus adds, **"Whatever you did for one of my brothers or sisters ... you did for me"** (verse 40).

Oh. When you serve others, you are serving Jesus.

You serve Jesus when you

- share your lunch,
- give Christmas presents to a child whose dad is in jail,
- bring your teacher flowers (or chocolate),
- visit your elderly neighbor,
- tell your friend she's beautiful when she claims she's ugly,
- sing at a nursing home, and
- do your chores without complaining.

Now think again; how did you serve Jesus today?

The best true story ever

You have rules at home about chores and Internet use. Rules at school tell you when you can talk and where you can run. Rules in your community tell you where you can and cannot skateboard. The last thing kids want are more rules. This is why I think sometimes you don't want to open the Bible. After all, some of God's most famous words are The Ten Rules!

When you open up the Bible, yes, there are rules that tell you things to do (and not to do) for your life to go well. But God's rules are a really small part of his book.

For those who like fairy tales, the Bible tells the *real* story of the Prince of peace who searches and searches for the one he loves. When he finds her, he rescues her and takes her to a beautiful kingdom with streets of gold and a spectacular castle where they live happily ever after.

For those who might be more into action stories, the Bible tells of a warrior who has rescued captives from the clutches of the Evil One. **"I saw heaven standing open. There was a white horse, and its rider is named Faithful and True. With integrity he judges and wages war. His eyes are flames of fire. On his head are many crowns"** (Revelation 19:11,12).

Open up the Bible today and hear the true story of the One who is powerful and loving, faithful and true, the one who obeyed all the rules so you could be in the eternal victory parade.

Character counts

I'm going to let you in on a secret: adults notice kids' character more than kids' achievements.

If you stop trying because you are losing a race, adults notice.

If you completely mess up your piano solo at the fine arts fair but pause and regain your composure, adults notice.

If your team is losing and you get a technical for disagreeing with the referee, adults notice.

If you spill paint all over your art project for the county fair but turn your mistake into something beautiful, adults notice.

It's true that adults love it when your team wins or you get a blue ribbon, that's because winning is fun and success feels good. What adults love even more is to see the way you handle yourself when things aren't going well. Do you finish strong even if you're in last place? Do you do your best no matter what? Do you get discouraged and quit a project or do you figure out a way to make it work?

All the adults that God has put in your life to help you grow up, to teach you about your God, and to show you what it means to become a responsible human being know that the person you are on the inside is far more important than earthly accomplishments. That's why they pay close attention to your character, more than your accomplishments.

Victories, ribbons, and money will come and go, but your character and reputation stick with you. That's why King Solomon tells you to focus on the inside: **"A good name is more desirable than great wealth. Respect is better than silver or gold"** (Proverbs 22:1).

Riding your bike*

Learning to ride a bike is not easy. You fall down many times, and your parent has to lift you up and put bandages on your scrapes. Your mom or dad runs right next to you, teaching you. It may take days, weeks, or months, but eventually you get stronger and fall fewer times.

Faith in God is like learning to ride a bike. At first you have many doubts and get hurt. God is always next to you, picking you up and teaching you through his Word. As you grow older, you become stronger, fall less, and go the right way. But you still aren't perfect, and there are obstacles in your way that can still cause you to fall. That is why God always keeps a close watch over you and helps you back up.

We don't have to be afraid because we know that no matter how many times we fall, God still loves us and will help us back up through his Word and promises. God loves us and has not, and will not, give up on us. We don't have to be afraid of the future or that God won't forgive us, because he already has. He promises, **"Don't be afraid, because I am with you. Don't be intimidated; I am your God. I will strengthen you. I will help you. I will support you with my victorious right hand"** (Isaiah 41:10).

Dear heavenly Father,

we know that you love us more than anything else and will always help us back up when we fall. Please help us always trust in you and stay on the right path.
In Jesus' name we pray. Amen.

This devotion was written by Max, a kid just like you.

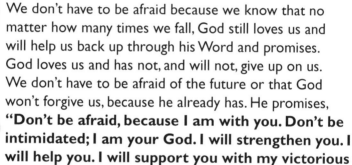

Pay it forward

You probably know all about the "Pay Me Back" concept. You give someone five dollars, and they have to pay you back. If someone hits you, you hit them back. If you clean out the dishwasher for your sister, she has to do a chore for you.

God is far more interested in the "Pay It Forward" concept. He's given peace, love, faith, hope, and joy to you as gifts. There is absolutely no way you can pay him back for all he has done for you. (After all, you don't give someone money to pay for the birthday gift he or she gave you.) Instead, you take the gifts God has poured into you and share them with the people in your life.

"Praise be to the God and Father of our Lord Jesus Christ, the Father of compassion and the God of all comfort, who comforts us in all our troubles, so that we can comfort those in any trouble with the comfort we ourselves receive from God. For just as we share abundantly in the sufferings of Christ, so also our comfort abounds through Christ" (2 Corinthians 1:3-5 NIV).

Jesus has given you peace. Pay it forward by helping a friend who is sad. Jesus has given you mercy. Pay it forward by forgiving your friend when he hurts you. Jesus has given you hope. Pay it forward by telling others about the joy that comes from knowing heaven is your real home.

Praise God for the privilege of paying it forward.

Cry; don't cry

If you've been to a funeral, maybe you felt a little awkward because you weren't sure how to act. If going to heaven is a good thing, am I not supposed to cry? But what if I'm sad?

Two stories in the Bible help us to see how Jesus reacted at two different funerals.

Funeral #1: Lazarus, one of Jesus' best friends, had just died. Jesus went for the funeral and to comfort Mary and Martha, Lazarus' sisters. **"When Jesus saw [Mary] crying, and the Jews who were crying with her, he was deeply moved and troubled."** When he went to Lazarus' tomb, the Bible tells us, **"Jesus cried"** (John 11:33,35).

When God created the world, death was not part of the plan. So every single death is a reminder that this world is not how it was meant to be. Death isn't natural; it's heartbreaking. It's okay to cry, like Jesus cried, when people you love die.

Funeral #2: One day Jesus saw a funeral procession. The only son of a widow was about to be buried. **"When the Lord saw her, he felt sorry for her. He said to her, 'Don't cry'"** (Luke 7:13). Then he told her son to get up—and he did!

If it's okay to cry, why would Jesus say, "Don't cry"? This woman's husband had died and now her son was dead too. Her family was gone, and she had no hope left. Jesus let her know that he had power over death; he gave her hope.

"We don't want you to grieve like other people who have no hope. We believe that Jesus died and came back to life. We also believe that, through Jesus, God will bring back those who have died. They will come back with Jesus" (1 Thessalonians 4:13,14).

It's okay to be sad and at the same time have the true hope that death has no power over us.

Worship God, not the Stars

"Don't let yourselves be tempted to worship and serve what you see in the sky—the sun, the moon, the stars, or anything else. The LORD your God has given them to all people everywhere" (Deuteronomy 4:19).

One of the best parts of camping is sitting around a campfire looking at the stars. Once you've gotten away from the streetlights of the city, it makes you feel small when you realize just how many are up there. It's fun to pick out constellations and to imagine how sailors navigated oceans and seas—using stars as their version of a GPS.

Did you know, though, that some people look to the sun, moon, stars, and planets to get advice on how to live their lives? Astrologists follow the patterns in the sky and, depending on when you were born, tell you if today will be a good day or bad day. Adults read their horoscopes to see if it is a good time to date someone or to make a financial decision or buy a house.

You know what God has to say about that? He thinks that's nonsense. Actually, it makes him angry. **"I am the LORD your God. . . . Never have any other god. Never make your own carved idols or statues that represent any creature in the sky, on the earth, or in the water. Never worship them or serve them, because I, the LORD your God, am a God who does not tolerate rivals"** (Exodus 20:2-5).

God made the stars. If you ever need any advice on how to live, go to the Creator, not to the creation.

Share the good news

You run around the water park screaming, "Come quick! Look!" Every slide and ride seems better than the next, and you just have to tell your friends how awesome each one is. That's how good news works. It's so great that you can't keep it to yourself.

In 2 Kings chapters 6 and 7, the king of Aram had surrounded the city of Samaria and the people of the city were starving to death. Four men who had skin diseases were banished outside the city walls and were starving too. They decided to head to the enemy's camp to see if maybe, just maybe, they'd find some food.

"So they started out at dusk to go into the Aramean camp. When they came to the edge of the camp, no one was there. The LORD had made the Aramean army hear what sounded like chariots, horses, and a large army.... So at dusk they fled" (2 Kings 7:5-7).

God, who doesn't need people to fight his battles, made four men walking sound like an entire invading army. When the men got to the camp, they found silver, gold, and clothes. They started eating and drinking.

"Then they said to one another, 'What we're doing is not right. This is a day of good news, and we're not telling anyone about it. If we wait until morning when it's light out, we'll be punished. Let's bring the news to the royal palace'" (verse 9).

So they ran back and told the men at the gates to let the whole city know that they had found a treasure.

You had a sin disease, but because of Jesus, you are healed. This is God's treasure to you. If you're keeping that news to yourself, what you're doing is not right. Every day is a day of good news, and it's your awesome job to tell everyone about it. Go take the news to everyone you know.

Jesus loves being around you

There is no country in the world where children are allowed to drive or vote. You have to wait until you're a grown-up. In God's kingdom, however, you are a full citizen.

"Some people brought little children to Jesus to have him hold them. But the disciples told the people not to do that. When Jesus saw this, he became irritated. He told them, 'Don't stop the children from coming to me. Children like these are part of the kingdom of God. I can guarantee this truth: Whoever doesn't receive the kingdom of God as a little child receives it will never enter it.' Jesus put his arms around the children and blessed them by placing his hands on them" (Mark 10:13-16).

The word *irritated* just doesn't seem to capture how Jesus was feeling. *Furious* would be a better word. Jesus absolutely hated that his disciples—the people closest to him—were trying to keep children, his little brothers and sisters, from getting close to him.

As little kids, you get to be close to Jesus, to spend time with him. You get the joy that being a child of God brings. You are as valuable to him now as you will be when you are 25 or 45 or 85.

The little children—the ones Jesus loved to be around—were God's children, just like you are.

Chomp on this!

God tells you that you are valuable to him. How can you spend more time with him?

The best part of heaven

Have you ever imagined what heaven will be like? When little girls in princess costumes hear that there are streets of gold and lots of gems, well, heaven sounds pretty great. Maybe you wonder if heaven is made of candy—and if you can eat all you want and never get sick. Some kids like to think about heaven because their friends here on earth hurt their feelings. Or maybe you wonder about who wins the basketball game in heaven if everyone has the perfect shot, the perfect block, the perfect rebound, and the perfect pass. Some kids hear that Jesus is preparing a place for them and they start designing their rooms right away.

As fun as it is to talk about heaven, because it is a real place, we easily gloss over the best part. In heaven we will be physically reunited with Jesus—the same Jesus who was once as old as you are now, the Jesus who loved you so much that he left that awesome heaven to come to our sometimes awesome but often sad earth to live in your place. This is the same Jesus who died on a cross and said to the thief next to him, **"I can guarantee this truth: Today you will be with me in paradise"** (Luke 23:43). This is the same Jesus who went to heaven where he is Lord of the universe.

So keep talking about heaven, but start with celebrating that we get to be with Jesus, God's Son. Because, ultimately, no matter what the other side benefits are, the best part of heaven is that each day we will be with him in paradise.

It's not too late

Luke Skywalker faced a final battle with his father, Darth Vader. He begged his dad to turn away from the dark side, but Darth answered, "You don't know the *power* of the dark side! I *must* obey my master."

Luke tried again, telling him there still was hope. Darth didn't believe him. "It is too late for me, son," he said.

As a kid like Luke, you think you have plenty of time. Adults, however, start to wonder if maybe their time is running out. Maybe it's too late for them.

As Jesus was taking the punishment for the sins of the entire world, the thief on the cross next to him realized that Jesus didn't deserve to be on a cross, but he, the thief did. He knew his time was running out when he said, **"Jesus, remember me when you enter your kingdom."**

Jesus, who knows that it is never too late, told him, **"I can guarantee this truth: Today you will be with me in paradise"** (Luke 23:42,43).

It's never too late for you or the people you know either. That's because Jesus is bigger than Satan. The Bible tells you that even when you sin a whole lot, God's grace covers it. **"But where sin increased, God's kindness increased even more"** (Romans 5:20).

You get to be like Luke and say, "It's never too late."

Remind yourself. Then tell your friends. Tell your family.

Dear Father,

thank you for reminding me that it is never too late. You are so kind and patient, and I don't deserve it. Yet you love me more. Your forgiveness covers every single one of my sins. You are so good to me. Thank you. Amen.

God gives us power

*Today let's **Dig In!** Read this section of Scripture, and then use the questions to talk about what God has to say in his Word.*

God didn't give us a cowardly spirit but a spirit of power, love, and good judgment. So never be ashamed to tell others about our Lord or be ashamed of me, his prisoner. Instead, by God's power, join me in suffering for the sake of the Good News. God saved us and called us to be holy, not because of what we had done, but because of his own plan and kindness. Before the world began, God planned that Christ Jesus would show us God's kindness. Now with the coming of our Savior Christ Jesus, he has revealed it. Christ has destroyed death, and through the Good News he has brought eternal life into full view. (2 Timothy 1:7-10)

Chomp on this!

What does God teach you in this passage?

What makes you say, "Thank you, Jesus"?

What makes you say, "I'm sorry, Jesus"?

Based on this reading, what would you like to ask God for?

Stand in awe

"The heavens were made by the word of the LORD
and all the stars by the breath of his mouth.
He gathers the water in the sea like a dam
and puts the oceans in his storehouses.
Let all the earth fear the LORD.
Let all who live in the world stand in awe of him.
He spoke, and it came into being.
He gave the order, and there it stood"
(Psalm 33:6-9).

Yosemite National Park in California makes you feel small. The park, which is the same size as the whole state of Rhode Island, has mountains, waterfalls, and enormous sequoia trees. Yet most people who visit see only one percent of the park—Yosemite Valley.

When you are there, you stand in awe of God. You see the vast sky in the daytime and what looks to be three hundred bazillion stars at night. God gathered the waters and made those lakes, rivers, and waterfalls. He formed the mountains and the hills. He made the trees.

You don't have to visit Yosemite to see God's creation. Even in the city, with all its streetlights, God's stars are powerful enough to shine through. The sunsets in the summer and the changing color of the leaves in fall—God did all of this so we would be in awe. He did this so that all seven billion people on earth would have a place to live that would always remind them of their Creator.

Look around you. Stand in awe.

Guard your heart!

Hello? Are you listening? Pay attention!

When your earbuds are in or you're playing a video game or the TV is on or you're reading a book or you just don't feel like listening, your parents have to work pretty hard to get you to focus on them. Still, they want your attention because they have something important to tell you.

Three thousand years ago, parents did the same thing to their kids. Solomon wrote the book of Proverbs to pass along wisdom to his son—and he told his son to listen up! **"My son, pay attention to my words. Open your ears to what I say. Do not lose sight of these things. Keep them deep within your heart because they are life to those who find them and they heal the whole body. Guard your heart more than anything else, because the source of your life flows from it"** (Proverbs 4:20-23).

You are given the Bible to tell you how God has saved you, to let you know that Jesus' work is finished and you don't have to worry at all about your future. That's why God wants you to pay attention. The more you listen up to what he has to tell you, the more you fill your heart with his good news. As you forget to focus on him, you fill your heart with junk. And here's what Jesus has to say about that: **"The mouth speaks what the heart is full of. A good man brings good things out of the good stored up in him, and an evil man brings evil things out of the evil stored up in him"** (Matthew 12:34,35 NIV).

Let Jesus fill your heart with good stuff—then guard it!

Time to Shine!

**"Do everything without complaining or arguing.
Then you will be blameless and innocent.
You will be God's children without any faults among
people who are crooked and corrupt.
You will shine like stars among them in the world"**
(Philippians 2:14,15).

In outer space, stars sometimes run out of fuel. They then collapse and get packed together super tightly. One theory is that they turn into something called a black hole. Black holes aren't really holes, though. The theory says that there's just so much no-longer-useful material crammed into a tiny space that a black hole pulls everything in from around itself. It "eats" the dust and gasses nearby, which means it gets bigger and bigger. It's so strong that no light can escape.

God tells us that this world is full of crooked and corrupt people; they are black holes. Complaining and fighting weighs them down. The more not-useful material they have inside of them, the more they attract other garbage. They keep growing and growing, and eventually no light can escape.

You, however, are God's child. He calls you to shine like a star in a world of black holes. When you fill up with God's Word and his promises, you have the fuel to shine. You use words that encourage people. You willingly agree to help others. You handle disappointments calmly.

You are God's star. It's time to shine!

Just a reflection

In Washington D.C. you can visit the Lincoln Memorial Reflecting Pool. Located in between the Lincoln Memorial and the Washington Monument, this long rectangle of water is designed to dramatically reflect the two majestic monuments.

The reflecting pool is an amazing site, but no one who goes to the United States capital says, "I saw the monuments' reflections in the pool, so I know exactly what they look like now." That's because people realize that as beautiful as a reflection might be, it's not the real thing. You have to turn around and look up to see the real beauty of the monuments.

This world is like that reflecting pool. We know God loves us. We can see his love for us, but because of sin, our view isn't completely accurate. Our knowledge isn't perfect. God tells us that the view in heaven is even better. When we are in his presence, we will turn around, look up, and see the real beauty.

"Now we see a blurred image in a mirror. Then we will see very clearly. Now my knowledge is incomplete. Then I will have complete knowledge as God has complete knowledge of me" (1 Corinthians 13:12).

Chomp on this!

How does sin blur your image of God and his love?

#1

When a team wins the championship, their fans start chanting, "We're #1! We're #1! We're #1!" Some fans will even wear giant foam fingers with #1 painted on them. They want everyone to know that they love their team the most.

What's #1 in your life? God, who is a jealous God, wants to be at the top in your life. He tells you to **"love the Lord your God with all your heart, with all your soul, and with all your strength"** (Deuteronomy 6:5).

How can you do that? I mean, really, that's a huge command from God. On your own, you can't. However, when you were baptized, the Holy Spirit came to live inside of you. So you do love the Lord with all your heart and with all your soul and with all your strength. It's just that sometimes you forget and put sports or school or electronics or friends first in your life. Because you were baptized, you are forgiven for when God comes in second or third or fourth place.

Today, remember that your most important job is to love God. When you love God most, it's like you are wearing a giant foam finger that points the way to heaven. People will see your life and will be able to tell that you are cheering, "God's #1! God's #1! God's #1!"

 ## Chomp on this!

What in your life has pushed God to second, third, or fourth place?

How can you do all the things you love to do and make sure that you love God most?

No need to beg

In the book *The Wonderful Wizard of Oz*, Dorothy, her dog, and her friends finally—finally!—get into the presence of the Wizard. The enormous head (with no body) sits in the giant, green marble throne and speaks, "I am Oz, the Great and Terrible. Who are you, and why do you seek me?"

Dorothy replies, "I am Dorothy, the Small and Meek. I have come to you for help."

After hearing Dorothy's request to take her to Kansas, the Head replies: "You have no right to expect me to send you back to Kansas unless you do something for me in return. In this country everyone must pay for everything he gets. If you wish me to use my magic power to send you home again, you must do something for me first. Help me and I will help you."

Your God is nothing like the Wizard of Oz. In fact, he is the complete opposite.

In Hebrews 4:16 we are told, **"Let us then approach God's throne of grace with confidence, so that we may receive mercy and find grace to help us in our time of need"** (NIV).

When God looks at you, he sees Jesus' perfect life and sacrifice. So when you approach your great God on his giant throne with your requests, he doesn't make you feel small and weak. He treats you like his child. He doesn't make you fight wicked witches to earn his help. When you ask him to use his power on your behalf, he says, **"For I am the LORD your God who takes hold of your right hand and says to you, Do not fear; I will help you"** (Isaiah 41:13).

Chomp on this!

What request do you have for God that maybe you've been afraid to ask about?

Walk On water

"I just want to be by myself!" You've said that, haven't you? After a busy day, sometimes you need time alone. Jesus had just fed five thousand people—that's a huge crowd—and he wanted some time alone. **"Jesus quickly made his disciples get into a boat and cross to the other side ahead of him while he sent the people away. After sending the people away, he went up a mountain to pray by himself. When evening came, he was there alone"** (Matthew 14:22,23).

By the time Jesus was ready to join the disciples again, there was a storm on the sea. Their boat was a couple of football fields away from the shore. That kind of stuff doesn't stop Jesus, however.

"Between three and six o'clock in the morning, he came to them. He was walking on the sea. When the disciples saw him walking on the sea, they were terrified. They said, 'It's a ghost!' and began to scream because they were afraid. Immediately, Jesus said, 'Calm down! It's me. Don't be afraid!' Peter answered, 'Lord, if it is you, order me to come to you on the water.' Jesus said, 'Come!' So Peter got out of the boat and walked on the water toward Jesus. But when he noticed how strong the wind was, he became afraid and started to sink. He shouted, 'Lord, save me!' Immediately, Jesus reached out, caught hold of him, and said, 'You have so little faith! Why did you doubt?' When they got into the boat, the wind stopped blowing. The men in the boat bowed down in front of Jesus and said, 'You are truly the Son of God'" (verses 25-33).

The Jesus you worship, who truly is the Son of God, uses his power to work in your life to help you do things you never thought you could do and to calm the storms in your life. Trust him.

God is watching

"I can't believe I made that goal! Did you see it?"

"Did you like my solo?"

"Watch my cannonball!"

Kids love to know that their parents are watching them. Parents love watching their kids. Sometimes, though, after about the 30th cannonball, parents get tired, stop watching, and go back to reading their books.

Your heavenly Father loves to watch you too, over and over and over. **"He who watches over you will not slumber. The LORD will keep you from all harm—he will watch over your life; the LORD will watch over your coming and going both now and forevermore"** (Psalm 121:3,7,8 NIV).

Satan, who loves to lie, wants you to think that God isn't watching you. Or maybe if he is watching you, he gets tired and starts reading a book instead. No way! God never gets tired of keeping his eye on you and protecting you from Satan. Even when you're sleeping, God is watching you and keeping you safe. He's concerned about where you go and what you do and he loves to work all of that for your good—for now and forever.

Don't you love knowing God is watching you?

Dear God,

sometimes I think I'm alone. I forget that you are watching over me, caring for me, and working to keep me close to you. Thank you for never sleeping and for being so very interested in my whole entire life. You are my awesome Father. Amen.

Be happy for your friends

When God chose Saul as his king, I bet Jonathan started thinking about how awesome it would be when *he* got to be king. That's because when a king dies, his son usually takes over. (Remember in *The Lion King* when Simba sang, "Oh I just can't wait to be king"? Kind of like that.)

Except it didn't turn out that way. When Saul didn't obey God, God rejected Saul and picked David to be the next king.

How would you take it if you were in line to be king and then someone else got it? You might expect Jonathan to have a huge temper tantrum. Instead, Jonathan watched David's faith in action as he killed Goliath and gave God all the credit. **"After that, Jonathan became David's closest friend. He loved David as much as he loved himself"** (1 Samuel 18:1).

Jonathan loved his God more than he wanted earthly glory. He saw that God was with David, and he wasn't jealous. Instead, he loved David and spent the rest of his life protecting his best friend.

When you see your best friend getting better grades or winning a class election or getting picked for a lead role in the play, you can be like Jonathan and celebrate. Sometimes other people get more earthly glory. We trust that our God has good plans for us too.

Jonathan—who wasn't jealous of his best friend—was God's child, just like you are.

Get plugged in

"Where's the power cord? My battery is about to die! What did you do with the charger?"

Everybody knows that a phone or tablet battery can only last so long before running out. Then you have to plug it in to charge. Without that power source, your electronics are as useful as rocks.

Without Jesus, you are as useful as a rock too. You start believing the voice that says, "You aren't good at anything. You're a failure. You're stupid. God doesn't notice you." Day after day those messages wear you down and drain your energy. Jesus, the great power source of all time, tells you to stop listening to those useless messages and look to him.

"The strength of those who wait with hope in the LORD will be renewed" (Isaiah 40:31).

You wait with hope in the Lord. You know this world and its mean voices are liars. You know Jesus loves you so much that he came for you. You know he thinks you are so valuable that he died for you. You know he will come back to take you to heaven.

As your battery wears down, read your Bible, go to church, spend time with Christian friends. Plug into God and get charged up.

Chomp on this!

What voices in the world wear you down?

What are some ways you can plug back into your power source—God?

You have a conscience

Yesterday, how much time did you spend thinking, "Okay, body, it's time to grow"? Obviously you didn't. You can't make your bones grow; you can't will your fingernails or hair to get longer either. It just happens, because God made you that way.

God also made you with a conscience. That's the part of you that knows some things are right and wrong. You know it's wrong to cheat. You wouldn't be sneaky about it if you thought it was okay. Your conscience lets you know that there is a God who is holding you to a high standard. Usually, though, your conscience only leaves you feeling guilty. **"They show that some requirements found in Moses' Teachings are written in their hearts. Their consciences speak to them"** (Romans 2:15).

Your conscience doesn't tell you that Jesus lived a perfect life for you. It doesn't tell you that he loved you so much he was willing to die a horribly painful death for you. Your conscience also doesn't tell you that Jesus came back to life. Unlike growing, learning about Jesus doesn't just happen.

You find that information in the Bible. That's why you read devotions like this one too—because sometimes you only remember that there is bad news and you need to hear, over and over and over, that there is good news. The best news.

 ## Chomp on this!

How does your conscience tell you that things are wrong?

Dear God,

thank you for giving me the good news about Jesus. Otherwise I'd only know about the bad stuff in my life. I'd feel guilty, and I wouldn't have any hope. Your Word lets me know that I am loved and that there is a very happy ending to what would be a very sad story. Amen.

The OutSide doeSn't matter

You get As. You get Cs.

You are in band. You play chess. You like jumping rope.

You have big ears. You are short for your age.

Your hair is curly. You have a huge birthmark on your arm.

You can barely swing a bat. You can dunk a basketball.

You sing off-key. You are the star of the show.

You race dirt bikes. You read for eight hours a day.

You wear glasses. You are in a wheelchair.

You love opera. You don't care for music.

You have autism. You started high school at age 11.

Your appearance and your interests set you apart. It's what makes you different from the kids around you. It's true that God made you the way he wants you to be. He doesn't look at you the way other people do. **"God does not see as humans see. Humans look at outward appearances, but the LORD looks into the heart"** (1 Samuel 16:7).

When God looks at every heart, he sees that on our own we don't like him; we aren't able to love him. Because he loves us and made us in his image, he sent Jesus on a rescue mission. Because Jesus kept his heart pure while he lived on earth and took God's punishment for our sins, we are forgiven and washed clean.

Like King David we get to say, **"Hide your face from my sins, and wipe out all that I have done wrong. Create a clean heart in me, O God, and renew a faithful spirit within me"** (Psalm 51:9,10).

Now when God looks at you, he looks inside and sees your clean heart—no matter how different you look on the outside.

The best kind of love

Everybody who joins the military takes an oath, which means they make a promise to "support and defend the Constitution of the United States against all enemies, foreign and domestic."

When they say these words, they are promising to do whatever it takes—to fight and to die—to protect this country.

The Bible says that giving up your life, being willing to die to protect someone else, is the highest act of love. **"The greatest love you can show is to give your life for your friends"** (John 15:13).

You face an enemy every day, whether it's the devil, the world, or even what the sinful part of you wants to do. God saw your enemy and knew you were powerless. So he sent Jesus as the soldier to fight this war for you. He ran to protect you from the punishment of your sins, and he gave up his life for you.

When he came to earth, he made a vow to do whatever it took to protect you. He did this because he calls you his friend. Think about that again: the Savior of the world is your best friend.

Dear Jesus,

thank you for calling me your friend. You came to earth to protect me, to fight for me, and to show me the best love of all time. Thank you for being my defender, and thank you for laying down your life so I can be God's friend. Amen.

God's name is on you

**"God establishes us, together with you,
in a relationship with Christ.
He has also anointed us.
In addition, he has put his seal of ownership on us
and has given us the Spirit as his guarantee"**
(2 Corinthians 1:21,22).

It's almost time to head back to school (get your groans out now). Before you go, you usually make sure to write your name inside your backpack, on your water bottle, and on your folders and binders. You need to let everyone know what supplies are yours.

God has claimed you too, just the way you've marked your school supplies. In today's passage he tells about all the ways he has said you are his.

He anointed you. He picked you and gave you the power to do the jobs he has for you.

He set his seal of ownership on you. At your baptism, God wrote his name on you. Satan can't have you because God owns you now.

He put his Spirit in your heart. He gave you the Holy Spirit to remind you that Jesus is coming back.

This coming school year, remember that you have God's name written all over your life. If anyone asks you about it, be sure to give God all the credit. You didn't choose to put God's name on you; he chose you. After all, no one thinks your jacket wrote your name on itself. That would be silly.

Go away, Satan!

*Today let's **Dig In!** Read this section of Scripture, and then use the questions to talk about what God has to say in his Word.*

Then the Spirit led Jesus into the desert to be tempted by the devil. Jesus did not eat anything for 40 days and 40 nights. . . .

The tempter came to him and said, "If you are the Son of God, tell these stones to become loaves of bread."

Jesus answered, "Scripture says, 'A person cannot live on bread alone but on every word that God speaks.'"

Then the devil took him into the holy city and had him stand on the highest part of the temple. He said to Jesus, "If you are the Son of God, jump! Scripture says, 'He will put his angels in charge of you. They will carry you in their hands so that you never hit your foot against a rock.'"

Jesus said to him, "Scripture says, 'Never tempt the Lord.'"

Once more the devil took him to a very high mountain and showed him all the kingdoms in the world and their glory. The devil said to him, "I will give you all this if you will bow down and worship me."

Jesus said to him, "Go away, Satan! Scripture says, 'Worship the Lord your God and serve only him.'"

Then the devil left him, and angels came to take care of him. (Matthew 4:1-11)

Chomp on this!

 What does God teach you in this passage?

What makes you say, "Thank you, Jesus"?

What makes you say, "I'm sorry, Jesus"?

Based on this reading, what would you like to ask God for?

How you build

Sand castles are awesome. You and your friends spend the morning digging, packing, and shaping your castle until you have the best sand castle ever.

Oh no! You turn around and realize that the tide is coming in. You watch the waves creep closer and closer. You try to build a moat, hoping to catch the water and stop the inevitable. But you can't. The waves are about to wash away all your hard work.

Living without God is like building a sand castle. **"Everyone who hears what I say but doesn't obey it will be like a foolish person who built a house on sand. Rain poured, and floods came. Winds blew and struck that house. It collapsed, and the result was a total disaster"** (Matthew 7:26,27).

When you think you are strong enough and can do everything on your own, you are fooling yourself. When trouble comes (and it will because this world is painful and hard and sinful), it will wash you away.

Living with God, however, is like building your castle out of concrete. Knowing his Word—and doing what it says—makes you strong when troubles come. **"Therefore, everyone who hears what I say and obeys it will be like a wise person who built a house on rock. Rain poured, and floods came. Winds blew and beat against that house. But it did not collapse, because its foundation was on rock"** (verses 24,25).

God is your foundation. Pay attention to how you build.

Can't get along!

Some plants are incompatible. That means they just don't like each other. They don't belong near each other. If they are planted by each other, neither one will grow well. You can't plant celery by corn because they both attract beetles. Do you like pumpkins and potatoes? Well, they don't do so well next to each other. Peas won't grow well if they are put next to garlic and onion.

Gardeners have to pay attention to their work, otherwise their gardens won't grow and all that hard work means nothing.

You are incompatible with this world. **"Stop forming inappropriate relationships with unbelievers. Can right and wrong be partners? Can light have anything in common with darkness? Can Christ agree with the devil? Can a believer share life with an unbeliever? Can God's temple contain false gods?"** (2 Corinthians 6:14-16).

God tells you to pay attention to your lives. If you hang out—plant yourself—too close to those who don't believe in Jesus, you won't grow as well. You can't just play a little bit with sin while being part of God's family. You can't bully and be kind. You can't use filthy language and praise God. You can't disrespect your parents and honor your Father. As a child of God, the light inside of you can't stand to be around the darkness of the world. The world will try to tell you that you need to fit in and look like them. God tells you, "Don't fit in. You are incompatible."

Chomp on this!

Are there people in your life whose choices are incompatible with being a believer in Jesus?

How can you share your faith with them but not let yourself get tempted by them?

In your Father's house

When Jesus was 12, his family went all the way to Jerusalem for the Passover. They wanted to worship at the temple. (Can you imagine walking 100 miles to church?) After they celebrated the Passover, it was time to go home.

Because there were lots of cousins and family and friends, they traveled in a huge group. Mary and Joseph thought Jesus was just walking with his friends and cousins. (It's the same as when you head to a park; you go and play while the parents talk.) After one day, they realized that Jesus wasn't actually with them. It took them another day to walk back to Jerusalem and then a third day to look around town. When they finally found him, he was back in church!

"He was sitting among the teachers, listening to them, and asking them questions. His understanding and his answers stunned everyone who heard him" (Luke 2:46,47).

Like most parents, they yelled at him because they were worried, but Jesus simply told them, **"Didn't you realize that I had to be in my Father's house?"** (verse 49).

Some people might be surprised to look for young kids in church. You know, though, that it's your Father's house too. There you get to hear just how much he loves you and how valuable you are to him. You hear that God cares more about who you are than what you do. (So it doesn't really bother him if you are short or tall or if you came in last at the track meet.) You hear that even when you sin, God still says, "I love you."

Jesus—who loved to be in his Father's house—was God's child, just like you are.

(By the way, in a little over 20 years, Jesus was in Jerusalem for the Passover again. Except this time was the time he would be tried, convicted, and crucified. He died for everyone, including kids just like you.)

The "bad" truth

It's hard to stay friends with someone who doesn't tell you the truth. After all, how can you trust a liar? Your God loves the truth and tells you the truth—even when it's hard to hear. Today's message is hard to hear.

"What your corrupt nature wants is contrary to what your spiritual nature wants, and what your spiritual nature wants is contrary to what your corrupt nature wants. They are opposed to each other. As a result, you don't always do what you intend to do. If your spiritual nature is your guide, you are not subject to Moses' laws. Now, the effects of the corrupt nature are obvious . . ." (Galatians 5:17-19).

Paul, the man who wrote these words from God, was writing to people who lived in a place called Galatia. (Today, it's the country of Turkey.) This was a personal letter to them, so he listed the sins the people who lived over two thousand years ago struggled with. Some sound an awful lot like ours today: hatred, rivalry, jealousy, angry outbursts, selfish ambition, conflict, cliques, and envy.

Then Paul continued, **"I've told you in the past and I'm telling you again that people who do these kinds of things will not inherit the kingdom of God"** (verse 21).

Did you really want to hear, "You aren't a good person and if you give in to the part that wants to do evil things, well, no heaven for you"? I didn't think so. Still, if it's in his Word, God thinks it's important for you to know because if you kid yourself and think you have any good in you on your own, you might think you don't need a Savior. And you really, really need a Savior. The good news is that you have one. His name is Jesus. He's changed your life. He's changed the way you live. (More on that tomorrow!)

Walk in Step with the Spirit

Three-legged races are a ton of fun. You find a partner and each put one leg into a burlap sack. Once you're connected to someone else, you realize you had better figure out—quickly—how to work and walk together. If you don't, you'll end up in a heap on the ground.

You and the Holy Spirit are in a three-legged race, working and walking together. **"Since we live by the Spirit, let us keep in step with the Spirit"** (Galatians 5:25 NIV).

How do you keep in step with the Spirit so you don't end up in a heap on the ground? (You remember the warning from yesterday, right?) God's Word tells you how.

"So I say, walk by the Spirit, and you will not gratify the desires of the flesh.... The fruit of the Spirit is love, joy, peace, forbearance, kindness, goodness, faithfulness, gentleness and self-control. Against such things there is no law. Those who belong to Christ Jesus have crucified the flesh with its passions and desires" (Galatians 5:16, 22-24).

The Holy Spirit is the one who sets the pace. He gives you the strength to walk with him, to say no to what your sinful heart wants to do. He changes you and gives you what he calls fruits. When all of these fruits are listed together, it's easy to read them too quickly and not think about each one. So, for the next nine days, we'll study each one, keeping in step with the Spirit.

Chomp on this!

Have a three-legged race at home. If you don't have a burlap sack (not many people do), use a towel and wrap it around your ankles.

Love

**"The spiritual nature produces *love*,
joy, peace, patience, kindness, goodness,
faithfulness, gentleness, and self-control"**
(Galatians 5:22,23).

The first thing the Holy Spirit works in you is love. That sounds super easy, doesn't it? Love. I love loving people.

Except that God asks you to do a hard kind of love—love everyone. Jesus was talking to a huge crowd of people when he told them, **"You have heard that it was said, 'Love your neighbor, and hate your enemy.' But I tell you this: Love your enemies, and pray for those who persecute you. In this way you show that you are children of your Father in heaven. He makes his sun rise on people whether they are good or evil. He lets rain fall on them whether they are just or unjust. If you love those who love you, do you deserve a reward?"** (Matthew 5:43-46).

Jesus is asking them, "You want a medal for loving your best friend or for loving your parents?" Sorry, that's not hard. Jesus says, "Love those who are mean to you. Love those who mock you. Love those teachers who make fun of you for your faith. Love the friends who think you are dumb for loving Jesus."

How? To be honest, you can't do this on your own, but remember that you are walking with the Holy Spirit. He helps you see your enemies through God's eyes: people who are lost, hurting, misguided; people who believe lies. Through Jesus' eyes you can see them as loveless people who need to be shown love. Through the Holy Spirit's strength, you can love.

That makes you different; that shows you are God's child.

JOY

**"The spiritual nature produces love, *joy*,
peace, patience, kindness, goodness, faithfulness,
gentleness, and self-control"**
(Galatians 5:22,23).

Feel free to sing along ...
If you're happy and you know it, clap your hands. <clap, clap>
If you're happy and you know it, clap your hands. <clap, clap>
If you're happy and you know it, then your face will surely show it.
If you're happy and you know it, clap your hands. <clap, clap>

(Sorry, now that song is stuck in your head, isn't it?)

That's a fun song to sing when you're in preschool, isn't it? But when
you get a little older, you probably feel foolish. Maybe you didn't sing
along now because you aren't actually happy. If you're reading this
in the morning, maybe it's too early to feel happy and you don't feel
like getting ready for school. If you're reading this at night, you're
probably worn out. That's okay. You don't have to fake being happy.

That's why this passage doesn't talk about happiness; it talks about
joy. And even God doesn't expect you to fake it. King David
didn't. When he was incredibly sad, it was then he found his joy.
He told God, **"Hear, O LORD, and have pity on me! O LORD,
be my helper! You have changed my sobbing into dancing.
You have removed my sackcloth and clothed me with joy
so that my soul may praise you with music and not be
silent. O LORD my God, I will give thanks to you forever"**
(Psalm 30:10-12).

God turns your crying into joy too. Because even through hard
times you know you have someone who cares about you so much
that he died for you. Someone who rose from the dead for you
and sits next to God talking about you. You have value. You have
someone on your side—forever!

If you're joyful and you know it, then your soul will surely show it.

Peace out

**"The spiritual nature produces love, joy, *peace*,
patience, kindness, goodness, faithfulness,
gentleness, and self-control"**
(Galatians 5:22,23).

Some people don't say, "Good-bye." They say, "Peace out."

When Jesus was eating dinner with his friends the night before he died, he gave them his own "peace out" message. He knew he was going to be crucified, so he started giving them the last important information he wanted them to know. Even though it didn't really sink in for them, he told them, **"I'm leaving you peace. I'm giving you my peace. I don't give you the kind of peace that the world gives. So don't be troubled or cowardly"** (John 14:27).

Jesus knew that these disciples' lives were about to get really hard. They were going to be laughed at, thrown in jail, mocked, beaten, and even put to death because of their faith in him. So he was telling them, "I'm giving you my peace, God's peace, which is a strong peace. Don't be afraid; don't hide when you're afraid people will think you're a dork for talking about God or maybe when you stand up to your friends to tell them to stop picking on others. You have this same peace. The peace that Jesus gives is a strong peace. It makes you brave, even when you feel like hiding.

Dear everlasting Father and Prince of peace,

you are the Lord of peace. Give us your peace at all times. Let your peace control us. Give us the strength to use your peace when people make fun of us for our faith or when we're tempted to hide our faith in you. Amen.

Pray for patience

"The spiritual nature produces love, joy, peace, *patience*, kindness, goodness, faithfulness, gentleness, and self-control"
(Galatians 5:22,23).

Have your parents ever asked, "How many times do I have to remind you to <fill in the blank>?!"

Maybe they asked you 4,231 times to pick up your socks. Maybe you fought too many times with your brother. Or maybe you interrupt when they are on the phone.

Over and over God tells us, "Don't be afraid; just believe." Over and over we worry anyway. The Bible tells us, "Your guilt is taken away"—and we keep feeling guilty for the sins he has forgiven. God tells us, "Be patient, bearing with one another in love"—and we keep fighting with each other.

Even though we can't seem to get it right, God doesn't say, "How many times do I have to remind you." Instead, because of his love, we get to say, **"I was treated with mercy so that Christ Jesus could use me, the foremost sinner, to demonstrate his patience. This patience serves as an example for those who would believe in him and live forever"** (1 Timothy 1:16,17).

God doesn't call us impatient and thickheaded; he simply gives us forgiveness and asks us to pass along his patience to others.

Chomp on this!

Work together to write a prayer that asks God to help you live patiently with each other.

Kindness

"The spiritual nature produces love, joy, peace, patience, *kindness,* goodness, faithfulness, gentleness, and self-control"
(Galatians 5:22,23).

"He hit me!"

"Well, she hit me first!"

"Well, he pushed me."

"Well, she ruined the Lego house I built!"

In kid logic, if someone ruins your stuff, you get to ruin theirs. Or at least make them pay for what they did. (To be fair, adult logic often works the same way.)

God's logic couldn't be more different. **"Make sure that no one ever pays back one wrong with another wrong. Instead, always try to do what is good for each other and everyone else"** (1 Thessalonians 5:15).

God's way of dealing with people doesn't often make sense to humans, though.

Christian kindness means watching out for other people. It means being kind to other Christians—maybe the people in your school or church or neighborhood. And it means being kind to those who don't know Jesus.

Why? For the same reason God is kind to you. **"Don't you realize that it is God's kindness that is trying to lead you to him and change the way you think and act?"** (Romans 2:4).

Be kind and lead others to Jesus too.

 ## Chomp on this!

What people in your life seem unkind?

How can you be kind to them?

Through God's eyes

"The spiritual nature produces love, joy, peace, patience, kindness, *goodness*, faithfulness, gentleness, and self-control" (Galatians 5:22,23).

Name five things that are good.

I'm betting pizza showed up on that list, or possibly a sports hero like Peyton Manning. Some people have really good dogs. If God made a "good" list, your name would be on it. Are you surprised? Don't be.

Because you are in the three-legged race with the Holy Spirit, the God who is good gives you all his good stuff too. **"May God, the source of hope, fill you with joy and peace through your faith in him. Then you will overflow with hope by the power of the Holy Spirit. I'm convinced, brothers and sisters, that you, too, are filled with goodness"** (Romans 15:13,14).

Here's how it works. God fills you with joy and peace. That gives you hope, so much hope that it overflows—it spills out all over the place in your life. Because you have all these good things in your life, your goodness spills out of you—and you share it with your classmates, your neighbors, your friends, your parents.

Every day you now get to hear God say, **"Good job! You're a good and faithful servant! You proved that you could be trusted with a small amount. I will put you in charge of a large amount. Come and share your master's happiness"** (Matthew 25:23).

Dear God,

you have made me good. Sometimes I just don't believe it, though. Or sometimes I forget it. I need your Holy Spirit to remind me every day that when you see me, you see Jesus. Thank you for filling me with your goodness and for sharing that goodness with others. Thank you for letting me share your happiness. Amen.

Be faithful

**"The spiritual nature produces love, joy, peace,
patience, kindness, goodness, *faithfulness*,
gentleness, and self-control"**
(Galatians 5:22,23).

In Yellowstone National Park, you'll find Old Faithful. This famous geyser erupts, well, faithfully. Each eruption has been tracked for so long that National Park Service employees can now predict—in a ten-minute window—when the next eruption will occur. Old Faithful got its name simply because it regularly, consistently does what it was made to do.

Philemon (pronounced fi-LEE-man) was God's Old Faithful. When Paul wrote him a letter he said, **"I always thank my God when I mention you in my prayers because I hear about your faithfulness to the Lord Jesus and your love for all of God's people. As you share the faith you have in common with others, I pray that you may come to have a complete knowledge of every blessing we have in Christ. Your love for God's people gives me a lot of joy and encouragement. You, brother, have comforted God's people"** (Philemon 1:4-7).

This is what faithfulness looks like: sharing your faith, learning more about your blessings, loving and comforting God's people.

As you study your Bible, you gain a complete knowledge of every blessing Christ gives you. Then you ask others if they know about Jesus, you encourage the people around you, and you comfort them when they are sad simply because it's what you were made to do. You overflow—you erupt—with the fruit of the Spirit. People can predict it simply because that's what you do.

And the people around you always thank God for you, because they hear about—and see—your faithfulness to the Lord Jesus. The best part? There's a reward at the end: **"Be faithful until death, and I will give you the crown of life"** (Revelation 2:10).

Gentle!

"The spiritual nature produces love, joy, peace, patience, kindness, goodness, faithfulness, *gentleness*, and self-control"
(Galatians 5:22,23).

What's your reaction ...

... if your coach yells at you for dropping the ball?

... if your parents yell at you for a bad grade on a test?

... if your friend yells at you for sharing her secret?

When people get angry or yell or shout, our natural reaction is to get defensive, because that's what a sinful nature does. It immediately comes up with reasons why your mistake isn't your fault: the pass was bad or you had so many chores that you had no time to study or she should have told you that you couldn't tell anybody.

When people react calmly and gently, your reaction changes, doesn't it? If your coach puts his arm around you or if your parents give you that horrible disappointed face or if you see the tears on your friend's face because of your betrayal, that's when you feel the weight of your mistake.

This is one of the reasons that the Holy Spirit wants you to produce gentleness. If you are trying to tell people about their Savior, yelling at them, calling them names, or putting them down for their horrible decisions isn't going to help them believe that God's family is a great thing to be a part of. That's why God tells you to **"be *gentle* in correcting those who oppose the Good News. Maybe God will allow them to change the way they think and act and lead them to know the truth"** (2 Timothy 2:25).

Your gentleness is one way that people can learn about God's truth, love, and mercy. Isn't that amazing!

Your Spiritual wall

"The spiritual nature produces love, joy, peace, patience, kindness, goodness, faithfulness, gentleness, and *self-control*" (Galatians 5:22,23).

The Great Wall of China is 13,170 miles long. (Want to know how long that is? The United States is only 2,900 miles across from east to west.)

The thing is, the Great Wall isn't actually one wall. It's a whole bunch of walls—some run parallel to each other and some are in sections all by themselves. Because of this, it didn't actually protect the country from being invaded by Genghis Kahn one thousand years ago—a time when citizens were slaughtered by the invading army.

Self-control is your spiritual wall. **"Like a city broken into and left without a wall, so is a person who lacks self-control"** (Proverbs 25:28). At your baptism, the Holy Spirit came to live inside of you, giving you a spiritual wall. A complete wall, not one that can be walked around or run over. Maybe it means not cheating to get an A or not yelling at your brother for coming into your room. Or maybe it means not rolling your eyes at your parents' "dumb" rules. You can't control that on your own. As God's child, you act differently all because God's kindness **"trains us to avoid ungodly lives filled with worldly desires so that we can live self-controlled, moral, and godly lives in this present world"** (Titus 2:12).

Dear Holy Spirit,

thank you for your gift of self-control. Amen.

God's love isn't random

It's National Random Acts of Kindness Day—in New Zealand. (That's the only country that has an official Random Acts of Kindness Day.) The whole point of the day is to do something nice for a stranger, simply because you want to be nice.

God celebrated National Random Acts of Kindness Day the day he sent Jesus to earth.

"At one time we too were foolish, disobedient, deceived and enslaved by all kinds of passions and pleasures. We lived in malice and envy, being hated and hating one another. But when the kindness and love of God our Savior appeared, he saved us, not because of righteous things we had done, but because of his mercy" (Titus 3:3-5 NIV).

God wasn't kind to us because we were kind to him. In fact, we were mean and hateful. Our nature was completely against him. When God sent Jesus—his kindness and love put into a body—he did it because he is full of mercy. He could have, and should have, punished us, but instead he had compassion. Not randomly, but on purpose.

Chomp on this!

What random acts of kindness have you done for people?

What are some ways you can share God's kindness with those around you?

VJ Day

From 1939 to 1945, over one billion people fought in World War II. Over 30 countries were involved in the war and had to pick which side they were on: the Allies or the Axis. Over 60 million people died in this brutal war.

By the summer of 1945, it was obvious that the Axis powers were going to lose—and on September 2, the Japanese formally surrendered. The war was over.

This world is in a Spiritual World War, and we hear about it in the book of Revelation. John was given a bunch of visions (kind of like dreams) about the world and its spiritual battles. John saw that "[ten kings] **will receive authority to rule as kings with the beast for one hour. They have one purpose—to give their power and authority to the beast.** (That's Satan.) **They will go to war against the lamb.** (That's Jesus.) **The lamb will conquer them because he is Lord of lords and King of kings. Those who are called, chosen, and faithful are with him**" (Revelation 17:12-14).

The whole world is involved in this war. The people on Satan's team have one goal: to serve Satan and wage war against Jesus. Sometimes is looks like they are winning, but God says that they will only have authority for one hour. (God just means that in the whole scheme of things, they have a very short time to look like they are winning.)

But the outcome is obvious. The Lamb will win. The day Jesus comes back, the beast's team will formally sign their surrender papers. They will lose.

Because you are on Jesus' team, you get to be part of the great victory celebration.

Breathing

Kids don't like to smell each other's breath. Parents actually hear complaints like, "He's breathing on me!" and "Her breath smells like death!" So you might be surprised to hear about two times in the Bible when people got breathed on, and they were both good things.

"Then the Lord God formed the man from the dust of the earth and blew the breath of life into his nostrils. The man became a living being" (Genesis 2:7).

When God created animals, he simply formed them and they started living. To create people, though, God chose to breathe into Adam. From that moment on, humans walked around with the breath of the living God inside them.

The second time happened after Jesus rose from the dead. He was about to go back to heaven (to get your room ready) and he told his disciples, **"'Peace be with you! As the Father has sent me, so I am sending you.' After he had said this, he breathed on the disciples and said, 'Receive the Holy Spirit'"** (John 20:21,22). The Holy Spirit gave them the strength and courage they would need to go to people in different cities and countries, telling them that their Savior had come.

The first time God breathed in a person, life began. When Jesus breathed on the disciples, he gave them the Holy Spirit. That kind of breath gives you life.

Chomp on this!

When you were baptized, the Holy Spirit put faith in your heart. How does the Holy Spirit use you now to spread the news about Jesus?

Walk the balance beam

Go get a ruler and find out just how long either 10 centimeters or 4 inches is. Go ahead. I'll wait. (In case you didn't get a ruler, I'll give you a visual: an iPhone is longer than 4 inches.)

Why is this important? Because that's how wide a balance beam is. When gymnasts are turning, hopping, leaping, and jumping on one, they only have 4 inches to make a solid landing.

On such a narrow beam, they have to stay focused. One wrong step and they fall.

Isn't that one of the reasons why we are fascinated by gymnasts? Be honest, most of us fall off just trying to balance on a curb on the side of the road. How they manage to accomplish those routines is amazing.

Following Jesus is like walking a balance beam. **"Let your eyes look straight ahead and your sight be focused in front of you. Carefully walk a straight path, and all your ways will be secure. Do not lean to the right or to the left. Walk away from evil"** (Proverbs 4:25-27).

Evil is all around you, wanting you to fall off of God's path. Use the Holy Spirit's power to stay focused and to keep your feet on the beam. Don't even think about leaning one way or the other, because falling hurts.

The best part of our balance-beam life? God is there helping us stay on the narrow way. And thanks to Jesus, we get a perfect score.

Forgive

**"As holy people whom God has chosen and loved ...
forgive as the Lord forgave you. Above all, be loving"**
(Colossians 3:12-14).

Forgiveness is hard, isn't it? I mean, really, if your brother hits you
and your dad is standing there making him apologize, do you say in
your calmest, most thoughtful voice, "Oh, my dear brother, I know
you could not possibly have meant to punch me. I know you must
feel horrible for your behavior. I want you to know that I forgive
you and I love you"?

Be honest; right now you're thinking that would be ridiculous.
Really you want to hit back—and maybe hit him a second time—
because you're so mad. You know you'd really get into trouble, so
instead you mumble, "I forgive you," but you don't really mean it.

We demand justice! If you hit me, I get to hit you. You should
never get away with anything!

That's not what God means when he says, "Forgive as the Lord
forgave you." God demands justice too, but he changed how it
works. You "hit" God with your sin. Instead of getting back at you, he
decided to punish Jesus. That way he could always be loving to you.

Because Jesus got punished instead of you, you get to hear God say,
"I forgive you"—completely, absolutely, fully, and forever. With that
peace inside of you, you get to forgive others the exact same way.

The bridge to heaven

**"Thomas said to him,
'Lord, we don't know where you're going.
So how can we know the way?'
Jesus answered him, 'I am the way, the truth, and the life.
No one goes to the Father except through me'"**
(John 14:5,6).

Over 75 years ago, people in San Francisco wanted a way to cross from one side of the Golden Gate Strait to the other. Unless they took a ferry, they couldn't do it. That's why the Golden Gate Bridge was built. Since the bridge opened on May 28, 1937, over two billion vehicles have crossed the 1.7-mile bridge.

God knows you need a way to get from this world to heaven and that you can't do it on your own. (There isn't a ferry.) So he built a bridge: Jesus. When Jesus came to this world, he bridged the gap between you and your God. By dying on a cross, he made it possible for you to "drive" to heaven.

But Jesus isn't simply *a* bridge to heaven, or *one of many* bridges. He is the *only* bridge. You can't go to heaven on a Buddha bridge or a Muhammad bridge or an I'm-a-good-person bridge. Jesus is the only way. No one gets to see the Father unless he or she goes through Jesus.

Dear Father,

thank you for sending Jesus to be my bridge, my way to life with you. Help me tell others about Jesus so they know the right way to take to heaven too. Amen.

You are marked

The Avada Kedavra Curse should have killed Harry Potter. Instead, though he was a defenseless one-year-old, the curse rebounded. All it left on Harry was a lightning-shaped scar.

From then on, Harry was marked. He didn't find out the reason for his scar until he was 11, when he left for Hogwarts. Over the course of all seven books, we follow Harry's battles against his mortal enemy—Lord Voldemort.

You, well, don't get the luxury of waiting until you're 11. Just like Harry, you have a mark on you. Because Jesus has claimed you, Satan has marked you as his prey, his mortal enemy—for life. In 1 Peter 5:8, God gives you some bad news: **"Your opponent the devil is prowling around like a roaring lion as he looks for someone to devour."**

So now, until you reach heaven, you will face battle after battle with him. Maybe you're wishing you had an invisibility cloak so you could walk around and your opponent couldn't see you. You have something way better than a cloak. You have Jesus. When Jesus died on a cross and came alive again, he defeated the devil. At your baptism, you put on his robe of righteousness. That, better than any invisibility cloak, tells Satan—"Back off! This one is mine!"

 ## Chomp on this!

How has Satan prowled around, looking for ways to devour you?

What temptations and troubles has he tried to use to get you away from God?

Dear Jesus,

thank you for giving me your robe of righteousness. Even though my mortal enemy, Satan, knows I'm yours, he still tries to get me, to hurt me, to pull me away from you. But he can't have me because you marked me as yours and I am safe forever. Thank you! Amen.

Blessed

*Today let's **Dig In!** Read this section of Scripture, and then use the questions to talk about what God has to say in his Word.*

[Jesus] went up a mountain and sat down. His disciples came to him, and he began to teach them:

"Blessed are those who recognize they are spiritually helpless. The kingdom of heaven belongs to them.

Blessed are those who mourn. They will be comforted.

Blessed are those who are gentle. They will inherit the earth.

Blessed are those who hunger and thirst for God's approval. They will be satisfied.

Blessed are those who show mercy. They will be treated mercifully.

Blessed are those whose thoughts are pure. They will see God.

Blessed are those who make peace. They will be called God's children.

Blessed are those who are persecuted for doing what God approves of. The kingdom of heaven belongs to them.

Blessed are you when people insult you, persecute you, lie, and say all kinds of evil things about you because of me. Rejoice and be glad because you have a great reward in heaven!" (Matthew 5:1-12)

Chomp on this!

What does God teach you in this passage?

What makes you say, "Thank you, Jesus"?

What makes you say, "I'm sorry, Jesus"?

Based on this reading, what would you like to ask God for?

God knows your plan

Walt Disney was fired from his first job because the editor said he "lacked imagination and had no good ideas."

Bill Gates, a computer genius, failed at his first business.

Albert Einstein, one of the smartest men ever, didn't talk until he was four and couldn't read until he was seven.

Abraham Lincoln, the president who freed the slaves, lost a number of elections and failed at starting up businesses.

Aaron Rodgers, a Super Bowl championship quarterback for the Green Bay Packers, was supposed to be drafted first. Instead, he had to wait until the 24th selection.

Theodor Seuss Giesel, you know him as Dr. Seuss, was told by 27 different publishers that his first book was no good.

What in your life makes you wonder, "Why is God letting this happen?" Maybe you can't figure out why your family had to move. Why did you have to break your wrist right when volleyball started? Why did your dad lose his job? Why did you have to repeat third grade?

Joseph, like you and all those people on the previous list, had a lot to wonder about. His brothers sold him into slavery. He was taken away from his home to Egypt. Potiphar's wife had him thrown in prison. His friend the cupbearer forgot to try to get him out of prison. Yet God used all of that, and Joseph became second-in-command of the whole country of Egypt. When he finally reunited with his brothers, he shared that he saw how God worked. **"Even though you planned evil against me, God planned good to come out of it"** (Genesis 50:20).

God will work for your good too. You'll see. Be patient.

Walls fall

It was time for the Israelites to defeat Jericho.

God talked to Joshua, the leader of the army, and said, "Here's how we're going to win. Have the people walk outside the city without talking once a day. Do that for six days. On the seventh day, walk around it seven times. Then shout and blow trumpets. Then the walls will fall and you will win."

That's not normally how the soldiers fought. Usually they used swords, and they chased and killed the enemy. No one would have blamed Joshua if he had said, "*Umm. What? That seems a little, well, weird.*"

Instead, Joshua went back to the people and did exactly what God told him to do and walked around the city.

"On the seventh day they got up at dawn. They marched around the city seven times the same way they had done it before. That was the only day they marched around it seven times. When they went around the seventh time, the priests blew their rams' horns. Joshua said to the troops, 'Shout, because the LORD has given you the city!' So the troops shouted very loudly when they heard the blast of the rams' horns, and the wall collapsed. The troops charged straight ahead and captured the city" (Joshua 6:15,16,20).

Why would God do that? To remind the Israelites that they had won because of his power, not because of anything they had done.

There are walls—problems and enemies—in your life too. Your God has the power to make those tumble without you doing a single thing. Then you can shout like Joshua that your God has given you the victory.

Terror doesn't win

On September 11, 2001, nineteen men hijacked four planes and flew them into the Pentagon in Washington, D.C., the World Trade Center towers in New York, and one crashed in a field in Pennsylvania. Nearly three thousand people died. Terror seemed to win.

King David felt that same way when he cried out to God about evil men who killed innocent people, even in his day.

"Why are you so distant, Lord? Why do you hide yourself in times of trouble? [The wicked person] waits in ambush in the villages. From his hiding places he kills innocent people. His eyes are on the lookout for victims. He lies in his hiding place like a lion in his den. He hides there to catch oppressed people. He catches oppressed people when he draws them into his net. His victims are crushed. They collapse, and they fall under the weight of his power" (Psalm 10:1,8-10).

Even though sometimes it seems like evil wins, David also knew that the Lord is still in power. **"You have seen it; yes, you have taken note of trouble and grief and placed them under your control. The victim entrusts himself to you. You alone have been the helper of orphans. You have heard the desire of oppressed people, O Lord. You encourage them. You pay close attention to them in order to provide justice for orphans and oppressed people so that no mere mortal will terrify them again"** (Psalm 10:14,17,18).

Terror didn't ultimately win in David's day. It doesn't ultimately win now. Our God is in control.

You can't bribe God

"Mom, if I clean my room, will you take me to the park?"

"Hey, Dad, if I help with dinner, can we have dessert?"

"Lauren, I'll clean out the dishwasher for you if you let me play with your birthday present."

Most of your life is spent negotiating, dealing, and telling people, "I'll do something nice for you if you pay me back." Sometimes it even works.

Do you ever try to play this game with God? Maybe you say, "God, I promise I will pray every single day if you just let me get an A on this test" or "Dear God, I won't ever hit my brother again if you let me get the new Xbox."

You can't bribe God. You can't do a good deed for him and then expect something in return. That's not how it works with him, because everything was, is, and comes from him in the first place. **"Who gave the Lord something which the Lord must pay back? Everything is from him and by him and for him. Glory belongs to him forever! Amen!"** (Romans 11:35,36).

Now this doesn't mean God is stingy. He's not sitting on some big throne handing out one itty-bitty blessing at a time. In reality, he loves to pour blessings into your life so much that you can barely keep track of them all. What it does mean is that you can't bargain your way to God's blessings. You can't earn them. You can't work for them. You can't bargain for them. You simply get to thank him for letting you use his stuff in this world to bring him glory.

Are you afraid?

What scares you? When you were younger, did you need a spray bottle filled with monster repellent to help you feel safe in your room? Maybe you can't stand spiders. Maybe you're afraid of bigger, serious, more grown-up concerns like your dad having cancer or your baby brother being in the hospital.

You know who wants to hear from you about all of your fears? Your God. **"Because you love me, I will rescue you. I will protect you because you know my name. When you call to me, I will answer you. I will be with you when you are in trouble"** (Psalm 91:14,15).

When you scream, "Dad! Come quick!" because you need him to kill a spider, he comes because you've called for him and he loves you. When you call out, "God! I need you!" he's there because you called for him and he loves you. He hurts when you hurt, and he promises that—no matter what—he is with you. You know, he already knows what's in your heart and mind. He already knows what scares you. I bet you'll feel better if you talk to him about it.

God, who made the whole entire universe out of nothing, cares about you. One of his favorite things is to watch over you, answer you, and protect you.

Call to him. He's ready.

 ## Chomp on this!

What things scare you at home? at school? with friends?

How do you think God can help with those scary things?

Dear God,

without me even saying it, you know what scares me.
Thank you for caring about me, for telling me that I can talk to you
about *everything*! Thank you for answering me all the time,
and for always being with me. Amen.

Be a loser!

When kids get really serious about their insults, one of the meanest things they can say is, "You're such a loser!" So it might surprise you that Jesus thinks being called a loser is the greatest compliment you can get.

"Those who want to come with me must say no to the things they want, pick up their crosses every day, and follow me. Those who want to save their lives will lose them. But those who lose their lives for me will save them. What good does it do for people to win the whole world but lose their lives by destroying them?" (Luke 9:23-25).

When you think about being Jesus' follower, it sounds like it will be easy—he did all the work of saving you and now you get blessed with forgiveness, peace, and joy. That is absolutely true. Jesus also gives a warning that following him is going to be hard. You are going to have to carry a cross—the things that can hurt you because you are a believer in Jesus.

The stuff that makes this world comfortable is not the stuff that God values. You might have to give up your stuff, your weekend sports, one or two of your six after-school activities, your free time, or your TV time if it gets in the way of serving Jesus by serving others.

When you give your time, your talents, and your money to bring glory to Jesus, you are a loser. And in God's world, being a loser makes you a winner!

Dear Jesus,

help me gladly be a loser so that I can be a winner in your kingdom! In Jesus' name. Amen.

Does God care?

"**A violent windstorm came up.
The waves were breaking into the boat
so that it was quickly filling up.
But he was sleeping on a cushion in the back of the boat.
So they woke him up and said to him,
'Teacher, don't you care that we're going to die?'
Then he got up, ordered the wind to stop,
and said to the sea, 'Be still, absolutely still!'
The wind stopped blowing, and the sea became very calm.
He asked them, 'Why are you such cowards?
Don't you have any faith yet?'**"
(Mark 4:37-40).

There are storms in our lives too. Parents get separated. Dads and moms deploy for the military. Older cousins die from drug overdoses. Wildfires, tornados, or mudslides threaten your house.

Just like the disciples, when hard times come, we sometimes think that God is sleeping, not paying attention to us. We wonder why God lets bad things happen to us. We ask him, "Don't you care?"

He does care. He's the God who knit you together. He's the God who sent Jesus to rescue you from Satan. He's the God who can calm storms with a word. He's the God who sends the Holy Spirit to guide you through this life. While all this happens, you still live in a sinful world and will still have bad things happen. Trust that he will use the storms in your life to bring you closer to him. Instead of saying, "Don't you care?" you get to say, **"God is my helper! The Lord is the provider for my life"** (Psalm 54:4).

 ## Chomp on this!

What storms have you faced?

How has God helped you and provided for you during them?

Tell the truth*

"**Peter was sitting in the courtyard.
A female servant came to him and said,
'You, too, were with Jesus the Galilean.'
But Peter denied it in front of them all by saying,
'I don't know what you're talking about.' ...
Peter remembered what Jesus had said:
'Before a rooster crows, you will say three times
that you don't know me.'
Then Peter went outside and cried bitterly"**
(Matthew 26:69,70,75).

When my friend Mandy and I were at the park, Mandy asked me, "Do you believe in God?" I knew that if I told her the truth, she might not be my friend anymore. So I didn't say anything.

I felt a lot like Peter, who denied that he knew Jesus. When we are afraid to confess our faith and cover it up or even lie about it, we are like him. God wants us to tell the truth about our faith and our love for Jesus. We don't hide it. We open our hearts and mouths and pour out our faith. We tell the truth about what Jesus did so our friends can know about forgiveness and eternal life with him.

After Peter denied Jesus three times, he confessed and was sorry for his sins. So when you commit a sin like I did, pray to God to forgive you. Then, when your conscience is at peace, you can tell the truth and spread the great news of Jesus.

Dear God,

please build up our confidence so we can spread your Word and the great news of what Jesus has done for all. In Jesus' name we pray. Amen.

*This devotion was written by Meghan, a kid just like you.

BY KIDS FOR KIDS

You get a trophy

**"Let the peace of Christ rule in your hearts,
since as members of one body you were called to peace.
And be thankful"**
(Colossians 3:15 NIV).

Time for a language lesson. In this passage, the Greek word for *rule* originally meant to "award prizes."

You know all about prizes. You get a ribbon for being in a spelling bee. The championship team gets a trophy. In the Olympics, the winner gets a gold medal.

The people who lived around Jesus' time understood prizes too. You might never have thought about it, but they had races and competitions too. They even had Olympics. Like today, the winners got the prizes. (Although their prizes were usually wreaths made from plant branches, which doesn't sound nearly as cool as gold.)

The games' organizers were the judges, and at the end of the day they handed out the prizes—they ruled! The more the Greek word was used, the more it meant less about the prize and more about the judge and ruler.

Today you let Christ's peace *rule* in your heart. It oversees your heart, and at the end of the day it gives you a trophy. It might not be wreaths or gold medals, but when you are at peace with Christ, when his peace "awards prizes" in your heart, you are showered with good things. You are content with what you have, you get along with the people around you, and you don't worry about school or friends or the future. When Christ's peace gives you a trophy, you win.

Say it with me, Christ's peace *rules*!

 ## Chomp on this!

What good things in your life are because Christ's peace *rules* in your heart?

Speak up!

Not even one hundred years ago, the Nazi party—a political party led by a man named Adolph Hitler—believed it had the right to determine who should live and who should die. Using the phrase "life unworthy of life," they decided to kill people simply because they were old, sick, had special needs, or belonged to other religions or countries. Today, some people believe they have the right to determine who should live or die. Using the words "pro-choice," they are willing to kill babies who are still living inside their mothers.

These things break God's heart. He's the God who tells us, **"The parts of the body that we think are weaker are the ones we really need"** (1 Corinthians 12:22).

God wants you to help spread the word that he designed each person and he thinks each person is valuable. He wants you to **"speak out for the one who cannot speak, for the rights of those who are doomed"** (Proverbs 31:8).

Look around you for people whom the world might consider to be weak. Maybe it's the one with autism who struggles to fit in. Maybe it's the elderly woman with the walker who takes forever to cross the street. Maybe it's the kid at school who always sits alone.

Smile at them; talk to them; walk with them. Reach out and let them know through your words and actions that they have a God who loves them, notices them, and thinks they are something special.

Chomp on this!

What people in your life seem "weak"?

How can you help them and be a friend to them?

You are God's letter

**"It's clear that you are Christ's letter,
written as a result of our ministry.
You are a letter written not with ink
but with the Spirit of the living God,
a letter written not on tablets of stone
but on tablets of human hearts.
By ourselves we are not qualified in any way
to claim that we can do anything.
Rather, God makes us qualified"**
(2 Corinthians 3:3,5).

Texts are fun, e-mails are fun, but every single person still loves getting a handwritten letter in the mail. A letter is a personal note from the author to the reader.

You are God's personal letter to the world. With the Holy Spirit inside of you, you walk around this world, letting people read you. They see what it looks like to be a believer in Jesus—how it changes your words, your actions, your attitude. It changes your entire life.

Yikes! Does that make you a little nervous? I mean, really, people will be watching you. Are you up for the job? Nope. Well, not by your own power. But with God, you absolutely are ready.

Dear God,

thank you for making me your letter. With the Holy Spirit inside of me, I walk around letting people know what it's like to be a member of your family. Help me communicate clearly how awesome it is to be your child. Amen.

Heaven is a dance party

Dance parties are fun. You get a bunch of friends together, crank up the music, then jump and dance and spin and shout and laugh.

The Israelites hadn't had that kind of fun in a long time. They had been held captive for a while when God talked to them, through the prophet Jeremiah, to tell them that he would bring them back home—and that there would be a dance party. **"I love you with an everlasting love. So I will continue to show you my kindness. Once again I will build you up, and you will be rebuilt, my dear people Israel. Once again you will take your tambourines, and you will go dancing with happy people"** (Jeremiah 31:3,4).

God loves you with an everlasting love too. He shows you his kindness and tells you that he is building you a room in heaven so you can be with him forever. So you, like King David, can say, **"You have changed my sobbing into dancing. You have removed my sackcloth and clothed me with joy so that my soul may praise you with music and not be silent. O LORD my God, I will give thanks to you forever"** (Psalm 30:11,12).

Until Jesus comes back, tell everyone you meet about what he has done for you. There is still plenty of room at God's dance party. Invite your friends.

Don't get tired

Sometimes you just want to misbehave, don't you? That's because it is exhausting to follow the rules every single day. You want to give in to all the temptations that tell you not to be kind or not to treat others with respect.

The apostle Paul wrote a letter to some Christians about two thousand years ago because they were tired too. He encouraged them—and he encourages you—**"We can't allow ourselves to get tired of living the right way. Certainly, each of us will receive everlasting life at the proper time, if we don't give up"** (Galatians 6:9).

If you're looking for how to live the right way, here are a few ideas:

Listen to your parents.

Obey your teachers.

Listen to your grandparents—even if you've heard the story before.

Give money from your lemonade stand to help the family who lost their house.

Write a thank-you letter.

In Mark 9:41, God says even the smallest act of kindness is living the right way: **"I can guarantee this truth: Whoever gives you a cup of water to drink because you belong to Christ will certainly not lose his reward."**

By the way, you don't do these things because you have to. These don't make God love you more. You do these things simply because this is why God made you—to share the love of Jesus and bring him glory. With the power of the Holy Spirit living inside of you, you don't get tired.

Keep your eye on the ball

"Keep your eye on the ball." Your volleyball coach says this over and over. If you get distracted and a serve comes your way, you're either too late to pass it, it flies over your head, or it might just smack you in the side of the face. You have to stay focused.

That's the same kind of focus we need to have on Jesus. **"We must focus on Jesus, the source and goal of our faith. He saw the joy ahead of him, so he endured death on the cross and ignored the disgrace it brought him. Then he received the highest position in heaven, the one next to the throne of God"** (Hebrews 12:2).

Jesus had laserlike focus when he walked on this earth. He defeated Satan's quick, easy temptations and stayed committed to the plan of defeating temptation for you. When he was on the cross, he saw past the pain and thought about rescuing you from your death. He ignored being humiliated, hanging naked on a cross, and having people mock him and spit on him. He kept focused on the joy ahead of him. You know what the joy is? You. Spending forever in heaven with you is his joy.

Today, fix your eyes on him. He is the One who started your faith, he makes it grow, he brings you joy and peace here, and he gets you to heaven.

Keep your eye on Jesus!

Dream big!

What's your dream job? Some kids grow up dreaming of being astronauts. Others want to be soldiers, princesses, moms, judges, dads, Olympians, doctors, presidents.

That's the fun part of being a kid—you get to dream big! The problem comes when you think things like this: "I'll never be able to escape my rough neighborhood" or "I'm too dumb" or "I don't have much to offer this world."

Your biggest problem—bring separated from God because of sin—got handled when Jesus died on a cross for you. Now you have eternal life. You are God's child, and he has big plans for you. Your brother, Jesus, said, **"I have come that they may have life, and have it to the full"** (John 10:10 NIV).

You were created to bring God glory through everything you do. As you dream big and live your overflowing-with-blessings life, you get to tell everyone you meet, **"I can do everything through Christ who strengthens me"** (Philippians 4:13).

Chomp on this!

Ask your parents what they wanted to be when they grew up. Astronaut? Chef? Pro basketball player?

Share your dream job. How can you reach your goals?

Talk about the ways you can glorify God and tell others about him through that job.

Dear Jesus,

thank you for strengthening me and giving me a full life. Help me dream big. Whatever I grow up to be, Lord, help me bring you glory so that more people want to know you and learn about your grace. Amen.

Keeping Score

Tell me if I'm wrong, but I think one of the most irritating things about kids' sports is when parents lie about the score. In some of my kids' basketball leagues, as soon as a team is up by ten points, the scorekeeper doesn't add points to the board because he doesn't want the losing team to feel bad about losing by a lot. Frankly, I think that's dumb. Every kid on that court knows the actual score, so the adults aren't fooling anybody.

God cannot lie, so he knows the score. At the same time, he isn't actually keeping track. In Psalm 130:3, we read, **"O Lord, who would be able to stand if you kept a record of sins? But with you there is forgiveness so that you can be feared."**

When Jesus died on the cross, he forgave your sins. There is no need for God to have a scoreboard tallying up all the times you hit your brother or lost your temper or rolled your eyes at your parents. All those sins were paid for when Jesus said, "It is finished." Now, when God looks at you, he's happy because you're on his team.

The only score that matters to him is Jesus: 1; Satan: 0.

You win!

Dear God,

thank you for not keeping score when it comes to my sins. I know I have a whole lot of them, but you see me as if I don't have a single one. Thank you for not keeping a record but for letting me claim Jesus' victory as my own. Amen.

Why worry?

*Today let's **Dig In!** Read this section of Scripture, and then use the questions to talk about what God has to say in his Word.*

So I tell you to stop worrying about what you will eat, drink, or wear. Isn't life more than food and the body more than clothes?

Look at the birds. They don't plant, harvest, or gather the harvest into barns. Yet, your heavenly Father feeds them. Aren't you worth more than they?

Can any of you add a single hour to your life by worrying?

And why worry about clothes? Notice how the flowers grow in the field. They never work or spin yarn for clothes. But I say that not even Solomon in all his majesty was dressed like one of these flowers. That's the way God clothes the grass in the field. Today it's alive, and tomorrow it's thrown into an incinerator. So how much more will he clothe you people who have so little faith?

Don't ever worry and say, "What are we going to eat?" or "What are we going to drink?" or "What are we going to wear?" Everyone is concerned about these things, and your heavenly Father certainly knows you need all of them. But first, be concerned about his kingdom and what has his approval. Then all these things will be provided for you. (Matthew 6:25-33)

Chomp on this!

What does God teach you in this passage?

What makes you say, "Thank you, Jesus"?

What makes you say, "I'm sorry, Jesus"?

Based on this reading, what would you like to ask God for?

Respect the authorities

**"Let everyone be subject to the governing authorities,
for there is no authority except that
which God has established.
The authorities that exist have been established by God"**
(Romans 13:1 NIV).

Maybe that passage made you think, "Blah, blah blah. The old guy who wrote these words never met my principal, my picky parents, or the police in my neighborhood."

Well, the author's name was Paul, and he understood better than you think. When he wrote these words, a leader named Nero was in charge. In the summer of 64 (not 1964, but actual 64), Emperor Nero set the city of Rome on fire. It burned for six days and seven nights, consuming almost three-quarters of the city. Obviously people were upset with him, so he started to blame Christians for the fire. He arrested believers and tortured them into blaming other believers. Tacitus, one of Rome's own news reporters, wrote, "Besides being put to death they were made to serve as objects of amusement; they were clothed in the hides of beasts and torn to death by dogs; others were crucified, others set on fire to serve to illuminate the night when daylight failed."

Even while he watched his friends tortured, murdered, and falsely accused, Paul—who was eventually beheaded by Nero—still wrote that God established authorities. God uses all sorts of rulers to ultimately work good for his people. The same goes for the authorities in your life.

You were a werewolf

Let's just get this out of the way. Werewolves are not real. You can't switch back and forth from a person to an animal. It can't happen because that's not how God created things to work.

That said, werewolves make for great characters in movies and television shows. If you want to make a movie extra creepy, you add a person howling at a full moon and transforming into a blood-thirsty creature. Werewolves prowl around, looking to bite humans—to turn them into werewolves too.

From the moment Adam sinned, he became like a werewolf. From then on, every person born would be bitten by that same curse: **"Sin came into the world through one person, and death came through sin. So death spread to everyone, because everyone sinned"** (Romans 5:12).

Werewolves can't do anything about their condition. The only way to stop them is to kill them. (Most movies show you need to use a silver bullet or drive a silver stake into their hearts.) You can't do anything about your sin condition either. The only way to cure you is to kill your sinful nature, which is exactly what Jesus did on the cross. When he died, he took your sinful nature and buried it with him. When he came back to life, he gave you a new nature, a spiritual nature that will live with him forever.

This isn't good news only for you. This is for all the sin-werewolves out there. **"Clearly, through one person's disobedience humanity became sinful, and through one person's obedience humanity will receive God's approval"** (verse 19).

Jesus came and changed you from a werewolf to a child of God. THAT is real.

Everything you need

How many Legos do you have? I bet the answer is, "Not enough."

Kids with one little Lego set want more. Kids with, let's say, 1,174,319 Lego pieces want more too. No child is ever content with the current amount of Legos.

Our whole lives are kind of like that too. Even though it would take us until tomorrow to even begin to list the good things God has given us, we want more. We look at all the good things God has given other people and think that maybe we don't have enough.

Learning how to be satisfied with what we have doesn't just happen. We need to learn how to do it. The apostle Paul wrote, **"I know what it is to be in need, and I know what it is to have plenty. I have learned the secret of being content in any and every situation, whether well fed or hungry, whether living in plenty or in want"** (Philippians 4:12 NIV).

Now, how many Legos do you have?

The answer is, "Just the right amount."

Dear Father,

thank you for how much you have blessed me and how many good things you've given me. Forgive me for when I wish I had more, when I haven't been content. Help me remember that you want what's best for me and sometimes stuff gets in the way. So, even though it's hard, please take away anything that distracts me from you. Help me learn more and more how to be content. Amen.

Show respect

"I can't STAND him!"

"I never get to play!"

"She's the worst teacher ever!"

"He's so unfair, and the homework is *so* stupid!"

At some point in your life, you are going to be majorly unhappy with your teacher or coach. When you rant, rave, and yell about the adults in your life, you act as if you have no control of your attitude. You forget what God says to you in Ephesians 4:26,27: **"Be angry without sinning.... Don't give the devil any opportunity to work."**

Believing that you can only be thankful if things go your way gives the devil a chance to work in your life. Instead, God tells you that your attitude is based on what *he* wants to work in you: **"Whatever happens, give thanks, because it is God's will in Christ Jesus that you do this"** (1 Thessalonians 5:18).

When you don't understand why the teacher seems harder on you than the other kids, give yourself a few minutes to calm down. Then give thanks. Let God know you are thankful for adults that volunteer their time to help make you better. Tell him thank you for the teachers whose job it is to push you and challenge you to grow. Trust that God will use every situation for your good, to bring you closer to him.

Maybe right now you aren't sure how he'll do this, but he promises he will.

 ## Chomp on this!

Have you ever disagreed with a teacher's decision?

How did you handle yourself?

How has God used teachers and coaches to push you and make you better?

God makes it right

Today is National Blasphemy Day. *Blasphemy* is a big word that means to put down or tell lies about God. Some blaspheme by saying there is no God. Others say they are their own god. Other people say that God is hate. Some say religion is only for stupid, weak people. Those may sound strange to you, but the people who truly believe that use this special day to criticize and hate religion—and make fun of people who believe in God.

Blasphemy is not a new idea. In the book of Malachi, we hear about people who **"have said, 'It's pointless to serve God. What do we gain if we meet his standards or if we walk around feeling sorry for what we've done? So now we call arrogant people blessed. Not only are evildoers encouraged, they even test God and get away with it'"** (Malachi 3:14,15).

Maybe you feel the same way: some kids cheat and get away with it. Sometimes bullies get away with beating others up. If so, then you need to hear the rest of this section.

"Then those who feared the Lord spoke to one another, and the Lord paid attention and listened. . . . 'They will be mine,' says the Lord of Armies. 'On that day I will make them my special possession. I will spare them as a man spares his own son who serves him. Then you will again see the difference between righteous people and wicked people, between the one who serves God and the one who doesn't serve him'" (verses 16-18).

When sometimes it seems like the blasphemers are winning, remember that God pays attention and listens. You are his special possession. He makes it right in the end.

You will do great things

**"I am the vine. You are the branches.
Those who live in me while I live in them
will produce a lot of fruit.
But you can't produce anything without me"**
(John 15:5).

Every fall, all across the country, people head out to pick apples, buy apple pies, and drink apple cider. Not one single person who goes to an apple orchard looks for fruit on branches that fell off a tree in a storm. You know, the branches that are on the ground. That's because everyone knows that if a branch isn't attached to a tree, you won't get any fruit. It just doesn't work that way.

Yet some people think they can cut themselves off from God, their Creator, and still expect to do good things in their lives. But it doesn't work that way. Jesus tells us that branches have to be attached to a tree to get the nutrition they need. Only then can they bear fruit. You have to be attached to Jesus to get your energy from him and to do anything that has true, lasting value. You might win championships, have a lot of friends, or make a lot of money, but none of that actually matters to God. Only when you are attached to Jesus will you bear real fruit: serving others and praising him.

Chomp on this!

What are the ways we can stay attached to Jesus?

What kind of "fruit" (good works) do we produce when we stay attached to him?

Dear Jesus,

you are the vine. I am a branch. I know that I can't do a single good thing without you. But I am connected to you. Because I get all my energy from you, help me be kind and do good things for the people in my life. Amen.

Thank a pastor!

October is Clergy Appreciation Month. Have you heard the word *clergy* before? Really, it's just a fancy word for a religious leader. Maybe you'd be more familiar with the word *pastor*.

This is the month when you get to **"give double honor to spiritual leaders who handle their duties well. This is especially true if they work hard at teaching the word of God"** (1 Timothy 5:17).

Maybe you don't realize just how hard it is to be a pastor. (*Pastor* is the Latin word for "shepherd.") As shepherds, they care for and watch over everyone in the church.

Maybe you don't necessarily think about it, but pastors are not only there for other people, they are there for you also. Does something in the Bible confuse you? They'll look with you to find God's answer. They'll pray with you if you are sad or hurt. Is there trouble at school or in your family? Pastors are there to pray with you and encourage you.

So this month follow God's command to **"obey your leaders, and accept their authority. They take care of you because they are responsible for you"** (Hebrews 13:17).

Chomp on this!

What things do you appreciate about your pastor?

What are some ways your family can show thankfulness?

Dear Good Shepherd,

thank you for giving us pastors as our shepherds. We appreciate that they do their jobs well and work hard at teaching your Word. Help us show them our respect. Please also be with their families who share them willingly with all of us. Amen.

A living sacrifice

Back when Isaac was a kid, he knew all about sacrifices. (Today you call it an offering and probably put money in a basket at church.) When Isaac lived, offerings were so much messier. Animals and blood were put on an altar to be burned and offered to God. (See where the term *offering* came from?)

One day, God told Abraham, Isaac's father, "Put Isaac on the altar." So he did. Isaac was about to be sacrificed as an offering!

Can you even imagine that God wants you to be sacrificed too? He tells you in Romans 12:1,2, **"In view of all we have just shared about God's compassion, I encourage you to offer your bodies as living sacrifices, dedicated to God and pleasing to him. This kind of worship is appropriate for you. Don't become like the people of this world. Instead, change the way you think."**

You are now a living sacrifice. God doesn't get the leftover time after you're done playing on the computer or phone. He doesn't get the scraps after sports. God wants you to stop thinking that the way the world lives is better than the life you've got. His compassion changes the way you think. God sacrificed his Son for you the way Abraham was willing to sacrifice Isaac. Now, God gets all of you. He gets the best of you.

 ## Chomp on this!

Read how the story of Abraham and Isaac ends. You'll find it in Genesis chapter 22.

You get what you get

"You get what you get and you don't throw a fit." I bet you heard that about 3,742 times when you were younger.

That's because little kids tend to pitch a fit about things that don't really matter. You know, like wanting a blue scissors but all that's left are the red ones. Or maybe someone else took the purple marker and you shouted, "THAT'S MY MARKER!"

As you grow up, though, you still pitch fits, don't you?

"Why can't I watch that movie when everyone else can?"

"Why can't I have those basketball shoes? Everyone else does!"

"But I *need* those clothes. I won't be cool if I don't have them."

In Philippians 4:11-13 the apostle Paul says, **"I've learned to be content in whatever situation I'm in. I know how to live in poverty or prosperity. No matter what the situation, I've learned the secret of how to live when I'm full or when I'm hungry, when I have too much or when I have too little. I can do everything through Christ who strengthens me."**

That's a nice way of telling you, "Look at your life. Be content. Be thankful. You get what you get and you don't throw a fit."

Dear Father,

sometimes I look around and want the things that you've given to other people. Help me be content with whatever blessings you give me. I know you give me exactly what I need and usually more than what I need. Make me grateful, Lord. Amen.

Out in the deSert

**"Later, John the Baptizer appeared in the desert of Judea.
His message was, 'Turn to God and change the way you
think and act, because the kingdom of heaven is near.'
Jerusalem, all Judea, and the whole Jordan Valley
went to him. As they confessed their sins,
he baptized them in the Jordan River"**
(Matthew 3:1,2,5,6).

In the middle of the Australian desert, you can find the world's
largest monolith, which is a fancy word for one gigantic rock.
Uluru* is 1,141 feet tall, which is taller than the Eiffel Tower in
Paris. If you wanted to go around it, you would have to walk for
almost six miles. Sometimes the color seems to change from red
to orange to almost light purple. It is so amazing that, even though
it is a five-hour drive from the nearest big city, almost 250,000
people visit each year.

John the Baptist was like Uluru. He stood in the middle of a desert,
but people traveled from all over the area to see him. His message
was as hard as a rock. After all, who wants to be reminded that
they are sinful and need to say they're sorry and turn back to
God? Still, his message was as beautiful as a color-changing rock.
That's because hearing "the kingdom of heaven is near," reminded
the people that a Savior was coming who would heal their broken
relationship with God.

Chomp on this!

Do you ever feel like Uluru or like John the Baptist? How
does believing in Jesus sometimes make you feel like you're
out in the wilderness?

How does your faith in Jesus make you stand apart? How does it
draw people to you?

*For parents: You probably know this as Ayres Rock. Uluru is the
Aboriginal and official name.*

You are God's flashlight

Whenever you go camping, you have to pack a flashlight. There's no way you can get from your tent to the bathroom in the middle of the night unless you can see the path. The flashlight stops you from tripping and falling over the logs and roots and tent pegs.

Without God, people are trying to find a path without a flashlight. King Solomon said, **"The way of wicked people is like deep darkness. They do not know what makes them stumble"** (Proverbs 4:19).

Because you know God, you have a light for your path. Now God has a job for you to do. Use your light to show others the way. **"You are light for the world. A city cannot be hidden when it is located on a hill. No one lights a lamp and puts it under a basket. Instead, everyone who lights a lamp puts it on a lamp stand. Then its light shines on everyone in the house. In the same way let your light shine in front of people. Then they will see the good that you do and praise your Father in heaven"** (Matthew 5:14-16).

Sing it with me, "This little light of mine, I'm gonna let it shine."

Chomp on this!

Talk about times you have let your light shine.

What are some ways you can shine this week?

Catch me when I'm guilty

"I am so happy I got a detention today!"

"My parents grounded me. They are the best!"

"I don't get to watch TV for a whole week. I think that's awesome!"

Raise your hand if you said one of these this week. Wait; raise your hand if you said one of these ever.

King David saw consequences a little differently. In Psalm 119:71 he writes, **"It was good that I had to suffer in order to learn your laws."**

Here's the deal. Kids who learn there are consequences learn how the world works—if you choose to disobey, you get grounded. If you don't do your homework, you get a detention. You may not like consequences, but they teach you that when you make poor choices, bad things happen.

Just like you, I'm sure David did not enjoy his consequences as they happened. But looking back over his life, he realized it was a good thing to be caught, to be disciplined, all so he could learn more about what God says. His troubles brought him closer to God. So will yours.

 ## Chomp on this!

What lessons have you learned from when you got caught?

Dear God,

help me do what you tell me to do. This is hard to say, but if I break your laws, please let me get caught. Use my mistakes to help me learn more about the way you want me to act. Amen.

Calls you by your name

"The LORD is my shepherd, I lack nothing"
(Psalm 23:1 NIV).

I'm sure that at some point you've been called the wrong name. Maybe your parents call you by your sister's name or your brother's name or—even worse—your dog's name.

One of the best songs about Jesus is a song you learned when you were a kid. (Although the song isn't only for kids; adults love it too.)

I am Jesus' little lamb.
Ever glad at heart I am.
For my Shepherd gently guides me,
Knows my needs and well provides me,
Loves me every day the same,
Even calls me by my name.

The Lord is your Shepherd. He loves you. He guides you. He completely provides for you. You have everything you need. When you're sad, you hear him gently say your voice, as if he is hugging you. When you're happy, the way he says your voice cheers along with you. When you are wandering away, there's a good chance he says your name with that little bit of warning . . . the same way your parents tell you to step away from a hot stove. No matter what, though, God is your Good Shepherd. You are his little lamb. Your heart is happy.

Dear Shepherd,

thank you for guiding me, knowing what I need, and giving it to me. Your love for me doesn't change from day to day, depending upon how I act. Instead, you call me, every day, by my name and remind me that I am yours. Thank you. Amen.

God determines where you live

If you've moved into a different house, you know it takes a while to feel "at home" in your new place. Some kids get sick to their stomachs just moving across town. Military kids move so often that they might have six or seven homes before they turn 18. Foster kids never actually have a home of their own and bounce from family to family.

No matter how much or how little you've moved, God wants you to know that he put you there. **"The God who made the universe and everything in it is the Lord of heaven and earth. . . . He has made every nation of humanity to live all over the earth. He has given them the seasons of the year and the boundaries within which to live. He has done this so that they would look for God, somehow reach for him, and find him"** (Acts 17:24,26,27).

The God who made this world decided where you'd live in this world—and how long you'd be in each place. Sure, maybe you moved because of your parents' job, but that was part of God's plan. He did not have you move because he enjoys seeing you struggle to fit in. He does not enjoy watching your heartache when you say good-bye to friends and neighbors. He did this because he wants you to look for him, to let him give you peace. When you don't feel at home, remember you have a real, eternal home waiting for you— and you'll never have to move once you're there.

By the way, every place you live provides opportunities to tell the ones around you about Jesus. Let your light shine so they look for him and reach out for him too.

Your Sibling's Keeper

How often do the kids in your family fight? Every day? Twice a day? Sixteen times a day? Have you lost track of the number of times you have yelled at or have thrown something at them?

You're not alone, you know. Jacob and Esau fought. Joseph really made his brothers mad. The first two brothers in the history of the world, well, that didn't end well either. Cain was so jealous of his brother Abel that he attacked and killed him.

That's when the heavenly Father intervened, **"The LORD asked Cain, 'Where is your brother Abel?' 'I don't know,' he answered. 'Am I supposed to take care of my brother?'"** (Genesis 4:9).

The answer was yes. He was supposed to take care of Abel. You're supposed to take care of your siblings too. That's why God put them in your family. Listen to the apostle Paul who tells you to **"be devoted to each other like a loving family. Excel in showing respect for each other"** (Romans 12:10).

When you are devoted to your family, you love each other most. You don't put each other down in front of your friends to look cool. Instead, you defend them and say nice things about them.

You are your brother's and sister's keeper.

Dear heavenly Father,

you put together our family the way you wanted it to be. Forgive me when I forget that these are the people you want me to protect and care about. Help me be devoted to this family, the same way my brother Jesus was devoted to me. Amen.

What makes you beautiful

Guys, today's devotion is going to sound more like it's for girls. Right now, you might think girls have germs or something, but someday—a long time from now—you might think about marrying one of them. God thinks it's important that you know, right now, what he values. Plus, if you ever have a daughter, it will be your job to teach her what true beauty is. So pay attention!

Girls, here's what the world wants you to do so you will be beautiful. Starve yourself so you will be skinny. Inject toxins into your face so you don't get wrinkles. Spend tons of money on clothes, makeup, and shoes made by famous designers. Show off as much of your body as possible so that boys will look at you.

The world is dumb.

The God who formed you, who decided how you would look on the outside, wants you to know what *he* thinks is beautiful. Here's a hint: it has nothing to do with anything on the outside. **"Beauty doesn't come from hairstyles, gold jewelry, or clothes. Rather, beauty is something internal that can't be destroyed. Beauty expresses itself in a gentle and quiet attitude which God considers precious"** (1 Peter 3:3,4).

God wants you to spend less time worrying about your outside shell so you can spend more time working on the person you are on the inside. When you believe God thinks you are so valuable that he sent Jesus for you, you care less about what other people think. The way your face glows because the love of Jesus pours out of you, that's what makes you precious. That's what makes you beautiful.

P.S. For the outgoing, talkative girls who might be reading this … please don't think that a gentle and quiet attitude doesn't mean you have to be a quiet person. It means that your heart is at peace because you know that God thinks you are stunning and wants you to use your energy and enthusiasm to bring joy to the people around you.

Invite them

**"How can people call on him
if they have not believed in him?
How can they believe in him
if they have not heard his message?
How can they hear if no one tells the Good News?"**
(Romans 10:14).

Your best friend throws a birthday party but doesn't invite you. At school you hear everyone talking about it, and he asks, "Why didn't you show up?"

Obviously you'd answer, "Well, I didn't know. You didn't invite me. Why didn't you tell me?"

Wouldn't you be hurt if he says, "I didn't think I actually had to tell you. I was just hoping you'd figure it out."

The whole time you would be thinking, "How can I come to a party that I don't know about?!"

Heaven is a celebration too! It's a forever victory party for God. But not all people know the party is going on because they don't know what Jesus has done for them.

That's why God has given you a job: invite people!

When Jesus told his followers to go and make disciples of all nations, it wasn't only a command for the disciples or for adults. He meant you too. You get to tell the people around you about the best party ever! Tell them the great things Jesus has done for them. Tell them the great things Jesus has planned for them. They can't figure it out on their own if they haven't heard the message. They won't know if you don't tell them the Good News! Invite them.

Dear Father,

I know that life with you is awesome here, but life in heaven will be even better. Help me not to be nervous but to invite all the people I know so they can know the good news too. Amen.

Heal people

**"The men there recognized Jesus
and sent messengers all around the countryside.
The people brought him everyone who was sick.
They begged him to let them touch
just the edge of his clothes.
Everyone who touched his clothes was made well"**
(Matthew 14:35,36).

Your little brother and sister believe a parent's kiss is magic. Moms or dads can kiss an owie and make it all better. You're getting more grown up, so maybe you don't believe that anymore. Yet when you're hurt, you still look to your parents for a hug or a gentle touch because somehow it does help you feel a little better.

That's how these people were with Jesus. Yes, Jesus was a human, but he was also God at the very same time. The same Jesus who was going to defeat death by God's power had power over sickness too. Just by touching him, people were healed. This same Jesus happens to be your brother, and he is still alive. Even though he is not here on earth, because he is in heaven preparing a place for you, he can and still does have the power to heal. Just ask.

Heal people—that's what your God can do.

Chomp on this!

Are there people in your life who are sick? Pray for them.

Dear God,

thank you for putting this story in the Bible.
Sometimes because I don't see you in person, I forget just how powerful you really are. You still have power over sickness; you still can heal people. We pray for our friends and family who are sick, and we ask you to heal them so they can tell more people about you and your power. Amen.

Bring your friends!

Yesterday we read about how Jesus' power healed people simply when they touched his clothes. There's another cool part to that story, so we need to read it again.

"The men there recognized Jesus and sent messengers all around the countryside. The people brought him everyone who was sick. They begged him to let them touch just the edge of his clothes. Everyone who touched his clothes was made well" (Matthew 14:35,36).

Some people recognized Jesus and couldn't wait to share that great news. Today, you'd probably text your friends, but these people didn't have phones or electricity or anything. So they sent some guys to run back to the town to tell everyone, "Jesus is here! The one who heals people is close by." The sick people wouldn't have known he was in the area if the healthy people hadn't shared the news.

There are people around you who might be physically sick too and need your prayers. There are probably more people around you, though, who are spiritually sick. You get to tell them, "Jesus is here! The one who heals your sins and your diseases came for you!" Invite them to church, pray for them, and share the stories about Jesus so they know that he can make them well.

Tell people that Jesus can heal them—that's what you can do.

Dear Jesus,

help me be as excited as the men in this story who recognized you. Let me be a messenger, telling people around me that you are with us and that you can heal both our bodies and also the hurts and illnesses on the inside. Amen.

Jesus loves kids!

*Today let's **Dig In!** Read this section of Scripture, and then use the questions to talk about what God has to say in his Word.*

At that time the disciples came to Jesus and asked, "Who is greatest in the kingdom of heaven?"

He called a little child and had him stand among them. Then he said to them, "I can guarantee this truth: Unless you change and become like little children, you will never enter the kingdom of heaven. Whoever becomes like this little child is the greatest in the kingdom of heaven. And whoever welcomes a child like this in my name welcomes me.

"Be careful not to despise these little ones. I can guarantee that their angels in heaven always see the face of my Father, who is in heaven.

"What do you think? Suppose a man has 100 sheep and one of them strays. Won't he leave the 99 sheep in the hills to look for the one that has strayed? I can guarantee this truth: If he finds it, he is happier about it than about the 99 that have not strayed. In the same way, your Father in heaven does not want one of these little ones to be lost." (Matthew 18:1-5, 10-14)

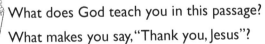

Chomp on this!

What does God teach you in this passage?

What makes you say, "Thank you, Jesus"?

What makes you say, "I'm sorry, Jesus"?

Based on this reading, what would you like to ask God for?

Troubles produce fruit

Uncle Gene's grapes wouldn't grow. He couldn't figure out why. The soil was good, he used fertilizer and watered them, and they had plenty of sun. The plants were beautiful and had bright green leaves, but no matter what he did, there was no fruit.

Then he learned that grapes actually need only sort-of-good soil. There can be some rocks, some clay, and you only need a moderate amount of nutrients in the soil. It turned out that Uncle Gene's soil was too good and actually stopped the grapes from producing fruit.

We all want to live like Uncle Gene's grapes. We want a life with good soil (a comfortable home with no chores), lots of fertilizer (full stomachs), sunshine (happiness), and plenty of water (money).

God knows, however, that sometimes if we have it too good, we get comfortable. Maybe like the grape plants we'd look good and healthy, but wouldn't actually be doing what we were made to do: to produce fruit.

That's why the apostle Paul said he actually was proud of having bad times. **"We also brag when we are suffering. We know that suffering creates endurance, endurance creates character, and character creates confidence. We're not ashamed to have this confidence, because God's love has been poured into our hearts by the Holy Spirit, who has been given to us"** (Romans 5:3-5).

The next time trouble comes, brag about it. God is using it to help you produce fruit—and not be ashamed.

ACTS

Does it make you nervous to pray? It's just itty-bitty you talking to a great big God. How in the world do you know what to say?

Jesus' disciples had the same question. **"Once Jesus was praying in a certain place. When he stopped praying, one of his disciples said to him, "Lord, teach us to pray as John taught his disciples"** (Luke 11:1).

After they asked, Jesus taught them the Lord's Prayer. But that's not the only prayer Jesus or the disciples ever said—after all, Jesus spent hours in the Garden of Gethsemane talking to his Father right before he was killed.

So what else can you talk about? Use the letters ACTS, and you'll find lots of things to pray about.

Adoration: Compliment God. Tell him why you adore him, why you think he is awesome!

Confession: Tell God about your sins. He already knows that you did them, but it is good for you to admit to the big ones and share the little ones—and apologize for the ones you don't even know you did.

Thanksgiving: Just like your dad makes sure you say thank you for your birthday gifts, you thank God for the good things he gives you each day. You can make it long or short, but list the things you were especially grateful for today.

Supplication: *Supplication* is a big, fancy church word for asking God to supply everything you need. You also ask God to supply the needs of your family and friends—and even people around the world.

ACTS isn't the way you *have* to pray. It's just an idea to help you pray. You can pray with your eyes open or closed, hands folded or not, out loud or in your head, or walking or lying in bed. God doesn't care if you use big words or little words. Just talk to him and be bold because **"the prayer of a righteous person is powerful and effective"** (James 5:16 NIV).

The race to perfection*

When a runner can't finish a cross country or track meet and a competitor carries her across the finish line, it makes the local news. Most runners are so focused on finishing that they may not notice the runners around them. So when someone stops to help out another person, that kind of sportsmanship stands out.

On our own, we have tripped and fallen at the start of the race and can't reach the finish line of perfection that God's law sets. Instead of ignoring us, God sent Jesus to run our salvation race for us. When Christ lived a perfect life and died on a cross, he took the place of the world. He started and finished the race for us. He did what on our own is impossible.

On the days you doubt that what Jesus did applies to you, remember this: God *promises* that Christ ran the race for you. Since Christ ran it for you, you do not need to worry.

Finally, as you get tired on your race in this life, remember that Jesus is still supporting and carrying you. He promises, **"Come to me, all you who are weary and burdened, and I will give you rest"** (Matthew 11:28 NIV).

Dear Father,

you sent Jesus to finish the salvation race we couldn't finish. Help us remember that you are still helping us when we are weak and weary. Amen.

This devotion was written by Isaiah, a kid just like you.

You are claimed

In *The Lighting Thief,* Percy Jackson learns that he is a demigod. That means he has one human parent and one parent who just happens to be a Greek god. Fortunately, Poseidon admits he is Percy's dad. (Not all demigods know who their parents are.) As 12-year-old Percy is on his quest to rescue Zeus' lightning bolt, mythological creatures and lesser gods try to stop him, to kill him.

Every time he is in trouble, he asks for his father to help him. The problem with Greek gods, though, is their children aren't sure if they will answer or be silent, if they will ignore them or help them.

Aren't you glad that your heavenly Father, who happens to be the real God, looks at you differently? **"Now, this is what the LORD says: Do not be afraid, because I have reclaimed you. I have called you by name; you are mine. When you go through the sea, I am with you. When you go through rivers, they will not sweep you away. When you walk through fire, you will not be burned, and the flames will not harm you. I am the LORD your God, the Holy One of Israel, your Savior"** (Isaiah 43:1-3).

You aren't Percy. You don't have to wonder if you are God's child; he claims you. He names you. As you face temptations and struggles, as you battle against Satan and this world, he is always—always—with you on your quest, no matter what.

Paint his name

Almost every park, county fair, or city festival offers face painting. Kids line up to wait for a chance to get a flower or tiger on their cheeks. Some get pretty detailed and ask for a tiger or a butterfly over their whole faces.

For the next few hours—or until it itches or their dads make them wash the paint off—they proudly show off the artist's work. They want everyone to notice what's on their faces.

When you get home to heaven, you are going to have some permanent face paint. **"The throne of God and the lamb will be in the city. His servants will worship him and see his face. His name will be on their foreheads"** (Revelation 22:3,4).

When Jesus left this earth to go back to heaven and prepare our home, he promised to come back for us. As we wait for him to take us to our real home, we get excited for the day there are no more tears, no more fights, no more loneliness. We know that we will see our God face-to-face and worship him. And his name will be on our foreheads—a sign that let's everyone know we are his.

While we wait for that day, we know Jesus has already called us—even now. Tell others about Jesus so he can paint their faces too.

 ## Chomp on this!

Do you have a question you want to ask God when you get to heaven? Share it with your family.

Heaven is guaranteed because of Jesus, who can you tell about that good news?

God's house is better

It is fascinating to learn how famous people live. We read about their fancy cars, their homes in Los Angeles and the Caribbean and New York, their indoor swimming pools, their maids and cooks and house managers and agents.

Let's be honest, if we had the chance, almost all of us would like to live that way. The God who created everything and actually owns everything in the whole world tells us to be careful about thinking that way. **"What good does it do for people to win the whole world yet lose their lives?"** (Mark 8:36).

When you have lots of money, you might start believing it is *your* money, not a gift from the God who provides everything you need. King David said, **"Better is one day in your courts than a thousand elsewhere; I would rather be a doorkeeper in the house of my God than dwell in the tents of the wicked"** (Psalm 84:10 NIV). This king, who had a whole bunch of servants and an entire army at his command said he would rather be a servant for God than have a mansion where evil was in charge. He would rather give away all his riches than walk away from God.

If a full bank account leads you away from Jesus, your life is actually poor. If being a celebrity surrounded by paparazzi leads you away from Jesus, it's time to be a servant instead. When your whole goal is getting a huge house for your life on earth, you've forgotten that Jesus has prepared a heavenly mansion for you.

Love each Other

When you're outside, sometimes it's sooooo easy to make fun of your brother so you can look cool in front of the other neighborhood kids. As he acts silly, it's tempting to roll your eyes and say, "He's *such* a doofus."

When you put him down instead of defending him, you are acting as if you need the other kids' approval to be cool, to be "somebody." Because of what Jesus did for you, laying down his life for you, God already approves of you. You don't need other people to make you feel better about yourself.

Now Jesus calls you his brother or sister and encourages you to love your brother the way Jesus loves you. **"I'm giving you a new commandment: Love each other in the same way that I have loved you. Everyone will know that you are my disciples because of your love for each other"** (John 13:34,35).

As you think about the words you use with your siblings, isn't it amazing that while Jesus grew up in a house full of brothers and sisters he never—not one single time—made fun of them or rolled his eyes at them. When Jesus died on a cross, he took the punishment for the times that your words hurt your family. Now when God looks at you, he doesn't see your hurtful words; he sees Jesus' perfection.

Chomp On this!

When have you put your brother or sister down? (If you're an only child, think about the times you've put down your friends or talked about your parents in a bad way.)

What are some things you can change, with the Holy Spirit's help, to love the people around you the way Jesus loves you?

Looking at the heart

King Saul wasn't going to be king for long. He had turned against his God, and God was doing something about it. He told Samuel, his prophet, **"I'm sending you to Jesse in Bethlehem because I've selected one of his sons to be king."**

When Samuel got to Jesse's home, he started looking for the next king of Israel. The oldest son came out, but he wasn't the one. God told Samuel, **"Don't look at his appearance or how tall he is, because I have rejected him. God does not see as humans see. Humans look at outward appearances, but the LORD looks into the heart."**

Samuel met ten sons—ten!—and still told Jesse, **"The LORD has not chosen any of these. Are these all the sons you have?"**

"There's still the youngest one," Jesse answered. **"He's tending the sheep."**

Samuel told Jesse, "Send someone to get him. We won't continue until he gets here."

When David got to the feast, **"The LORD said, 'Go ahead, anoint him. He is the one.' Samuel took the flask of olive oil and anointed David in the presence of his brothers. The LORD's Spirit came over David and stayed with him from that day on.**

Are you the youngest? Do people compare you to your brothers or sisters? God doesn't look at the outside like other people do. No matter how big (or small) you are, God sees your heart, and he has plans for you.

Chomp on this!

Read the whole story in 1 Samuel chapter 16.

Don't be Scared!

Do you dress up for trick or treat? It's fun to be a princess or a ninja or maybe a cowboy or a ballerina. Maybe you even like the creepy stuff, like a monster or mummy. This is the week when people think it's okay to scare others or have others scare them, all because they know it's for pretend.

What about real fears, though? At some point everyone has a scary problem, one that isn't just part of an active imagination.

Are your parents fighting? Do you get bullied at school? Is your neighborhood a little dangerous? Is someone in your family sick? What other problems do you have that make you scared?

This was a problem for God's people thousands of years ago.

When the Israelites were going up against their enemies, God told them he wasn't only *with* them, but he'd do the fighting *for* them. **"Do not be fainthearted or afraid; do not panic or be terrified by them. For the LORD your God is the one who goes with you to fight for you against your enemies to give you victory"** (Deuteronomy 20:3,4 NIV).

Whatever problem you have, do not be afraid or panic. God wants you to know that he is with you. He loves you and watches over you; he helps you when you're afraid. But he does even more than that. He fights FOR you. He tells you not to worry. He's got this.

 ## Chomp on this!

What things scare you right now?

How do you think God might fight your fears for you?

What you need

When your family asks you what you *want* for your birthday, the list is incredibly long. Legos, earrings, gift cards, a trip to a water park, electronics, a new bike, fancy clothes, a puppy, and every single toy in the dollar bin.

If they ask what you *need*, you might make the same list. When an adult named Paul wrote a letter to a young man named Timothy, he said the list of things he needs is actually very short. Food. Clothes. That's it.

"If we have food and clothing, we will be content with that. For the love of money is a root of all kinds of evil. Some people, eager for money, have wandered from the faith and pierced themselves with many griefs. But you, man of God, flee from all this, and pursue righteousness, godliness, faith, love, endurance and gentleness" (1 Timothy 6:8, 10, 11 NIV).

When you look around your bedroom and see all the things you think are missing, you focus on the stuff the world thinks is important. When that happens, Paul told Timothy to *flee*, to run like you're being chased by bees!

When you know your parents can't afford it but you still beg, "I'm the only one who doesn't have a phone. I *need* a phone," run away!

If you think kids will like you better because there's a brand name on your hoodie, flee!

When you believe expensive clothes on the outside means you are more valuable on the inside, get away!

As you run away from thinking that stuff will make you happy, start chasing the things God says will bring you real joy: living God's way, hanging in there when you're discouraged, giving away the toys and books and clothes that you don't need, loving people who are mean. Be content, and you'll be thankful for the blessings you already have.

The hiding place

In her book *The Hiding Place*, Corrie ten Boom shares the story of her life. In a horrible time in the world's history, she and her sister, who believed in Jesus, were among hundreds of thousands of people put into a big prison called a concentration camp.

Their sleeping area was only supposed to hold 400 people, but there were 1,400 women crammed inside. Their beds were straw-covered platforms—and 9 people shared a bed. The first night Corrie felt things biting her ankles and realized they were fleas! Her sister, Betsie, reminded her that the Bible says to **"always be joyful. Never stop praying. Whatever happens, give thanks, because it is God's will in Christ Jesus that you do this"** (1 Thessalonians 5:16-18).

Corrie believed she would never, ever, ever be thankful for biting fleas. Over the next few weeks, she and her sister read their Bible (which they had to hide so guards wouldn't take it away). They studied the Bible with other prisoners and encouraged them even though everything looked hopeless. Later they found out that because of the fleas, guards wouldn't step into that room. That's why they had so much freedom to read and share the Bible with prisoners. That's when Corrie saw how God used even horrible situations to work for good. She now was thankful for the fleas.

Even in the middle of a depressing prison, Corrie and Betsie knew that God doesn't say, "Give thanks only in happy times" or "Be joyful only when things are going your way" or "Pray when you remember to, you know, maybe every three or four days." Instead he says, "Be joyful—always. Pray—always. Give thanks—always."

Chomp on this!

What in your life seems like fleas? What bothers you or makes you sad? What have you been complaining about?

How do you think God can use that for your good?

Baa baa black Sheep

There's a term for people who don't fit in: *black sheep*. These are the people who are so very different from everyone else that they stand out like a black sheep in a flock of white sheep. Maybe you're the black sheep in the classroom—the one who can't seem to get along with the teacher and always gets into trouble. Maybe you have a black sheep in your family—an older sister who got caught doing drugs or a dad who bailed when he found out your mom was pregnant. Sometimes family members are embarrassed, almost ashamed, by the black sheep. They think that one person's choices are a bad reflection on them.

In Jesus' family there are no black sheep. Jesus became one of us so that no one would have to be left out. **"Jesus, who makes people holy, and all those who are made holy have the same Father. That is why Jesus isn't ashamed to call them brothers and sisters"** (Hebrews 2:11).

When Jesus gave you his perfection and holiness, he gave you the permission slip to call the all-powerful, all-knowing, all-holy God "Dad." When Jesus talks about you, he doesn't shake his head and say, "I can't believe what she has been doing lately" or "I'm so embarrassed he's in the family." Instead, Jesus puts his arm around you and says, "Hey, sis! What's up, bro! I'm happy to see you!"

By the way . . . there are still plenty of black sheep in this world who don't know that Jesus has given them the right to be in his family. Tell them the good news. Let them know they belong.

Math Problems?*

Have you ever had a hard time doing math? All those fractions and division problems and equations and graphs can be pretty confusing. Sometimes you need a tutor to figure it all out. With Jesus, there's one math problem that doesn't make sense to our minds, but the Holy Spirit tutors us so we can understand it. It looks like this:

Jesus' perfect life + Jesus' innocent death + faith = eternal life in heaven.

It doesn't make sense to us because we know we don't deserve it. We sin all the time and are not perfect in any way. We don't deserve God's love either, but he still chose to love us enough to send his only Son to be mocked, ridiculed, and put to death in a horrible fashion. Because of that love we get to live forever. **"You were once dead because of your failures. . . . But God made you alive with Christ when he forgave all our failures"** (Colossians 2:13).

This passage explains God's math problem perfectly. God made us alive because of Jesus and forgave all our sins. Faith in Jesus Christ is your only way to eternal life.

In God's math, Jesus is always the right answer.

Dear God,

we all have trouble with math sometimes, but help us see that one math problem will save us. The math problem that is Jesus Christ. Help us look to you in times of trouble. In Jesus' name we pray. Amen.

This devotion was written by Kirstyn, a kid just like you.

Pester God

"Mom, can we have dessert?"

"Just a minute, I'm on the phone," she says.

Twenty seconds later, you ask again—even though you can see she's still on the phone.

She tells you to wait—and you wait what seems like six hours, but really was only seven minutes, until you ask again.

You ask and ask and ask until she just says, "Fine, yes, whatever."

You know that's how to get what you want. You pester your parents until they give in. That might drive your parents bananas, but that's actually how God wants you to talk to him.

He wants you to come to him, to talk to him, to ask him for good things. He wants you to **"ask, and you will receive. Search, and you will find. Knock, and the door will be opened for you"** (Luke 11:9).

When you pray, you keep talking and asking, never giving up. As much as God loves to hear your prayers for a baby sister or a new outfit or to get an A on a test, he also wants you to ask for the things he loves to give you: joy, kindness, wisdom, compassion, and a forgiving heart.

No matter what you pray, God promises that he hears you and will work everything for your eternal good.

Chomp on this!

What things have you been praying about lately?

How can you "pester" God with your prayers?

You aren't a zombie

In Haitian culture, a zombie is a dead person who is animated by magic or witchcraft. They aren't really alive; they're just the walking dead.

In popular culture, people pretend they are zombies—also called the undead—by wearing torn clothes, putting on pretend blood, and walking around mindlessly while moaning.

In the Bible, it turns out that people who do not believe in Jesus are zombies—and you were a zombie too!

"You were once dead because of your failures and sins. You followed the ways of this present world and its spiritual ruler. This ruler continues to work in people who refuse to obey God. But God is rich in mercy because of his great love for us. We were dead because of our failures, but he made us alive together with Christ. (It is God's kindness that saved you.) God has brought us back to life together with Christ Jesus and has given us a position in heaven with him" (Ephesians 2:1,2,4-6).

When you follow the world and Satan, you are walking through this world spiritually dead. There is no hope, no peace, no joy. But God loves us and hates to see us in that condition. So he sent Christ to pay for your sins—and to truly raise you from the dead.

Now instead of being the walking dead, you are alive and will rule along with Jesus in heaven!

Dear Father,

help me look for those who are spiritual zombies in this world. Help me tell them that Jesus has made them alive. Help them believe it so they can truly live. Amen.

Knock, knock

Today is National Knock-Knock Jokes Day, so I have one for you:

Knock, knock

Who's there?

Car.

Car who?

Mountain.

That's a horrible knock-knock joke, isn't it? A three-year-old made it up. Usually, though, knock-knock jokes are funny. Once you get started, everyone tells one—and everyone ends up laughing.

The Israelites did the same thing, except it wasn't with jokes. As they'd walk together to worship, they'd sing: **"Then our mouths were filled with laughter and our tongues with joyful songs. Then the nations said, 'The Lord has done spectacular things for them.' The Lord has done spectacular things for us. We are overjoyed"** (Psalm 126:2,3).

If you were just told you'd won a million dollars, you might be stunned for a minute. Then you'd laugh and tell everyone. After being held captive in Babylon for 70 years, the Israelites had won the lottery: they could go home to Jerusalem. From then on as they went to worship, they'd laugh and praise God and tell stories of the awesome things he did.

You can do the same thing. Sing loud, happy songs. Be overjoyed. Your God has done spectacular things for you too!

Chomp on this!

Okay, get it over with. Everybody tell a knock-knock joke. Then tell a story of how God works in your life. One that makes you happy. One that makes you feel like you won the lottery. One that fills your mouth with laughter.

November

Give thanks

"Give thanks to the LORD because he is good, because his mercy endures forever.

Give thanks to the Lord of lords because his mercy endures forever.

Give thanks to the only one who does miraculous things—because his mercy endures forever.

to the one who made the heavens by his understanding—because his mercy endures forever.

to the one who spread out the earth on the water—because his mercy endures forever.

to the one who made the great lights—because his mercy endures forever.

He remembered us when we were humiliated—because his mercy endures forever.

He snatched us from the grasp of our enemies—because his mercy endures forever.

He gives food to every living creature—because his mercy endures forever.

Give thanks to the God of heaven because his mercy endures forever" (Psalm 136:1,3-7,23-26).

Chomp on this!

Make a list of the blessings in your life. List the people in your life. Be sure to include miracles, creation, his power and protection from Satan, how he provides for you, and anything else he has given you that brings you closer to him.

Dear Lord,

this whole month as we think of all the reasons we have to be thankful, help us remember that every good and perfect gift comes from you. Your mercy, kindness, goodness, and faithfulness endure forever. Thank you. Amen.

Follow your Leader

**"God used his power to give Jesus
the highest position as leader and savior.
He did this to lead the people of Israel to him,
to change the way they think and act,
and to forgive their sins"**
(Acts 5:31).

You've played Follow the Leader, right? One person gets to be the leader, walking around the playground weaving back and forth, tiptoeing on stepping-stones, balancing on curbs, hopping over cracks on the sidewalk.

God and the Israelites played the longest ever game of Follow the Leader. When God decided that the Israelites had been slaves in Egypt long enough, he shared his rescue plan. He'd get them out of Egypt and he'd lead them to the Promised Land—even though it took them 40 years.

"By day the LORD went ahead of them in a column of smoke to lead them on their way. By night he went ahead of them in a column of fire to give them light so that they could travel by day or by night. The column of smoke was always in front of the people during the day. The column of fire was always there at night" (Exodus 13:21,22).

When Jesus says, "Follow me!" he's inviting you to play Follow the Leader too. He's telling you, "I know the way to go. I will protect you when it's dangerous, I will watch over you, and I will help you know which path to take."

The best part? He doesn't just lead you here on earth. His whole goal is to get you to the Promised Land. Heaven is the finish line. Follow him.

He keeps track

After trick-or-treating you know exactly how much candy you have, and you keep track of it. You don't even have to write it down to know that you have 9 pieces of licorice, 14 mini peanut butter cups, 42 pieces of taffy, 37 pieces of gum, 13 chocolate bars, and 3 each of 7 other kinds of candy bars. (This mental list also is what gets your parents into trouble when they snitch the candy from your bucket after you go to bed.)

God knows you just as well as you know your candy bucket. He tells you, **"Even every hair on your head has been counted. Don't be afraid!"** (Luke 12:7).

God pays attention to the tiniest of details in your life and keeps track of them. He knows the big stuff, like when you're afraid to start a new school. When you feel alone, crying yourself to sleep because of a fight with a friend, he's there. When you wonder if he's listening, he is. When you are anxious about making a mistake in a game, he knows.

God paid attention to your biggest problem—being separated from him because of sin—and he took care of it by sending Jesus. You are his child now, and he cares about every single piece of your life.

Don't be afraid. He's keeping track of you.

Build each other up

At home my kids have been known to intentionally bicker and annoy one another. At school, however, the oldest one has marched up to schoolmates and declared, "No one picks on my little brother but me!"

Are you guilty of the exact same thing? Do you defend your brother and sister in public, but in private look for all the things that drive you bananas? Or do you poke and poke at them to try to get them upset? The place where we should love one another deeply is actually the place where we often judge each other harshly.

The apostle Paul had an important message for the members of churches who lived two thousand years ago, and it still fits your life today. **"All of Moses' Teachings are summarized in a single statement, 'Love your neighbor as you love yourself.' But if you criticize and attack each other, be careful that you don't destroy each other"** (Galatians 5:14,15).

Part of your job in a family is to love, not to criticize and attack. Let's make it our goal to use words to **"encourage each other and strengthen one another"** (1 Thessalonians 5:11). Satan prowls around looking for people to devour. Let's not do his job for him—especially in our families.

Chomp on this!

What are some things you'd like for your family to say and do to build each other up?

Dear Father,

you tell us that we are to love one another the same way we love ourselves. When we are tempted to criticize and attack, let the Holy Spirit remind us to love each other most. Amen.

Facing the giant

David was just anointed king, but that didn't mean he was the king yet. He was still out tending sheep while his brothers were fighting a war against the Philistines.

He was running an errand for his dad—taking food to his brothers—when he heard Goliath, a 9-foot-tall giant, shouting for someone to fight him. The losers would be slaves for the winners.

All the Israelites were terrified, except David. He was the smallest guy there, but he knew he had the biggest God on his side. David said to King Saul, **"No one should be discouraged because of this; I will go and fight this Philistine."**

With a stick, five small stones, and his sling, David walked toward Goliath. Goliath called for his fake, nonexistent gods to curse David. Instead, David said, **"You come to me with sword and spear and javelin, but I come to you in the name of the LORD of Armies, the God of the army of Israel, whom you have insulted. Today the LORD will hand you over to me. . . . Then everyone gathered here will know that the LORD can save without sword or spear, because the LORD determines every battle's outcome. He will hand all of you over to us."**

David was right; the Lord didn't need a sword or spear. David killed Goliath and gave all the credit to God. Whatever challenges you face, God faces them with you.

Chomp on this!

Read the whole story in 1 Samuel chapter 17.

Escaping the prison

**"The God who is in his holy dwelling place ...
leads prisoners out of prison into productive lives,
but rebellious people must live in an unproductive land"**
(Psalm 68:5,6).

In San Francisco Bay, California, only 1.5 miles from shore, is the island of Alcatraz.

Though it has a rich history, Alcatraz is most famously known for its maximum-security prison. This cold, damp, harsh prison was the last stop for our nation's most notorious criminals.

Throughout its history, thirty-six men (including two who tried to escape twice) were involved in fourteen separate escape attempts. Twenty-three were caught, six were shot and killed during their escape, and two drowned. Five are listed as missing or presumed drowned. Only 1.5 miles away from the shore, yet there are no recorded successful escape attempts.

Sin and death made you a prisoner—and there was no escape. Until, that is, God sent Jesus. He brought the keys that opened up your cell and set you free.

Now that you are free, your job is to talk to people who are still prisoners of sin, people who don't know Jesus. Tell them about the freedom that Jesus offers.

"Thanks be to the Lord, who daily carries our burdens for us. God is our salvation. Our God is the God of victories. The Almighty Lord is our escape from death" (Psalm 68:19,20).

Your Safe Spot

All sorts of drills at school prepare you in case of an emergency. You practice walking outside for a fire drill, you head to the gymnasium or the basement during a tornado drill, and you know which safe spot in the classroom is yours during a stranger-danger drill.

What about emergencies in your life? The book of Psalms tells you over and over where to go in case of trouble.

"He hides me in his shelter when there is trouble. He keeps me hidden in his tent. He sets me high on a rock" (27:5).

"You are my hiding place. You protect me from trouble. You surround me with joyous songs of salvation" (32:7).

"Hide me from the secret plots of criminals, from the mob of troublemakers" (64:2).

When you are feeling scared by problems in your family; when you are afraid of moving to a new school; when you live in a dangerous neighborhood; when you are hiding because of fire, tornados, or hurricanes, God wants you to run to him and hide in his protection. Talk to him about what scares you. **"Then God's peace, which goes beyond anything we can imagine, will guard your thoughts and emotions through Christ Jesus"** (Philippians 4:7).

Chomp on this!

What in your life scares you?

Choose one of these passages (or another one that you like) and memorize it. Think of it and remember to hide in God's protection whenever you are scared.

You are a weirdo

**"The Father has given us his love.
He loves us so much that we are actually called God's
dear children. And that's what we are.
For this reason the world doesn't recognize us,
and it didn't recognize him either"**
(1 John 3:1).

This world has no idea who you are. No matter how often you introduce yourself, it'll never recognize you. That's because being God's child actually makes you a stranger, a weirdo. The world didn't know who Jesus was, and he is God.

Just because God says he loves you, he doesn't say he'll make all your problems disappear. But being his child helps you deal with it. All the good stuff that comes along with being part of God's family is yours—right now. Maybe you don't feel like you belong in this world, but you belong to God. He tells you, "Maybe nobody else knows who you are, but I do. You aren't a weirdo to me. You're mine. I love you so much."

Chomp on this!

How does the world not recognize you?

What things make you seem like a weirdo to unbelievers?

Dear God,

thank you for loving me so much that you call me your child.
I get to live in your house. I get to know I belong.
I get your inheritance. Amen.

Goodness and mercy hunt you down

"Surely goodness and love will follow me all the days of my life, and I will dwell in the house of the LORD forever"
(Psalm 23:6 NIV).

Bloodhounds are fascinating dogs. They have such a sensitive sense of smell that they can distinguish smells at least a thousand times better than humans. Once a bloodhound smells a scent, it needs to track. It doesn't give up until it finds the source. Some bloodhounds have been known to stick to a trail for more than 130 miles. This sense of smell is so good, and the dog is such a reliable tracker, that lawyers can use that information when they are in a court in front of a judge.

Goodness and love are called the hound dogs of God. When King David says, "Surely goodness and love will follow me all the days of my life," really he is saying, "Surely goodness and love will hound me." You can't run away from God's goodness; you can't escape God's kindness. When Jesus lived his whole life without sinning and then took the punishment you deserve, he gave you peace with God. God can now hound you with goodness and love. The blessings in your life aren't random; they aren't accidents or luck. You don't stumble around and accidentally find them.

God's goodness and love are a choice. He hunts you down and tracks you in order to give them to you. They won't ever stop following you.

 ## Chomp on this!

How have you seen God's goodness and love hunting you down like a hound dog?

Time to brag

When some other kid tells you about her awesome new house with a pool, you wish you had a pool. When you hear about the laser tag birthday party, you wish you had been invited. You'd be really mad if your brother told you he got to go out for ice cream while you had your trumpet lesson.

You get jealous when other people get good things; you wish you had them too. Face it; nobody wants to listen to someone else brag.

In Psalm 106, King David asked for good things from God: **"Remember me, O Lord, when you show favor to your people. Come to help me with your salvation so that I may see the prosperity of your chosen ones, find joy in our people's happiness, and brag with the people who belong to you"** (verses 4,5).

David was asking God to show favor to him, to allow him to see all the ways God was blessing the people with good things and happiness. David wanted to be able to brag with all the believers about how good their God was.

As part of God's family, you ask God to be good to you and then you can brag about his blessings. When you brag, you tell people about all the good things that come from being in his family. Pray then that others get a little jealous and want to learn how they can be part of God's family. Then tell them, so they can brag with you.

How will God use you?

**"Our bodies are made of clay,
yet we have the treasure of the Good News in them.
This shows that the superior power of this treasure
belongs to God and doesn't come from us"**
(2 Corinthians 4:7).

Jonah did NOT want to love the people God had told him to preach to. So he ran away and had to get swallowed by a giant fish. Then he followed God's plan.

David had a man killed and then took the man's wife to his house. Still, the Bible calls him a man after God's own heart.

Rahab was a sinful woman and had a bad reputation in her town. Yet she helped the Israelites and became a believer. She is actually one of Jesus' great-great-great-great-great- (you get the idea) grandmothers.

Peter claimed over and over that he loved Jesus best. Just a few hours later, he swore he had never even known him.

Paul, who had previously been called Saul, approved as Stephen was stoned to death for believing in Jesus. Paul ended up becoming one of the greatest missionaries of all time.

What about you? What sin do you struggle with? Still, how has God used you to serve the people in your life?

What's amazing about God is that he uses all sorts of people from all different backgrounds to share his message with the world. He uses you to share his message. He puts his treasure inside of you, knowing that you are only made of dust, and gives you the privilege of telling the story.

You were designed

When your mom was pregnant, she had an ultrasound. This machine gives doctors a picture of you so they can make sure you are healthy. Every parent is thrilled to see you for the first time, to watch your heartbeat or see if you suck your thumb already. Your parents may have used the ultrasound to find out if you were a boy or a girl.

God didn't need an ultrasound to see you. Even before you were born, he kept an eye on you. Psalm 139:13-15 says, **"You alone created my inner being. You knitted me together inside my mother. I will give thanks to you because I have been so amazingly and miraculously made. Your works are miraculous, and my soul is fully aware of this. My bones were not hidden from you when I was being made in secret, when I was being skillfully woven in an underground workshop."**

While you were growing inside your mom, God was actually the one knitting you together. He saw every detail. He watched your bones being made. He planned for your hair color, your knees, your eyes, your toes, your laugh, your walk. He wanted to bless the world with you—exactly who you are.

Thank God that you have been amazingly made. You are miraculous.

Don't you feel special?

Chomp on this!

How can we remember that we are miraculously made?

How we can avoid the temptation to be like a movie star who starves to be skinny?

How do we work hard to be our best, but not idolize a baseball player or cyclist who took drugs to be bigger, faster, stronger?

You aren't an Orphan

Poor Annie. When she was two months old, she was left at an orphanage with a note: "Please take good care of our little darling. Her name is Annie. . . . We have left half of a silver locket around her neck and kept the other half so that when we come back for her, you will know that she's our baby."

Annie spent the next 11 years with the cruel and horrible Miss Hannigan. A visit by Daddy Warbucks' staff changed everything. She got to move into a mansion with a maid, a cook, and more servants than she could count.

When Jesus was talking to his disciples right before he was going to be crucified, he knew they would be worried, so he said, **"Do not let your hearts be troubled. You believe in God; believe also in me. My Father's house has many rooms; if that were not so, would I have told you that I am going there to prepare a place for you? And if I go and prepare a place for you, I will come back and take you to be with me that you also may be where I am"** (John 14:1-3 NIV).

Sometimes when we can't see Jesus, we feel like Annie, that we're left on the doorstep of a horrible place. We have the Holy Spirit inside of us—like Annie's locket—to let us know we are God's child. We know that Jesus is preparing our mansion for us, and he is coming to take us back. Just a few verses later, Jesus said, **"I will not leave you as orphans; I will come to you"** (John 14:18 NIV).

You won't be—you aren't—an orphan.

Jesus is for everyone

*Today let's **Dig In!** Read this section of Scripture, and then use the questions to talk about what God has to say in his Word.*

Then Peter said, "Now I understand that God doesn't play favorites. Rather, whoever respects God and does what is right is acceptable to him in any nation. God sent his word to the people of Israel and brought them the Good News of peace through Jesus Christ. This Jesus Christ is everyone's Lord. You know what happened throughout Judea. Everything began in Galilee after John spread the news about baptism. You know that God anointed Jesus from Nazareth with the Holy Spirit and with power. Jesus went everywhere and did good things, such as healing everyone who was under the devil's power. Jesus did these things because God was with him. We can testify to everything Jesus did in the land of the Jews and in Jerusalem. People hung him on a cross and killed him, but God brought him back to life on the third day. God didn't show him to all the people. He showed Jesus to witnesses, apostles he had already chosen. We apostles are those men who ate and drank with Jesus after he came back to life. He ordered us to warn the people, 'God has appointed Jesus to judge the living and the dead.' In addition, all the prophets testify that people who believe in the one named Jesus receive forgiveness for their sins through him." (Acts 10:34-43)

Chomp on this!

What does God teach you in this passage?

What makes you say, "Thank you, Jesus"?

What makes you say, "I'm sorry, Jesus"?

Based on this reading, what would you like to ask God for?

HomeSick

You know what it's like to be homesick. Maybe you were away at camp for a week and were having fun, but you really wanted to sleep in your own bed and eat your mom's food. At your first sleepover you had to call just to hear your mom or dad say goodnight. Even on vacation with your family, the noises scare you, the sleeping bag is uncomfortable, and you just want to go home!

Christians—even young Christians your age—know what it's like to be homesick.

St. Augustine, a church leader who lived more than one thousand years ago, was homesick too—for heaven. He said, "You have made us for yourself, O Lord, and our hearts are restless until they rest in you."

The trouble you face now makes you restless. You are uncomfortable and just want to be where nothing will ever hurt again. You struggle to fit in, you move back and forth from your mom's house to your dad's house, or you wonder why God couldn't have made you like everyone else. All of these remind you that this sinful world isn't how God planned for it to be.

That's why we are thankful for hope. We remember that this world only lasts for a little while. **"We don't have a permanent city here on earth, but we are looking for the city that we will have in the future"** (Hebrews 13:14).

 ## Chomp on this!

What things about this world make you homesick for what God promises you in heaven?

Just a little can kill you

Peanut allergies have gotten worse. Peanut dust can cause severe reactions, and eating a tiny bit of peanuts can kill someone with severe allergies. Because it's a matter of life and death for some students, many schools have peanut-free tables or are completely peanut-free zones. They know they have to keep kids completely away from what will kill them.

Just like a little bit of peanut butter can make a kid sick, a little bit of lies about God can hurt you just as much.

In Galatians chapter 5, Paul wrote a letter to some Christians who were in danger. These Galatians had been told they had to follow certain rules to be believers, that Jesus' salvation wasn't enough.

Paul sent them a warning, **"A little yeast spreads through the whole batch of dough"** (Galatians 5:9). He was telling them, "You're starting to believe a dangerous lie." Believing that Jesus' life and death aren't all you need for salvation will hurt your faith. Thinking you have to earn your own salvation can be deadly. Any teaching that doesn't match what God's Word says can hurt your faith too. That's why you need to make sure that what you read and hear matches what God says.

Kids with allergies carry an EpiPen. They always have this little container of medicine nearby because it will save their lives if they accidentally eat the wrong foods. God's Word is your EpiPen. In it you'll find the medicine you need to save you when you start believing lies. Carry it with you wherever you go.

Ask your Dad

**"Ask, and you will receive.
Search, and you will find.
Knock, and the door will be opened for you.
Everyone who asks will receive.
The one who searches will find, and for the one
who knocks, the door will be opened.
If your child asks you for bread,
would any of you give him a stone?
Or if your child asks for a fish, would you give him a snake?
Even though you're evil,
you know how to give good gifts to your children.
So how much more will your Father in heaven
give good things to those who ask him?"**
(Matthew 7:7-11).

Have you ever asked your mom for a snack and she gave you sawdust instead? Or have you asked your dad to play catch and he made you play with a ball made out of nails?

Obviously not. Your parents love you. They aren't going to give you something that will hurt you. (Before you say anything, vegetables as a snack won't actually hurt you!)

You trust that they are going to protect you because they love to take care of you.

So why when you ask God for something, do you feel like you have to cross your fingers and hope that maybe, just maybe, he might listen to itty-bitty you?

God is your Father, and it makes him happy to take care of you. He loves it when you ask him to watch over you. He loves to give you good things. So go ask your Dad.

Good and evil?

It's impossible to hope that both Harry Potter and Lord Voldemort win. You can't cheer for both the Boston Red Sox and the New York Yankees. You can't dress up like a Sith and a Jedi at the same time.

When it comes to rivalries, you have to pick which side you're on. It's the same with your life and faith. **"Can right and wrong be partners? Can light have anything in common with darkness?"** (2 Corinthians 6:14).

Right and wrong—God's light and Satan's darkness—are so opposite from each other that they can't stand to be near one another. Satan will try to trick you into thinking you can serve yourself while still following Jesus. He'll tempt you to think it's okay to cheat on your social studies test so you can get a better grade. He'll make you think you can use your mouth to lie, swear, and hurt people's reputations during the week and then sing praise to God on Sunday. But you know the truth. You can't have anything to do with Satan's darkness because Jesus has made you a child of the light.

Satan even tried to get Jesus to fall for the same lies. Jesus was smart enough to say, **"Go away, Satan! Scripture says: 'Worship the Lord your God, and serve only him'"** (Matthew 4:10).

When Satan comes tempting, tell him to get away. You only serve your God.

Burn water

One of my favorite parts of camping is the campfire. Mainly because I love s'mores: marshmallows, chocolate—yum!

When it comes time to build the fire to make the s'mores, you'd think I was ridiculous if I piled up all the wood and then dumped buckets and buckets of water over it, filling the fire pit until it ran around all over the ground.

When Elijah wanted to show that he worshiped the real God, he challenged 450 prophets of a fake god named Baal to a fire competition. Each side would build an altar, place a bull on top, and then pray. Elijah told them, **"You call on the name of your gods, but I will call on the name of the Lord. The god who answers by fire is the real God"** (1 King 18:24).

The other prophets tried and tried, but their god never did a thing. (Duh, because he was fake.)

When it was Elijah's turn, he built his altar and a big moat around it—and then dumped so much water over it that it was soaking wet! **"The prophet Elijah stepped forward. He said, 'Lord God of Abraham, Isaac, and Israel, make known today that you are God in Israel and that I'm your servant and have done all these things by your instructions. Answer me, Lord! Answer me! Then these people will know that you, Lord, are God and that you are winning back their hearts.' So a fire from the Lord fell down and consumed the burnt offering, wood, stones, and dirt. The fire even dried up the water that was in the trench"** (verses 36-38).

Today, people might think you are ridiculous for believing in a God who can do awesome things in your life, even as he rules from heaven. But the God who can start water on fire is the same God who can heal your brother, who helps you sleep when you're afraid, who can help your confusion when your parents lose their jobs.

To him, it's a piece of cake.

God watches over you

What do you want to be when you grow up? (Feel free to answer now, if you'd like.)

Do you ever get sick of people asking you that?

I mean, really, you have no idea what your future looks like, do you? Still, don't you think it would be nice if God sent you an e-mail or a text telling you? In his Word, not an e-mail, God reminds us that we don't have to worry about anything in our future—and anything in our lives right now. He already accomplished living a perfect life (so you can take credit for that), dying a painful death (so you don't have to), and rising from the dead (so you can live with him forever).

"Don't ever worry and say, 'What are we going to eat?' or 'What are we going to drink?' or 'What are we going to wear?' [Or even 'What am I going to be when I grow up?'] **Everyone is concerned about these things, and your heavenly Father certainly knows you need all of them. But first, be concerned about his kingdom and what has his approval. Then all these things will be provided for you"** (Matthew 6:31-33).

The God who has already taken care of your biggest need— choosing you to be his own child—will take care of your smaller needs. He knows what your future looks like.

The next time someone asks you, you can say, "I don't know, but I know that God will take care of me."

Worry about yourself

It's so hard to worry only about yourself, isn't it? When the teacher says, "Study your spelling words," you don't immediately get your own list but instead lean over and tell the daydreaming kid next to you, "Hey! He said to study your spelling words!" The whole time you're forgetting that you aren't exactly doing what the teacher asked either.

Maybe you get in the car and say, "You would not believe what so-and-so said in class!" The whole time you forget that you are gossiping about a gossiper.

After dinner, when your parents ask you to clean the kitchen, you don't think to say, "Sure!" Instead you run to your brother's room and shout, "Hey! Mom says we have to clean the kitchen! I'm not doing it by myself!" The whole time you're so worried that he might get out of work that you don't even realize that you aren't doing what your mom asked either.

It's so very easy to see the flaws in other people and not so easy to see them in ourselves, isn't it? Jesus knew that people tend to worry more about what other people do wrong. So he told them, **"The standards you use for others will be applied to you. So why do you see the piece of sawdust in another believer's eye and not notice the wooden beam in your own eye? How can you say to another believer, 'Let me take the piece of sawdust out of your eye,' when you have a beam in your own eye? You hypocrite! First remove the beam from your own eye. Then you will see clearly to remove the piece of sawdust from another believer's eye"** (Matthew 7:2-5).

Let the Holy Spirit work in your heart to make sure you pay attention to your behavior first. Then, as someone who recognizes your own sins, you can help others along.

Gifts from God*

Are you the best speller in your class?

Can you do long division in a split second?

Do you have a hard serve in volleyball?

Can you play a four-part Chopin nocturne on the piano?

Some people have all of these gifts. Maybe you don't have any of these, but God says in the Bible that everyone has gifts. Whether you are talented in music, sports, computer coding, academics, listening well, art, or being a good friend, I Corinthians 10:31 tells us, **"Whether you eat or drink, or whatever you do, do everything to the glory of God."**

When Jesus lived and died for you, he brought you into God's family. As part of God's family, you use your unique gifts to do the jobs he has set for you to do. Use your talents to serve the people in your life so they see how awesome God is.

It's not so much which gift you get that matters to God; it's how you use the ones he does give you.

Chomp on this!

What talents has God given you?

How can you use those talents to talk about God and his glory?

Dear God,

thank you for the many gifts and abilities that you give to us. Help us use them to our best ability so that we show how thankful we are for everything that you do for us. In Jesus' name we pray. Amen.

This devotion was written by Jenna, a kid just like you.

God's adopted children

**"Before the creation of the world,
he chose us through Christ to be holy and perfect
in his presence. Because of his love
he had already decided to adopt us through Jesus Christ.
He freely chose to do this so that the kindness he had
given us in his dear Son would be praised and given glory"**
(Ephesians 1:4-6).

People who are adopted know they were handpicked. Their adoptive families couldn't help themselves; they were so excited to add another child to their family. They said, "We want them!" and cried for joy when the papers were signed.

Before you were even born, before the world was even created, God handpicked you and me. But sin keeps us out of his family, so God came up with a plan: Jesus.

"God sent him to pay for the freedom of those who were controlled by these laws so that we would be adopted as his children" (Galatians 4:5).

Our adoption papers were signed when Jesus lived a holy and perfect life for us, died for us on a cross, and rose from the dead. We are now part of God's family, and when he looks at us, he sees holiness and perfection.

When you're feeling lonely, if you think you don't belong, remind yourself, "I am God's child. He picked me!"

Dear Father,

thank you for adopting me, for handpicking me. Thank you for bringing me into your family and letting me call you Dad. Amen.

Jesus understands you

Chomp on this!

Discuss how you picture Jesus when he was on this earth.

When you pictured Jesus, did you see him as a baby in a manger? Or did you see him walking on water? Or did you picture him hanging on a cross? Raise your hand if you saw him as a kid just like you.

Yes, Jesus was a baby and, yes, he was an adult, but the Bible doesn't talk about him much as a kid. Well, except for the time he was 12 years old and went to the temple. So we don't often think about the fact that Jesus had to grow—and grow up. There's one passage, however, that reminds us: **"Jesus grew in wisdom and maturity. He gained favor from God and people"** (Luke 2:52).

Jesus had to learn to walk and talk, just like toddlers do. His dad taught him how to be a carpenter, so that meant Jesus had chores to do. He had friends and cousins, which is why his parents didn't know he was missing when he had stayed at the temple. They thought he was hanging out with the kids his age. He was tempted to get angry with his brothers and sisters. As a teenager, he had to learn and become more mature.

Because Jesus went through every stage of life that you do, he understands you completely. As you grow in wisdom and maturity too, you can talk to him about everything.

Jesus raises the dead

A 12-year-old girl was dying. Her dad was desperate. Even though he was one of the leaders at his synagogue, there was nothing he could do to save her. Then he saw the man who could.

"When he saw Jesus, he quickly bowed down in front of him. He begged Jesus, 'My little daughter is dying. Come, lay your hands on her so that she may get well and live'" (Mark 5:22,23).

As Jesus was walking to his house with him, someone else came and told the man that the girl had died. But Jesus—who knew how the story would end—told him, **"Don't be afraid! Just believe."** (verse 36).

They got to the house and saw everyone sobbing. Jesus asked, **"'Why are you making so much noise and crying? The child isn't dead. She's just sleeping.' They laughed at him. So he made all of them go outside. Then he took the child's father, mother, and his three disciples and went to the child. Jesus took the child's hand and said to her, 'Talitha, koum!' which means, 'Little girl, I'm telling you to get up!'"** (verses 39-41).

Because of sin, everybody will die. Only some people, though, believe that Jesus defeated death when he rose on Easter. (The ones who don't might laugh at you the way they laughed at Jesus.) You know the truth: death doesn't have eternal power over you anymore. Someday Jesus will take your hand and say, "Little child, get up. It's time to go home."

Chomp on this!

Read the whole story in Mark 5:21-23, 35-43.

Trust in God*

Sometimes, no matter how hard you try, things just don't seem to go your way. You can't hit a shot in basketball or throw a strike in baseball. You have to start your art project over six times. It might be about more serious things. No matter how often you ask the teacher for help, it still just doesn't make sense. Your parents keep fighting. You try to get your parents to listen to your side of the story, but they just don't get it.

It's hard not to get discouraged. It's hard not to feel alone. It's hard not to be scared.

When that happens, God wants you to **"be strong and courageous! Don't tremble or be terrified, because the Lord your God is with you wherever you go"** (Joshua 1:9).

Wherever you go, whether it's church or across the country, God will be with you wherever you go and whatever you're doing. Whatever you're going through, whether it's problems with your friends, family, or school, he is with you. He uses everything that happens in your life to make your faith stronger so you grow closer to him. His strength will make you strong. His power makes you courageous. His hope helps you not be discouraged.

Chomp on this!

What things in your life make you feel scared?

What discourages you?

How does today's passage help you face those things?

This devotion was written by Weston, a kid just like you.

Sometimes cheaters win

"Help, Lord, for no one is faithful anymore;
those who are loyal have vanished from the human race.
Everyone lies to their neighbor;
they flatter with their lips
but harbor deception in their hearts"
(Psalm 12:1,2 NIV).

Sometimes cheaters win, don't they? You know it. You've seen the classmate who looked at your paper during the spelling test. Or you've seen the kids who showboat when they score and everyone thinks they're cool. Or maybe you've had money stolen from your locker and no one admitted taking it.

It works that way for adults too. The people who cheat sometimes get the raises and the promotions. Neighbors who are angry and bitter make life miserable. Celebrities mock God—and are even more popular.

Are you ever tempted to take the easy way out? Doesn't it seem like cheating, lying, and stealing might actually make your life better? Making good choices, being honest, and working hard seems like a waste of time when you see other people being lazy and dishonest and not getting caught.

God sees what's going on, and he wants to remind you that he will act when the time is right. **"You, Lord, will keep the needy safe and will protect us forever from the wicked, who freely strut about when what is vile is honored by the human race"** (Psalm 12:7,8).

Cheaters might win here on earth. Believers, however, will win forever in heaven!

Chomp on this!

How do you feel when cheaters win?

How can you be sure to work hard and be honest when others aren't?

Be the best

"How am I supposed to guard *her* in practice? She's so much faster and better than I am!" Megan asked.

"Well, if you want to be the best, you have to play the best," answered her dad.

Megan's dad knew that playing against someone faster, tougher, bigger, and stronger would make her play harder. You watch that person, learn from her, and get better because of her. Without a challenge, you never get better at sports. I mean, really, would eighth graders get better at soccer if they played a team of first graders? Probably not. Winning would come too easily. There wouldn't be a challenge and the eighth graders would probably goof off.

King Solomon knew that to become the best person you can be, you need to be challenged too. **"As iron sharpens iron, so one person sharpens another"** (Proverbs 27:17 NIV).

If you hang around kids who complain about their parents, who talk bad about other kids, who don't care how they do in school, you'll easily fall into that same kind of talk. You'll goof off and start picking up their bad habits.

If you have friends who tell you, "Hey, we shouldn't be making fun of him" or "Let's get our homework done first; then we can play," they are encouraging you to get better. You may not like it because you'd rather goof off. Still, it's better for you. You're getting sharper every day.

 ## Chomp on this!

Have you ever had a friend who sharpened you, who helped you get better?

How have you encouraged your friends? Name a situation in which you helped someone get sharper, to be the best person he or she could be.

Can you only talk to God in church?

When you head to church on Sunday, you might hear the pastor say, "Welcome to God's house." God's house sounds like a great thing, doesn't it? We like to go to our church home where we hear about God and worship him with our friends. Sometimes, though, you might think that because it's God's house, he never leaves there. That *you* have to go see *him*.

The people who lived in the Old Testament thought that too. They believed that God lived only in the temple in Jerusalem. So they went at least once a year to show that they loved him. God loved their worship, but he also wanted them—and you—to know he is too big to live in one church building. **"However, the Most High doesn't live in a house built by humans, as the prophet says: 'The Lord says, "Heaven is my throne. The earth is my footstool. What kind of house are you going to build for me? Where will I rest?"'"** (Acts 7:48,49).

The whole world is God's house. No matter where you are, he is there. You don't have to wait until Sunday to pray to him or worship him. Talk to him when you're about to take your math test. Bring him glory by taking your elderly neighbor's dog for a walk. Thank him for being with you when you are nervous on the school bus.

He sees you. All the time.

Dear God,

you are with me all the time. Help me find comfort in that and help me remember that I can talk to you in prayer whenever I need to and you will listen. Amen.

Your photo is on God's fridge

Throughout the country, every grandma's refrigerator looks almost identical. It's filled with an abundance of "Grandma" magnets made by toddlers, photos of grandchildren, and newspaper clippings about her favorite people in the world.

Grandmas are so incredibly proud of their grandchildren and love them so deeply that they love to see their faces and handiwork every single day. Every time they grab some milk, their hearts fill up with a little more love.

In Zephaniah 3:17, you hear that God loves you as much as your grandma loves you—more, actually. **"The LORD your God is with you. He is a hero who saves you. He happily rejoices over you, renews you with his love, and celebrates over you with shouts of joy."**

If Jesus hadn't come for you, God would have had to hate you and your sins. Instead, God sent Jesus as your hero. He loved you enough to come find you and rescue you from Satan's evil clutches. Now, God knows you, is proud of you, and his heart fills with a little more love every time he sees you. The Father, Son, and Holy Spirit do fist bumps because of you.

Whenever you think that maybe God is mad at you, remember what Jesus did for you. Now your photo is hanging on God's refrigerator.

You get the victory

Never in the history of the Olympics has the skier who won the gold walked off the podium and given the medal to a person who crashed halfway down the hill. We'd be stunned if it happened. I mean, really, who would be crazy enough to do that, to give someone else his or her medal?

Jesus would, that's who. God knew we had crashed and didn't even stand a chance at winning a medal, which is getting to heaven. So he sent Jesus to race the course for us. Jesus came, was tempted like we are, and lived a perfect life. Then he took your sins on a cross and died, burying them with him. When he rose, he defeated Satan.

Jesus hands you the gold medal and says, "I know you crashed, but here you go, take my medal. Heaven is waiting for you."

Aren't you stunned that you get to say, **"Thank God that he gives us the victory through our Lord Jesus Christ"** (1 Corinthians 15:57)?

Dear Jesus,
thank you so much for skiing my race for me. You set the world record, and even though I crashed, you gave me your gold medal. Thank you, God, for giving me the victory. Amen.

Your Christmas tree Story

About this time, most people are busy getting Christmas trees set up in their houses. What's your favorite part of the tree? Maybe it's the lights that brighten up the darkness or the smell of the fresh needles (if you get a real tree). Maybe you like the ornaments best because some are yours: the handprint made out of modeling clay, the one that reads, "Baby's 1st Christmas," or the one you made last year in art class. Whatever you like best, the Christmas tree tells a story about your family. You can also use a Christmas tree to help tell a story about your Jesus.

Tree: The green reminds you of the new life Jesus has given you. The tree points up to heaven, reminding you to point others to heaven too.

Lights: Jesus, the Light of the world, is about to be born. You can shine your light by showing Jesus to others in the way you speak and act. As the lights sparkle, you remember to share your light with a dark world.

Tree topper: A star reminds you of the one that led the wise men to Jesus. A bow reminds you that the best gift of all time is lying in a manger. An angel reminds you to tell the same message the angels sang: "Glory to God in the highest!"

Ornaments: As you look at the ornaments that tell you about your life, you can think of Jesus' life: his miracles, his words, his love. They can also remind you to tell the story of the good things that God has done in your life: how he watches over your family, gives you everything you need, protects you, and is always there for you.

Your Christmas tree is one way to **"always be prepared to give an answer to everyone who asks you to give the reason for the hope that you have"** (1 Peter 3:15 NIV).

Crying yourself to Sleep

Bad things happen in this world. Sometimes the trouble is so bad that you cry yourself to sleep. (You don't have to be embarrassed to admit it.)

You cry yourself to sleep when your pet dies, when your friends say horrible things about you, when you get suspended and disappoint your parents, or when you feel so sick that medicine doesn't make you feel better.

David, who was the king of an entire country, had lots of reasons to cry himself to sleep. He was sick, he felt guilty about his sins, and his enemies were mocking him. All he could do was cry. **"I am worn out from my groaning. My eyes flood my bed every night. I soak my couch with tears. My eyes blur from grief"** (Psalm 6:6,7).

The one thing David didn't do, though, was forget about God and his goodness. He prayed for God to help him—and God answered. David ends his psalm confidently: **"The Lord has heard the sound of my crying. The Lord has heard my plea for mercy. The Lord accepts my prayer"** (verses 8,9).

When you cry in bed at night, God hears you. Ask him for his mercy; he loves to listen. He accepts your prayers because Jesus has washed away your sin and given you the right to call God your Daddy. Talk to your Father and sleep in peace.

Chomp on this!

What has made you cry yourself to sleep?

What kind of prayer can you say when you feel so sad that you can't sleep?

Dear God,

when I cry, I feel so alone. Remind me that you see me, listen to me, and hear my prayers. You accept my prayers because Jesus has given me peace with you. Thank you. Amen.

Start fresh

I love playing with an Etch A Sketch. You turn the knobs this way and that and create an awesome piece of art. If you get bored with it or make a mistake, you just shake it to erase it. The aluminum powder cleans the screen and you can start over.

Maybe you've played with a Magna Doodle. You draw with the pencil that's attached and, when you want to start over, you just slide the little handle across the screen and—voilà—good as new.

The author of Lamentations knew how awesome a clean screen is: **"The reason I can still find hope is that I keep this one thing in mind: the LORD's mercy. We were not completely wiped out. His compassion is never limited. It is new every morning. His faithfulness is great"** (Lamentations 3:21-23).

God easily could have wiped us out because of sin. Instead, he chooses not to punish us, but his mercy wipes us clean. Each morning we see how God is faithful. He keeps his promises, even when we break our promises to him.

Each day is a new day for you, a new day to say, "Thank you, Jesus, for forgiving my sins. Thank you for making it so that God isn't angry at me, but loves me."

You are his Sculpture

"For we are God's handiwork, created in Christ Jesus to do good works, which God prepared in advance for us to do" (Ephesians 2:10 NIV).

In the 1920s, when people looked at a mountain in South Dakota, they saw, well, a mountain. Sculptor Gutzon Borglum, however, saw faces.

Using many courageous workers and lots of dynamite, he started blasting away and carving off everything that did not look like Presidents Washington, Lincoln, Roosevelt, or Jefferson.

Each year over three million people visit Mount Rushmore, and not a single one of them says, "Wow! Isn't it amazing how that mountain sculpted itself?" Instead, they are astonished by the man who had the vision to see what wasn't there.

You are God's Mount Rushmore. He sees not just what you are—a mountain—but he makes you into what you will be. You are unique, handcrafted, and carved by him. He made you and has plans for you to bring him glory.

Just like the mountain can't take credit for what it became, neither can you. You are God's handiwork, his masterpiece. You couldn't do that on your own. Now, when people tell you how awesome or helpful or intelligent or strong or thoughtful you are, you just say, "My Sculptor did all the work!"

Dear God,

we know we are your handiwork. You created us to bring you glory. Help us do the good works that you want us to do. Amen.

Love means you protect others

The Israelites were slaves in Egypt. Pharaoh was worried they were getting too powerful, so he declared that every baby boy born to an Israelite should be killed or thrown into the Nile River to drown.

When Moses was born, though, his mom couldn't bear to kill him, so she hid him instead. This only worked for three months, and eventually she made a waterproof basket and put him in the river. Miriam, Moses' sister, loved him and was worried.

"The baby's sister stood at a distance to see what would happen to him" (Exodus 2:4).

Pharaoh's daughter found the crying baby and felt sorry for him. That's when Miriam got the courage to walk up and ask Pharaoh's daughter, **"'Should I go and get one of the Hebrew women to nurse the baby for you?' She answered, 'Yes!' So the girl brought the baby's mother"** (verses 7,8).

Miriam—the protective, older sister—was God's child, just like you are. If you're an older brother or sister, you get to keep an eye on the younger ones in the family. With your bigger size and more years of experience, you get to help them when they are in trouble and protect them when they get picked on.

P.S. If you have an older brother or sister, be sure to thank them. God's given them an important job to love you. Make it an easy job for them!

 ## Chomp on this!

Read the whole story in Exodus 1:8–2:10.

Don't be Surprised

**"You know very well that the day of the Lord will come
like a thief in the night.
When people say, 'Everything is safe and sound!'
destruction will suddenly strike them.
It will be as sudden as labor pains
come to a pregnant woman. They won't be able to escape.
But, brothers and sisters, you don't live in the dark.
That day won't take you by surprise as a thief would.
You belong to the day and the light
not to the night and the dark"**
(1 Thessalonians 5:2-5).

In the early morning of December 7, 1941, the Japanese led an attack on the naval base in Pearl Harbor, Hawaii. People were caught by surprise as they looked into the skies and saw the fighters and bombers. If the Americans had been prepared, maybe two thousand people wouldn't have died.

The day that Jesus is going to come back for all of us is going to be a surprise too. **"Look! He is coming in the clouds. Every eye will see him, even those who pierced him"** (Revelation 1:7). Except that you won't be surprised. Because you belong to him, you belong to the day. For people who don't know him, though, this surprise attack will be terrifying and there will be no place to hide.

You can make a difference. Tell people about Jesus' life. Tell them he earned forgiveness for them. Tell them that he is coming back. Don't let them be caught by surprise.

A boy who shared his lunch

People just couldn't leave Jesus alone. Here was God, in person, and they followed him everywhere.

"As Jesus saw a large crowd coming to him, he said to Philip, 'Where can we buy bread for these people to eat?' Jesus asked this question to test him. He already knew what he was going to do. Philip answered, 'We would need about a year's wages to buy enough bread for each of them to have a piece.' One of Jesus' disciples, Andrew, who was Simon Peter's brother, told him, 'A boy who has five loaves of barley bread and two small fish is here. But they won't go very far for so many people.' Jesus took the loaves, gave thanks, and distributed them to the people who were sitting there. He did the same thing with the fish. All the people ate as much as they wanted" (John 6:5-9, 11).

Five thousand men were at this meal, and Jesus fed all of them with five loaves of bread, two small fish, and a thankful prayer.

Maybe you think your gifts and offerings to Jesus can't make a difference. The money you give seems to be so very little. The prayers you say seem small. The God who owns everything in the world doesn't see them as little at all. Instead, he takes them and accomplishes great things.

 ## Chomp on this!

Read the whole story in John 6:1-15.

Dear Jesus,

I'm just a kid! Sometimes I think I can't do great things because I'm young and don't have much to give. Remind me that you worked a HUGE miracle with that little boy's fish and bread. You can take my small offering and do great things with that too! Amen.

Don't you catch on?

Yesterday we learned about the boy who shared his lunch—with five thousand people.

Not too many days later, "[Jesus] **got into a boat again and crossed to the other side of the Sea of Galilee. The disciples had forgotten to take any bread along and had only one loaf with them in the boat. Jesus warned them, 'Be careful! Watch out for the yeast of the Pharisees and the yeast of Herod!' They had been discussing with one another that they didn't have any bread. Jesus knew what they were saying and asked them, 'Why are you discussing the fact that you don't have any bread? Don't you understand yet? Don't you catch on? Are your minds closed? Are you blind and deaf? Don't you remember? When I broke the five loaves for the five thousand, how many baskets did you fill with leftover pieces?' They told him, 'Twelve'"** (Mark 8:13-19).

The disciples had just watched their Teacher work miracles—and yet they were still focused on finding food. They hadn't caught on that everything they needed here on earth would be provided. Jesus was telling them to pay attention so they wouldn't believe the lies the Pharisees were telling.

Sometimes, even though we know God provides for us, we forget to trust him. We worry more about our clothes and our food and our broken toys than we do about the temptations we face.

Let's focus more on Jesus so we can say, "We understand. We caught on. We remember. Thank you, Jesus, for providing for us."

Wash Out Your Mouth

When you wash your face at bedtime (I hope you wash your face at bedtime), sometimes you get soap in your mouth. Isn't that gross? No amount of spitting seems to get rid of that taste.

So maybe you can understand Ralphie's misery in the movie *A Christmas Story*. When Ralphie used a really "dirty" word, his mom made him sit in the bathroom and bite on a bar of soap. She felt it would wash out his mouth and remind him to choose cleaner words. Ralphie was a slow learner, though. As he narrates the movie, he says, "Over the years I got to be quite a connoisseur of soap." (*Connoisseur* is a big word that means he was an expert.)

As disgusting as that would taste, Ralphie's mom was teaching him that she was absolutely interested in the words he used. God is just as interested in the words you use. Your mouth is the mouth he gave you. He wants you to use it to share his words too.

"With our tongues we praise our Lord and Father. Yet, with the same tongues we curse people, who were created in God's likeness. Praise and curses come from the same mouth. My brothers and sisters, this should not happen!" (James 3:9,10).

God does not want your mouth to sing praises on Sunday and to swear at kids on Monday. The mouth he gave you to encourage people shouldn't be used to be sarcastic. The mouth God gave you is for praising him, not for bragging about yourself. Today, use your mouth for good.

Dear Jesus,

I'm so sorry. I have used my mouth to hurt people. I say mean things and put people down. I know this should not happen. Remind me that you gave me my mouth to praise you. Help me only use my mouth for good. Amen.

God loves it when you're loud

Is your first name Shh? You know, because your parents say, "Shh" before they say your name, you wonder if your name is actually Shh-Hannah, Shh-Ben, Shh-Emma, or Shh-Ryan.

Did you know that your God loves it when you're loud? Well, when you praise him loudly. Psalm 150, in fact, tells you to make a loud noise before the Lord:

"Hallelujah! Praise God in his holy place. Praise him in his mighty heavens. Praise him for his mighty acts. Praise him for his immense greatness. Praise him with sounds from horns. Praise him with harps and lyres. Praise him with tambourines and dancing. Praise him with stringed instruments and flutes. Praise him with loud cymbals. Praise him with crashing cymbals. Let everything that breathes praise the LORD! Hallelujah!" (verses 1-6).

When you get home to heaven, it's going to get even louder. You and every single believer from every single country who has ever lived will praise God in one big group. And this is what it will sound like: **"I heard what sounded like the noise from a large crowd, like the noise of raging waters, like the noise of loud thunder, saying, 'Hallelujah! The Lord our God, the Almighty, has become king. Let us rejoice, be happy, and give him glory'"** (Revelation 19:6,7).

When it comes to praising God here on earth, let's practice now. Rejoice! Be happy! Give him glory.

(By the way, when your parents do shush you, you still need to obey them.)

Help each Other

"Go carry Grandma's suitcase in."

"Help your coach carry those bats."

"Please help me carry in the groceries."

"Help carry each other's burdens. In this way you will follow Christ's teachings" (Galatians 6:2).

Wait, that last one didn't sound like something you hear every day. Yet God tells you that you *do* need to help other people carry their troubles. Maybe that means you help a friend with his homework. Or maybe you help your classmate pick up her books after someone knocked them out of her hands. Or maybe it means visiting people in nursing homes and sitting with them because they are lonely. Or listening to and praying for a friend whose parents are getting a divorce.

One thing you shouldn't forget, though, is that your family and friends have been told to help *you* carry *your* burden too. You don't have to be strong all the time or hide what you are feeling. When you share the things that make you sad or scared, other people get to follow Christ's teachings too.

In Ecclesiastes 4:10 God reminds us, **"If one falls, the other can help his friend get up. But how tragic it is for the one who is all alone when he falls. There is no one to help him get up."** Thanks to your family and friends, you are surrounded by people whom you get to help, and who are ready and willing to help you too.

 ## Chomp On this!

What problem or fear or concern do you have that you've been keeping to yourself?

Say a prayer as a family and be sure to add the concerns that you have just shared with each other.

God Spills Out Good Things

Piñatas make birthday parties better. You're with friends, you get to hit something with a stick without getting yelled at, and you look up to see the ultimate reward—candy!—showering down on you. You mob the ground, gathering up every piece you can. There's so much that it falls out of your hands and you have to roll up the bottom of your shirt just to carry it all. You have so much that you are actually willing to share with the kid who didn't get as much.

God and his blessings are like that piñata. In 2 Corinthians 9:8, we hear that **"God is able to bless you abundantly, so that in all things at all times, having all that you need, you will abound in every good work"** (NIV).

The God who owns the whole entire world loves it when you pray to him. He can't wait to spill out good things into your life. His blessings are inexhaustible. (That means they never get used up; they just keep coming.) You have every single thing you need all the time. Now when you see just how full your life is, you look for the people around you who don't have as much and you gladly share.

Chomp on this!

How can we share God's blessings?

Here are some ideas:

- give your toys to a shelter
- donate backpacks at the beginning of the school year for foster kids
- send your candy from trick-or-treating to people in the military
- give the money you made on your lemonade stand to missionaries.

What are other ways you can share with people who live by you or who live far away?

Make water walls

The next time you take a bath, try to separate the water. Think really, really hard and see if you can make half the water go to your right, half to your left, and you stay dry in the middle. If that doesn't work, just raise your hands. Do you think that would help? No? You're right. There's no way you can divide water like that.

That's the problem the Israelites had. They were being chased by the big bad Egyptian army with its chariots and horses—and now there was a sea in front of them. They thought for sure they were doomed. They forgot that their God was the real, living, active God who had promised to fight for them—and he did!

God, in a cloud, moved behind the Israelites and hid them from the Egyptians. Then he told Moses to lift up his hand. **"Then Moses stretched out his hand over the sea. All that night the LORD pushed back the sea with a strong east wind and turned the sea into dry ground. The water divided, and the Israelites went through the middle of the sea on dry ground. The water stood like a wall on their right and on their left"** (Exodus 14:21,22).

As soon as the Israelites made it to the other side, God-the-cloud moved and the Egyptians went racing onto the dry path. That's when God had Moses raise his hand again—and the walls of water came crashing down, killing all the Egyptians. **"When the Israelites saw the great power the LORD had used against the Egyptians, they feared the LORD and believed in him and in his servant Moses"** (verse 31).

If your God can make water walls to protect his people, you know he can absolutely protect you too. When people hurt you or cause drama or tell you they think you're a loser, you know that your God will give you a way out. His Word reminds you that he will watch over you and use his power to protect your heart and your mind when you're being attacked.

God is better than Santa Claus

Many people are getting ready for Santa Claus to come to town. There are plenty of television shows that tell you how the whole Santa thing works. He keeps track of your behavior all year. Then when Christmas comes around, if you've been good, he'll give you the things on your list. If you've been bad, well then, it's a giant lump of coal for you.

He sees you when you're sleeping. He knows when you're awake. He knows if you've been bad or good so be good for goodness' sake.

God sees you when you're sleeping. He knows when you're awake. And he definitely knows about the choices you make. Still, he doesn't want you to worry about the gifts he's planning to give you anyway. **"Don't ever worry and say, 'What are we going to eat?' or 'What are we going to drink?' or 'What are we going to wear?' Everyone is concerned about these things, and your heavenly Father certainly knows you need all of them. But first, be concerned about his kingdom and what has his approval. Then all these things will be provided for you"** (Matthew 6:31-33).

You can stop making a list of the things you need. God has that taken care of. Instead, be concerned about God's kingdom. Share the good news. Let your neighbors and your friends know that Jesus Christ is coming to town.

God's rules

*Today let's **Dig In!** Read this section of Scripture, and then use the questions to talk about what God has to say in his Word.*

Then God spoke all these words:

"Never have any other god. Never worship them or serve them, because I, the LORD your God, am a God who does not tolerate rivals. I punish children for their parents' sins to the third and fourth generation of those who hate me. But I show mercy to thousands of generations of those who love me and obey my commandments.

"Never use the name of the LORD your God carelessly. . . .

"Remember the day of worship by observing it as a holy day. You have six days to do all your work. The seventh day is the day of worship dedicated to the LORD your God. . . .

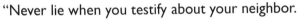

"Honor your father and your mother, so that you may live for a long time in the land the LORD your God is giving you.

"Never murder.

"Never commit adultery.

"Never steal.

"Never lie when you testify about your neighbor.

"Never desire to take your neighbor's household away from him.

"Never desire to take your neighbor's wife, his male or female slave, his ox, his donkey, or anything else that belongs to him." (Exodus 20:1,3,5-10,12-17)

Chomp on this!

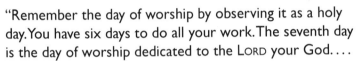

What does God teach you in this passage?

What makes you say, "Thank you, Jesus"?

What makes you say, "I'm sorry, Jesus"?

Based on this reading, what would you like to ask God for?

Be different

Out of all the Olympic bobsledding teams, one team always draws a crowd—the Jamaicans. Everybody is fascinated because nobody expects people from the Caribbean to leave the sun, sand, and ocean life for training in freezing temperatures and flying down an icy track at almost 90 miles per hour.

The difference sets them apart. So does yours. **"Do not conform to the pattern of this world, but be transformed by the renewing of your mind"** (Romans 12:2 NIV).

When you put God first and not you first, you are not conforming to the pattern of this world.

When you are generous to others without expecting them to do nice things for you in return, you are not conforming to how the world works.

When you start to draw a crowd of people (or just one or two) who are fascinated by what makes you different, **"be ready to defend your confidence in God when anyone asks you to explain it. However, make your defense with gentleness and respect"** (1 Peter 3:15).

Chomp on this!

What is the pattern of this world? How do people of this world live and act?

List three things that set you apart from the world.

Dear God,

please help me stand out from the crowd. Help me gladly be different. When I attract as much attention as a Jamaican bobsled team, help me use that chance to tell people about you and the hope that I have. Amen.

Take a TRIP

It's time for the dreaded class presentation on your science fair exhibit. You are sick to your stomach just thinking about it. What if you mess up and the class laughs? What if your mind goes blank? It's a good thing you have notes or you surely would get a failing grade *and* die from embarrassment.

Some people are as nervous to pray as they are to make a presentation. What if God laughs? What are you supposed to talk about? Sometimes it's helpful to have your conversation planned. Today, you can use the word *TRIP* to help you make notes on your prayers.

Thanksgiving: **"I will give thanks to you with all my heart, O Lord my God"** (Psalm 86:12). God has given you a bazillion blessings. Say thank you.

Repentance: **"Various sins overwhelm me. You are the one who forgives our rebellious acts"** (Psalm 65:3). Be honest, you know you were mean, talked back, or chose to be lazy. Talk to God about your specific sins.

Intercession: **"Make petitions, prayers, intercessions, and prayers of thanks for all people"** (1 Timothy 2:1). God loves it when his children pray for each other. Talk to him about your friends and family—and even strangers in other countries—and their health, faith, problems, and relationships.

Petition: **"Ask, and you will receive. Search, and you will find. Knock, and the door will be opened for you"** (Matthew 7:7). God loves giving you both physical and spiritual blessings. Ask him to dump them all out into your life.

Enjoy your TRIP.

December 19

Born in a barn

**"While they were in Bethlehem,
the time came for Mary to have her child.
She gave birth to her firstborn son.
She wrapped him in strips of cloth
and laid him in a manger
because there wasn't any room for them in the inn"**
(Luke 2:6,7).

Kids can't seem to close doors behind them. I never did when I was a kid either, and when I left the back door open, I'd occasionally get asked, "Were you born in a barn?" My mom obviously knew I wasn't. We both knew the question meant, "We don't live like animals. Please close the door."

When Jesus decided the time was right, he was born in a barn, a place more suited for animals than babies. When you look in his manger, you see the one true God who loves you so much that he was willing to give up the glory of heaven to come live in our dirty, smelly world. He was willing to be connected to humans by being born of a human mom. He lived his whole life knowing that he would end his life on a cross, suffering the punishment we deserved. He was born in a barn, so he could prepare a mansion for us in heaven.

Dear Jesus,

thank you for being born in a barn willingly. You are the God of all creation and yet you chose to be born in a room full of animals. When we forget how much you love us, help us look at your manger to remember just how good you are to us. Amen.

Don't brag

**"Praise should come from another person
and not from your own mouth,
from a stranger and not from your own lips"**
(Proverbs 27:2).

"I'm the best!"

"You can't beat me!"

"I'm so smart!"

"Bring it on!"

Whether they are smack-talking, showboating, or just simply being conceited, it's hard to be around people who are constantly telling you that they are the best. (If they aren't the best, they think they are better than you.)

If you walk around constantly telling people that you're the fastest, smartest, strongest, coolest, or prettiest—did I miss anything?—pretty soon nobody really wants to hang around with you. That's because true friends are kind, interested in others, and helpful.

If you end up with no friends around you, you make it a lot harder for God to use you in his plan. Who will believe what you have to say about God if they can barely stand to listen to you talk about yourself? Bringing God glory is way more important than telling others how awesome you are. When you're tempted to brag about yourself, tell them, "Let me tell you how awesome God is."

By the way, if you do happen to be the fastest, smartest, strongest, coolest, or prettiest, let someone else brag about how they see God working through you. Let other people praise you.

Dear Father,

you have given me many talents and abilities, but I didn't do that on my own. They are gifts from you. Help me give you glory in every situation. Amen.

When God calls, listen

Samuel lived at church. His mom had desperately wanted a child, so when she finally had one, she promised God that this baby would serve the Lord his whole life. When he was old enough, she took him to the temple to live and serve there.

"The boy Samuel was serving the Lord under Eli. In those days a prophecy from the Lord was rare; visions were infrequent.... Samuel was asleep in the temple of the Lord where the ark of God was kept. Then the Lord called Samuel. 'Here I am,' Samuel responded. He ran to Eli and said, 'Here I am. You called me.' 'I didn't call you,' Eli replied. 'Go back to bed.' So Samuel went back and lay down.... Samuel had no experience with the Lord, because the word of the Lord had not yet been revealed to him (1 Samuel 3:1,3-5,7).

This happened again—and again. Finally, Eli realized what was happening, told Samuel the Lord was calling him, and sent him back to his room.

"The Lord came and stood there. He called as he had called the other times: 'Samuel! Samuel!' and Samuel replied, 'Speak. I'm listening'" (verse 10).

For the rest of his life, Samuel listened to what God said and then spoke his words to God's people. You listen to God's words too and want to share that message with others.

 ## Chomp on this!

Read the whole story in 1 Samuel chapter 1 and 1 Samuel chapter 3.

You're so spoiled

About now there might not be any more room around your Christmas tree because it is overflowing with all the gifts. The huge box from your parents might have a tiny envelope with plane tickets to see your best friends. Your grandparents are generous because they love to see your face light up. Your cousins love to pick out something they know you really want. However, as you open up gift after gift, it gets a little embarrassing because there are so many. You start to feel spoiled.

As God's child, when people look at you, they see there is no more room around you either because you are overflowing with God's gifts. Psalm 31:19 says, **"How abundant are the good things that you have stored up for those who fear you, that you bestow in the sight of all, on those who take refuge in you"** (NIV).

Because Jesus bought you back from the devil and hell, you are now in God's family. The God who created and owns everything in this world loves to be generous with you. It makes him happy to surprise you with good things. He loves to see your face light up when you realize just how much he treasures you. He picks out exactly which physical and spiritual blessings in your life will help you bless others.

Dear God,

sometimes I feel so spoiled when I realize all the good things you have put in my life. My home, clothes, food, toys, and books are far more than I need. You also spoil me with spiritual gifts that are even better. You give more love, joy, peace, patience, kindness, goodness, gentleness, self-control, and faithfulness. Amen.

Time to listen

At almost every family holiday, reunion, or get-together, the kids run off and play while the adults sit around and talk. (Talk. Talk. Talk. Boring. Boring. Boring.) If you do sit still long enough to chat, usually the older people ask you about your day, how school is going, and what hobbies you are into. As soon as you're done talking, you run off to play again.

Job (*pronounced Jōbe*), who lived about four thousand years ago, knew that kids need to listen to people who are older than them: **"Ask the people of past generations. Find out what their ancestors had learned. We have only been around since yesterday, and we know nothing. Our days on earth are only a fleeting shadow. Won't their words teach you? Won't they share their thoughts with you?"** (Job 8:8-10).

While you are having fun with your cousins, which is super fun, be sure to include your elders. The next time you see your grandparents or aunts and uncles, be sure to take a few minutes to learn from them. It's a time to listen and to get instruction and understanding.

 ## Chomp on this!

Don't know what questions to ask? Live too far away and don't get to see your elder relatives in person? Call them or send them a letter and use these questions to listen to their wisdom:

What is your favorite Bible passage?

Who first told you about Jesus?

What chores did you do as a kid?

What was your most embarrassing moment?

What's the most important lesson you have learned?

What is your favorite family tradition?

Whom do you admire and why?

Humiliation

One of my favorite dinner topics is, "What's your most embarrassing moment?"

That's because we all talk about the time that we tripped and fell in front of everyone or when our shorts almost fell off at recess or the time we almost walked into the wrong bathroom. I'm sure you have an embarrassing moment too. Now that it's over we can look back and laugh, but at the time all we could think was, "I'm so humiliated!"

Jesus' whole life—from the time he came to earth until he died on a cross—is called his humiliation. Jesus **"made himself nothing by taking the very nature of a servant, being made in human likeness. And being found in appearance as a man, he humbled himself by becoming obedient to death— even death on a cross!"** (Philippians 2:7,8 NIV).

God, who lives in light, was willing to put aside that glory to grow as a baby inside his mother. Jesus left the mansion of heaven to be born in a manger. The God who has always existed and always will exist was willing to die on a cross.

Jesus was willing to suffer all of this humiliation for us so that we wouldn't have to be humiliated when we stand in front of God on judgment day. Instead, God will hug us and say, "It's good to have you home."

A baby just like you

Chomp on this!

If you were God, how would you have come to the world?

"Today in the town of David a Savior has been born to you; he is the Messiah, the Lord. This will be a sign to you: You will find a baby wrapped in cloths and lying in a manger" (Luke 2:11,12 NIV).

I think if I were God, I'd come with lightning or thunder. Something that's loud, bright, spectacular—and just a little bit scary. Instead, God became a baby, born in the middle of the night when everyone was sleeping. Doesn't that sound like a weird way to save the world?

Because of the gap between us and God, we can't lift ourselves up to him, so he decided to become a baby and bring himself down to us. He could have picked any way—maybe even the way you thought you'd do it. Still, he chose to become a baby, a baby who needed feeding and holding, who needed to learn how to walk and talk. He was a baby like you, except that he was nothing like you. He was perfect and holy. He was God with us.

This is the way God *chooses* to give us heaven.

God sent Jesus—his only Son—as a baby, just like you!

Jesus—who came to be perfect and holy—lived so that we can be called God's child, just like him!

Jesus never missed*

How many of you have seen someone playing basketball and it seems that he can't miss a shot? He hits everything he puts up . . . or so it seems. Even though this guy is on fire, he still misses some shots. He isn't perfect. God tells us in James 2:10, **"Whoever keeps the whole law and yet stumbles at just one point is guilty of breaking all of it"** (NIV). God demands that we be perfect, and we know all too well that we aren't. We fight with our siblings, talk back to our parents, and we grumble when we receive a lot of homework.

God sent a solution, however. This solution was Jesus' death and resurrection in our place. In Isaiah 53:5 we hear, **"He was pierced for our transgressions, he was crushed for our iniquities; the punishment that brought us peace was upon him, and by his wounds we are healed"** (NIV). Christ paid the price for every single one of your sins.

Even on the best of nights, a basketball player will miss a shot. Even on our best days, we miss the shots we take in life. But Jesus hit every one of the shots and never missed. We win.

Dear Jesus,

thank you for coming to be pierced and crushed in our place. Please help us always trust and rely on this truth. In Jesus' name we pray. Amen.

*This devotion was written by Ben, a kid just like you.

Mix in the yeast

Bread is yummy. French toast is delicious. Almost everybody loves cinnamon rolls. And, let's face it, pizza without the crust just isn't the same.

Nobody, however, wants to eat bread that's flat and hard. That's why bread makers add yeast. They mix just a little bit of yeast through the dough, and the whole loaf rises and becomes light and fluffy.

God says the way he works is a lot like yeast in bread. **"[Jesus] told them still another parable: 'The kingdom of heaven is like yeast that a woman took and mixed into about sixty pounds of flour until it worked all through the dough'"** (Matthew 13:33 NIV).

Sixty pounds of flour is, well, about as much as some of you weigh. All it takes is a few tablespoons of yeast worked and worked through all of that flour to make the bread rise. That's some pretty powerful stuff.

God's kingdom is like that. His Word is so powerful that all it takes is a little bit to work through this whole world. As part of God's kingdom, no matter where you go, God is using you to work his Word into his world. As you tell others about him, let his love shine through you. You mix his Word into their lives.

When it seems like there are so few believers working to share his love with such a big group of people who don't know him, know that your God's Word is powerful. The Holy Spirit works through your little message and makes a big change.

 ## Chomp on this!

How can your family work God's Word through the neighborhood?

How can you share Jesus with others?

How to make your life better

"My dad doesn't understand me!"

"My mom is so embarrassing!"

"Their rules are so stupid!"

You could probably come up with a whole list of other reasons why you don't really have to listen to your parents, couldn't you? That's why today's passage can be tough to hear. Ephesians 6:1-3 tells you, **"Children, obey your parents in the Lord, for this is right. 'Honor your father and mother'—which is the first commandment with a promise—'so that it may go well with you and that you may enjoy long life on the earth'"** (NIV).

Wouldn't that command be so much easier if your parents were perfect? It sure would be. But your parents are sinful. They punish you when it wasn't actually your fault, they yell when they are tired, and they don't always listen when you try to tell your side of the story.

God knows that and he says, "I know. Obey them anyway. Your life will go so much better."

Do you want to know the best thing about being in your family? The same Jesus who forgives you for not obeying perfectly is the same Jesus who forgives your mom and dad for not parenting perfectly either. You are being raised by forgiven sinners. Obey them anyway. It's the right thing to do.

Chomp on this!

Conduct an experiment. For one day, do every single thing your parents ask you to do—right away, even if you think it's dumb. Then do it for another day. Then try a third. See if it goes well with you.

Search, Search, Search

**"My son, if you take my words to heart
and treasure my commands within you,
if you pay close attention to wisdom,
and let your mind reach for understanding,
if indeed you call out for insight,
if you ask aloud for understanding,
if you search for wisdom as if it were money
and hunt for it as if it were hidden treasure . . ."**
(Proverbs 2:1-5).

You have spent three hours building your amazing Lego city. You know exactly which piece you need to finish your building and no other piece will do. Even though it takes you another hour, you will search through your 42 bazillion Legos in a container the size of a laundry basket because it has to be the right one.

God wants you to search for wisdom the same way you search for your Legos. He wants you to pay attention, to read your Bible, to ask your parents for advice, to pray to him for the ability to understand his Word.

Why do you do all this? King Solomon, the wisest man on earth, tells you, **". . . then you will understand the fear of the Lord and you will find the knowledge of God. The Lord gives wisdom. From his mouth come knowledge and understanding. He has reserved priceless wisdom for decent people"** (Proverbs 2:5-7).

Wisdom helps you know God better. It's time to start looking.

Your inheritance

Most parents and grandparents have a will. That's a big pile of papers that lets people know who gets what when they die. Most of the time, everything gets left to their children and grandchildren. (That's you!) Maybe you've been given some jewelry or money or a dollhouse or furniture or toys. Those things are called an inheritance.

When Jesus lived on this earth, he called all believers his brothers and sisters. If you are his brother or sister, that means you are God's child. **"If we are his children, we are also God's heirs. If we share in Christ's suffering in order to share his glory, we are heirs together with him"** (Romans 8:17).

As God's child, you are in God's will. He has an inheritance waiting for you. It's better than money; it's better than a car or a house or furniture or jewelry. You have glory waiting for you. You get to reign with Jesus in heaven.

When God tells you that it's time to go to your heavenly home, this is what it's going to sound like: **"Then the King will say to those on his right, 'Come, you who are blessed by my Father; take your inheritance, the kingdom prepared for you since the creation of the world"** (Matthew 25:34 NIV).

When you get to heaven, you will hear, "Welcome home!" That's the best inheritance ever.

New Year blessings

Today is the last day of the year. Do you have your party stuff ready? Are you staying up until midnight to celebrate? Everybody is so excited for the new beginning, for the fresh start, that the new year has to offer. As you end this year and start another, let God give you his blessings. (This blessing from Numbers 6:24-26 is the same blessing that the priests gave to the Israelites five thousand years ago, and it still applies today.)

"The Lord will bless you and watch over you."

God the Father guards, shelters, and protects you. He pays attention to your spiritual protection.

"The Lord will smile on you and be kind to you."

God the Son's face lights up when he sees you, and your face reflects that joy. He lovingly meets your heart's needs.

"The Lord will look on you with favor and give you peace."

God the Holy Spirit lives inside of you, blessing you and giving you the security that comes from knowing you are always loved.

This is what's going to make next year a happy new year.

Chomp on this!

How did God bless and watch over you last year?

How did you see God smile on you and be kind to you?

How did God give you peace?

About Time of Grace

Time of Grace is an international Christian outreach media ministry that connects people to God's grace through Jesus Christ so that they know they are loved and forgiven. The ministry uses television, print, social media, and the web to share the gospel with people across the U.S. and around the world. On the weekly *Time of Grace* television program, Pastor Mark Jeske presents Bible studies that are understandable, interesting, and can be applied to people's lives. The program is broadcast on more than 150 local stations; 4 satellite networks, including American Forces Network; and airs on ABC Family, which is carried by virtually all cable providers in the U.S. For a complete broadcast schedule, visit timeofgrace.org. Watch *Time of Grace* or visit timeofgrace.org, where you will find the program via streaming video and audio podcasts, as well as study guides, daily devotions, blogs, a prayer wall, and additional resources. You can also call 800.661.3311 for more information.

P.O. BOX 301
MILWAUKEE, WI 53201
800.661.3311 | 414.562.8463
info@timeofgrace.org
timeofgrace.org